DIARY OF A CRACK ADDICT'S WIFE

CYNTHIA D. HUNTER

Dafina Books

KENSINGTON PUBLISHING CORP.
http://www.kensingtonbooks.com

Additional praise

"I know the book will be awesome and inspiring. God has ordered all of our steps and He has allowed you to live through and to tell an inspiring and motivational story of your personal life. Thanks!!"
—Denise W. Burrow

"This book has changed my life. I am so happy Cindy has decided to step forth and speak on our behalf. It is a masterpiece!"
—Regina Givens

"Congratulations, Cindy! I can't wait to read your book!"
—Karen E. Quinones Miller,
Author of the best sellers
I'm Telling and *Satin Doll*

"Sister Cindy, you know that God had a plan for your life, and He allowed you to live it and tell it! I know your book will be a great success! It is something that will touch the lives of so many others who have lived it, are still living with it, and will die with it. Be blessed and continue to use your wisdom by encouraging others.
This book is a #1 best seller!"
—Saundra K. Perkins

"I cannot wait to get your book and dive on in. I'm sure it will be fantastic!"
—Tracy Allen

"I am the founder of The Divine Sisterhood Book Club. BRAVO on your efforts to make a difference."
—Edwina Jackson

Praise for
Diary of a Crack Addict's Wife

"Riveting! A compelling story that succeeds in telling the day-to-day drama of hardships that an entire family must deal with whenever it is exposed to the crippling effects of drugs. Through this account, it becomes easier to see the devastating effect on the individual as well as the person who loves them the most. To watch someone else change before your eyes is a terrible shame, but to have the strength to relay those thoughts and feelings to paper is an awesome feat of courage and strength! This book is a groundbreaking testimony that will be heralded as the most revealing biography written in years! No one has ever written with such commitment and personal conviction! After reading this book, you won't feel the same about those who use drugs and their struggle to survive. You will have an amazing insight and understanding of how hard it is to deal with the changes a family has to endure before finally growing strong enough to simply say, 'enough is enough.' This book is truly addictive! It should be applauded for its truthful exploits and read time and time again. Finally, we can understand what it really means to be the wife of a crack addict!"
—Sean C. Robinson, Publisher, GFA Magazines

"Powerful! A must-read for all women! It leaves you with an inner hope and gives you strength to continue to strive for God's goodness, because after reading this diary, you know you can make it, too!"
—Thelma Jones

"BRAVO!!! A commendable effort by a rising literary genius. Your words have touched the minds and hearts of those who live in the shadows and cannot be heard."
—William C. Johnson, Jr., Esq., M.B.A., LL.M

"This book indeed shows that drugs tear apart the family structure as characters deal with life-changing circumstances such as drugs, alcohol, death, children, and love. I was moved with the spirit of the character, Cee. Her devotion to God and her 'right' living never falters, and it proves that opening your heart to God is never in vain."
—Preston Wilson

"This book will touch many people's interest. I believe this book will motivate and inspire many women. I would love to post this book at my online store at cbbookdistribution.com. Please feel free to visit our site. Thank you for sharing yourself with us."
—Brenda Piper, C & B Books Distribution Center

Dedication

I dedicate this book to my precious and special girlfriend, Geraldine Charles, who lost her husband to crack cocaine. Geraldine, you were there for me many, many days and nights, even though you were going through your own situation. I just want you to know that it was through your strength that I found hope. Without your love and support, where would I be? To me, you are a very precious and rare gem, one to be treasured for many more years to come. I'm so honored that God chose you to be a part of my treasure chest. True friends such as you are hard to find, and I feel so blessed to have you in my life!

Special Thanks

To the world's greatest jazz artist, Ms. Bobbi Humphrey. Thanks for all your unconditional love, words of wisdom, and shared moments. Every time I listen to your wonderful CD entitled "Passion Flute," it inspires me to excel above, beyond, and over. Not only does it enlighten my spirit, but it moves my soul to a place called serenity. Bobbi, your zest for life and your willingness to give back and embrace others show that you have compassion, and to me you're a Class Act to follow! I feel so honored and blessed to be graced with your presence in my life. Thanks a million!

Acknowledgments

First of all, before I get too carried away, let me start out by giving thanks and honor to God for entrusting me with the insight and fortitude to pursue my passion (which is writing) with much love, inspiration, and determination so that I can help others in hopes that they, too, will learn from my true-life experiences and apply it to their own everyday lives. Also, I would like to give thanks to each of the following gemstones that God has placed into my life to help me stay focused and to persevere; without them this book would have been impossible.

To my two wonderful children, Terrance and Tiquan. I know God is real because He blessed me with you; your understanding and support mean the world to me, and I could not have asked for any better. To the love of my life, Mr. Tyrone O. Black, Sr. Thanks for all your wonderful words of encouragement and patience in helping me to strive for greatness. To my mentor and editor, Karen Thomas—thanks from the bottom of my heart for all your belief in me and warm words of wisdom that kept me strong in the midst of the storm. To the greatest manager and best girlfriend anyone could ask for, Regina Givens, for all the many, many years of unwavering support and belief that I could soar; your words, filled with much love and inspiration, gave me the wings I needed to fly. To my sweet Aunt Micki—thanks for all your tender love and support and dear words of inspiration; you mean the world to me. To my very, very gifted and talented childhood friend Buster Davis for utilizing his vivid imagination to create such a captivating cover for this book, one that is so stunning it will touch the hearts of many for years to come. No one else could have done it better; you are the master at your craft, and remember you're "stuck with me" for life. To the magnificent Theresa Bush for all her everlasting support and for utilizing her unique gift to add just the right splash of color to the cover to make it sparkle. To Sherry Poole-Clarke and family—from day one you always showed how much you cared and have continued to support me no matter what; thanks for all your words of inspiration and love. To my dynamite friend Cherly Brandon, for believing in me before I ever put pen to paper when we were both penniless. To my very dear and special friend Lamon Hamilton for all your encouraging words and acts of kindness. To my precious friend Mrs. Barbara Moone, who taught me life is only a journey if you live it and reach for the stars. To my special, special friend Sywanda Gray for her vision about the title for this book and her constant overall support from day one. To my childhood friend Felicia Word—I'll never forget the words of inspiration you said to me that changed my life forever. To my genuine girlfriend Dale Lee for the many days we spent strolling through the park daydreaming about what it was going to be like when God blessed us to bless someone else. To my friends Teresa Mcrae and Pamela Martin for always being there when I needed a listening ear. To my favorite cousins, Tracie, Sidney, Fred, William, Ike, Lenice, Joan, and Pep. I love you for all your words of encouragement and faith. To my sweet friend and co-worker Paulette Mcintosh. From the first day we met, I knew God had placed you in my life for all the right reasons; all your love and words of wisdom have given me the strength to persevere. To my beautiful and precious Aunt Janice Gee, who was always there with a good word to keep me striving for greatness. To my Aunt Dot for her insight and wisdom in keeping the faith to overcome obstacles. To my wonderful mother, Ida Mae Abraham, who believed in me at a time when no one else did and continued to pray for my success every day. To my brother, Charles, who stood by my side through thick and thin. To my brother, James Abraham, for believing in me at the tender age of twelve and encouraging me to write from my heart. To my one and only precious sister, Deloris Abraham, who always had the faith that someday I would make it. To my wonderful loving manager and friend, Angela Stringfellow, for her everyday moral support and belief in me as a person; without you I would be lost. To my loving and witty editor of the self-published version of this book, Mary Martin, who had the ability to bring out the best in me as a writer; your keen eye and sharp sense of purpose made me strive to fulfill my mission to get the word out; I could not have done it without you. To my special mom at work, Betty Barton. Your love and inspiration, filled with words of encouragement, gave me the strength to move mountains and keep on climbing nonstop; I'm so blessed to have you in my life. To my sweet friend Arlene Thompson. Your willingness to lend a listening ear at the drop of a dime and your level of confidence in me are just beyond any words I can describe. To my traveling buddy and road manager, Mr. Nelson Cross—thanks for all your genuine support, dedication, and understanding. To my partner Henry Parker for his genuine sense of humor and keeping it real. To my coworker Will Harris for his genuine support and words of encouragement, constantly reminding me to keep my eye on the prize. And to my precious team leader at work, Menia Peguese, for her genuine concern and belief in me as an individual. Being a part of your team has been a true blessing; your kindred spirit and willingness to support me in my quest for greatness made me realize that I was fortunate to have you in my life! And to all my coworkers and teammates at Amex—thanks for your generous support and many, many words of encouragement. They helped fuel the fire that kept me going; I feel honored to have been a part of a team so rare and special. And to all my other family members, friends, and generous fans who have supported me on my journey with this book. I just want to say thank you from the bottom of my heart for everything. I could not have made it without you.

I would personally like to give many thanks to a few fellow writers who have inspired me and encouraged me in this labor of love:

Denise Campbell—*Spanish Eyes. Love Thy Sister . . . Watch Thy Back* and C.F. Hawthorne—*For Every Black Eye.*

Prelude

In your very wildest of dreams, at the least, can you imagine yourself not just being involved with an addict, but "marrying" a CRACK
addict, thinking and hoping that he will change? Sometimes we already know the truth, but refuse to believe it. If we would only listen to that little voice deep down inside of us, this world would be
all the better for it. When we pretend we don't hear it, we get
caught up in a vicious cycle, and before you know it, every person
we meet or greet is a crack addict. So many times I have often heard
my girlfriends talk about how their husbands were alcoholics, or
that their husbands smoke too many cigarettes, but never have I
heard one say, "Guess what? My husband's smoking crack!" Talking
about something as disgusting as CRACK COCAINE was taboo and
nothing to talk about, much less telling the embarrassing truth that
it was a part of your everyday life and that your man was doing it!

After many years of careful research and not being able to find
any books that I could relate to for answers on crack cocaine and
spousal abuse, I decided to tell my own story, in hopes of reaching
other women and men who were just like me: in an abusive
relationship with a crack addict and with nowhere to turn. I guess
you may be saying to yourself, "What an introduction!" . . . and
guess what? You are so right, and that's because I have lived it, just
like some of you have and still are. I only hope and pray that
through my expressions of true-life experiences—some joyful, but
mostly heartfelt sorrow, disappointment, hurt, and pain (the kind

you could only imagine if you, too, were in my shoes)—that this book will give you the motivation, courage, determination to succeed and willingness to excel in all aspects of your life. Dealing with a crack addict has given me the strength and determination to live the dreams inside of me, and dare to reach out to help others to see their own future through all of their trials and tribulations, and to learn God's true purpose for their lives. Sometimes it takes bad things to happen for us to realize that we are not in this world by ourselves and that there is a greater being and that is God our Creator.

September 16, 1985

Dear Diary,

I remember it as though it was yesterday. I'll never forget a hot, summery day in August. I had so much fun just strolling along the streets of downtown Paterson, New Jersey, enjoying window-shopping, reminiscing. Going into boutique shops, trying on the most expensive outfits, pretending I was Mrs. Royalty. Back then I was happy, full of life, ambitious, determined, and filled with the will and desire to be a success. So I thought.

I had just met the man of my dreams, everything I needed and wanted in a man. This new man of mine had a caramel complexion with baby-smooth skin and stood about six feet tall. You knew from looking at his lean, fit physique that he believed in working out. By the way all of his clothes flowed onto his tight-framed body you could tell they were custom-made, fitting him to a tee, making him appear as though he had just stepped out of *GQ* magazine. Just looking at him with his jet-black wavy hair and those big, beautiful brown eyes made me yearn for his touch. No matter how hard I tried to resist him, the temptation of his touch was there, piercing my soul with every thought and emotion; I knew he was the water I needed to quench my thirst. Mark had much charm, good looks, wit, and a way with words that would make you weak in the knees, so smooth you would melt like butter. This man was one of the most intelligent brothers I had ever encountered that was on my wavelength. Mark's gregarious smile and charming personality made him stand out in a crowd. He was street smart, business savvy, and very ambitious; at one time he had even worked on Wall Street. Any woman would have thought she had hit the jackpot.

As I strolled along Main Street, I couldn't help but think about my newfound love and the way he made me feel. Thinking back, it was the end of May this year when we first met, and from the very first day we laid eyes on each other, I knew that there was something very special about Mark. Walking home from the bus stop about five blocks from my house, my feet were starting to ache and swell; the closer I got, the more my feet started to ache. That day it seemed as if I would never reach my front door.

Before I could reach the block where I lived I could see Darrel, my stepsister Joyce's husband, across the street, waving at me. Usually Darrel was a loner, but this particular day he had someone else with him. Looking at Darrel from afar, the gentleman with him appeared to be rather charming and cute, I must say. With my feet aching the way they were, today was not the day for me to be introduced to anyone, let alone a man of this magnitude. And yet no matter how hard I tried to convince myself, here was Darrel crossing the street with his friend. For a moment I wanted to pretend like I didn't see him, but I knew it was too late to try that trick. All I could say to myself was please, please do not cross that street and come over here. The corn on my pinky toe was acting up something awful, throbbing like no tomorrow. And nevertheless, here it was. I had just gotten off from work and was dressed to the hilt with my white-and-navy blue pinstriped skirt suit with the split in the back and my navy blue-and-white spectators to match. You couldn't tell me that all eyes weren't on me, even though I wished they weren't, for right at that moment my feet were killing me, and being too cute to relieve the pain by trying not to limp wasn't helping, either.

Remember how it felt when someone was staring a hole straight through you? This is how I felt as I continued to walk toward my house, blushing all the way, pretending that no one was behind me. Here I was, almost at the point of praying and begging not to let Darrel come anywhere near my house with his friend, and deep inside hoping that he would at the same time. It was too late. I stopped dead in my tracks when I heard someone call out my name. I could feel my heart skipping a beat and my mouth freezing up on me. I was too afraid to respond for fear that I might say something that I would regret later. I turned around, trying not to appear surprised, thinking that it was Darrel who called out my name. However, I was shocked to learn the truth: it wasn't Darrel, but instead it was his friend Mark. By this time I was speechless. Usually I had so much to say when spoken to, but this day was far different than any other. Standing there, face-to-face with this handsome man in front of me, gave me goose bumps from head to toe. And for the first time "Cee," for a change, did not have one word to say. I mean, nothing. Finally Darrel broke the ice and introduced me to Mark. Dimples graced his cheeks as he smiled from ear to ear, appearing to be shy.

"Are you always in a hurry?" Mark asked. Before I had a chance to answer his first question, he floored me with another. "I'm not trying to be rude or anything," he said, "but do those shoes hurt your feet?" By this time I was annoyed and felt that he was being rude. In my mind this man thinks it's all about him and is very arrogant, I thought to myself as my blood started to boil. He really had some nerve; how dare he insult me this way. Who did he think he was?

"Are *you* always this rude and straight to the point?" I asked. "And what happened to manners? Like, 'how are you today, young lady' for starters?" I asked with a pinch of anger in my voice.

"Well, first let me start off by asking you to forgive me for being so rude," he said. "You look so lovely and charming, I didn't know what else to say. If I appeared to be rude it is only because I'm dazzled by your beauty. To me you're a chocolate princess. I begged Darrel to introduce me to you against his wishes and, may I add, I love your style," he said. "Let me get it right this time," he said, chuckling under his breath, as he asked what kind of work I was into and if I was a secretary. Watching him squirm while trying to make conversation made me feel good and gave me the upper hand. Darrel's face lit up with laughter as he watched his friend fumble over his words trying to think of something to say, right after he had just made himself look like a fool. While answering Mark's questions, I felt relaxed; it had been a long time since I'd had any stimulating conversation with a man. The more we chatted, the more comfortable I felt, almost as if he was someone I had known for a very long time. We must have stood in front of my house and talked for about two hours before he finally worked up enough nerve to ask me out on a date.

"Moving kinda fast, aren't you?" I asked.

"Well, you never said you had a boyfriend or anything," he implied.

"Just because I didn't say so doesn't mean I don't."

"Well, do you?" he asked blushingly.

"No, I don't, nor am I looking," I replied. Here I was, trying to appear to be Miss Tough Lady (the one who didn't really need a man and felt they were a dime a dozen, knowing good and well in my mind that this was a lie) with a wide smile plastered on my face almost to the point of laughter as I joked with him.

"Will it be okay if I come by to see you tomorrow?" he asked sincerely, "Or are you going to be busy since you are so single and don't have anybody?" he said jokingly.

"I have no idea what I'll be doing tomorrow, but I'm sure I can fit you into my schedule," I laughed.

"Fit me into your schedule? Girl, you got it going on," he said as he laughed openly. "Well, since you have to fit me into your schedule, what time do you think you'll be available?"

"What about eight tomorrow night?"

"Oh, by all means, please pencil me in that slot. Better take it while you can fit me in, so to speak," he said, being sarcastic. "Darrel told me a lot of nice things about you as we were walking to the store. When he waved at you I told him I didn't care what he did as long as he introduced me to you. I had to meet you, if nothing else."

Staring at him in a daze like a puppy that needed a drink of water, I couldn't help but wonder what it would be like to kiss this man. In my mind I was caressing and kissing him and he didn't even know it. Today, I was as cool as a cucumber and forever proud of myself. As the saying goes, never let them see you sweat, and this day I didn't. "Cee, it was nice meeting you, and, by the way, I work third shift on my night job, so right now I need to go home so I can catch a quick nap. Hopefully you won't forget me tomorrow night. After all, you did pencil me in for 8:00 p.m., correct?" he asked, being smart again.

"Yes, I did," I replied. "Are you always so silly?"

"If being silly is going to make you change your mind about our date, then no, I'm a serious man with serious plans," he said, laughing as he turned around to walk away. "Well, guess I'll see you tomorrow. Have a nice evening."

"I shall," I replied. If looks could kill, I guess he would have dropped dead. As I watched him walking down the street, I noticed that he was slightly bowlegged.

He had no idea of how turned on I was—I couldn't wait until the next day. No matter how hard I tried to sleep, it didn't come easy and without a price; I tossed and turned all night, wondering what my first date with Mark was going to be like and fantasizing about all the possibilities. Did this man have a girlfriend, and if so, where was she? Why hadn't Darrel mentioned anything about Mark to me before? Where had he been hiding himself?

All those questions ran through my mind while I scurried to get home from work the next day, trying to figure out what I was going to wear and how I was going to fix my hair. I asked myself if I wanted to be sexy, or just plain Jane; sophisticated lady, or if nothing else, just throw on a pair of my form-fitting jeans, as I continued to look in the mirror. Pulling out about six outfits, nothing satisfied me. Here it was, almost 7:30, and I didn't have one candle lit, no soft, mellow music on, and standing in front of the mirror looking like Raggedy Ann, and wishing Raggedy Andy would appear just once to tell me what to wear and what I should do. I made my brother play lookout man (I guess he is as close to Andy as I'm going to get) while I continued to contemplate what to wear for the evening. At last I finally settled on an outfit that I felt comfortable with, sliding on a nice, slinky royal blue dress that reached my ankles and had a small but sexy slit on the side, hitting just above my knee, giving me a soft and subtle look. My see-through, open-toed sandals had a glassy look with their low, sexy heels, and my hand-carved African accessories gave my outfit just the right flair, if I do say so myself. I felt great, and my brother told me I looked fabulous. Sipping on a glass of red wine, trying to hold my composure until the moment he would arrive, I could feel my palms starting to sweat as I sat in my bedroom listening to the radio and adding the finishing touches to my outfit. Anticipating what the night was going to be like gave me the jitters and made me feel a little nervous. Opening my bedroom door for a breath of fresh air, I could overhear my brother talking to someone, and from the sounds of everything I recognized a familiar voice, none other than Mark's. When he stepped around the corner of the porch leading away from the balcony, I could tell he did not see me peeking at him. Watching him move about the way he did, I just knew he had to be a great dancer. Not wanting to appear over-anxious or desperate, I waited patiently for my brother to guide him inside, greeting him at the door with a gracious smile. The expression on his face spoke a thousand words. Inside my mind I was thinking, this man looks so good I could eat him for breakfast, lunch, and dinner, and maybe even brunch. Tugging at the collar on his cream-colored silk shirt, you could see the tiny hairs on his chest peering out. Looking down at the floor, you couldn't help but notice the gray Stacy Adams shoes that adorned his feet, with the gold tassels attached to the end of his shoelaces, which matched his charcoal gray cuffed slacks, making them stand out. Without further ado he reached out for my hand and held it up to his lips, kissing it ever so gently. Mark's lips were so soft they felt like cotton to me. I once again was speechless and smiled, letting him know how much I approved of what he was doing. My brother took it upon himself to put on some soft, mellow music and lit my favorite scented candles for me, something I should have already had set up well in advance. But no, I had to get ready for Mr. *GQ*.

Our first date went like a cinch. We must have talked until 3:00 in the morning; the time went by so fast, and neither one of us wanted to call it quits. The more we talked, the more we realized how much we had in common. To be honest, his conversation stimulated every fiber of my being. Reflections from the candles danced on the wall as we sat in the living room on the floor, laughing hysterically at the shadows that appeared from the flames and making fun of one another while sipping on a bottle of red wine I had opened earlier, the same wine I sipped on to calm my nerves before he arrived. It felt so good knowing that this man was interested in me, and I in him.

That first date led to many, many more, each better than the last, and as time went on, eventually we were destined to fall in love with each other as was evident in everything we did or dared to say. [We always say to ourselves, if only I knew then what I do now, this would have never happened. Sometimes in life we go around and over the bumps in the road, but it's not until we hit the bump head-on that we open our eyes and realize what God is trying to show us.]

September 18, 1985

Dear Diary,

Today is a very special day. Mark and I finally realize we both feel the same way about each other. Even though we haven't been dating for a long time, I think I'm falling in love with this man, and maybe someday in the future, would not mind having his child. I believe he would be a good father. At least I pray he will. He seems to be all I could ever want in a man. He is so tall, charming, and has looks to die for. For the first time in my life, I can truly say I'm ready to give my whole heart and soul to someone whom I know, without a shadow of a doubt, I can have a real future with.

September 19, 1985

Dear Diary,

Mark came over last night and brought me the prettiest bunch of roses that I have ever seen. When I opened the door, lo and behold, there he was standing proud, handsome, and smelling good, of course. Well, gotta go! Oh, by the way, he really turns me on.

September 23, 1985

Dear Diary,

I'm thinking about letting Mark move in with me so we can buy this house together. They always say two heads are better than one. At least we could save some money. (By the way, he has a good job and, it looks like, a bright future.) I believe we can have something together. Even though I haven't told my big brother what my intentions are, I feel it will be okay. You see, my brother, Chad, has always spoiled me ever since we were kids. When we were small, he would always protect me and ward off the bullies. He didn't care if they were girls; his only concern was that I was his baby sister and nobody was going to mess with me, even though he was the main one to beat me up after my grandmother went to work. He was always the ambitious one, at a very early age. I can remember when he got his first job at the age of ten. On Saturday morning, he would jump out of bed and rush to get ready for his boss man, Mr. Campbell. His boss was a very witty and charming older white man in his mid-fifties who stood about six feet, two inches tall, with the most distinguished salt-and-pepper hair you have ever seen. He was a fun-loving, kind-spirited person. His genuine concern about the children in our neighborhood assured everyone that he was a man to be trusted and loved. Every weekend, he would come over and give the neighborhood kids a ride on his pickup or bring watermelon and share it with everyone. There was always something to do when he was around. He was always interested in what we children were doing in school and encouraged us to always strive for greatness within ourselves. It was through his caring and concern that we, as children, learned to excel. When he would come to get my brother for work in that old, raggedy pickup truck, you could hear it coming down the road for about two miles. That's just how loud his muffler was. My brother, with his little, tight blue jeans, was always so neat and his shirts well crested as if he had a real, real job. You would have thought this young man was working in someone's office the way he dressed. Even though his little pants were twisted above his ankle, it didn't matter; he was neat as a pin. So to him, nothing else mattered. There would be days he would come home with bags and bags of candy; those days felt like heaven to me.

September 25, 1985

Dear Diary,

My mind is made up. I'm going to let Mark move in. Let's face it, I don't want to live without you, baby.

September 26, 1985

Dear Diary,

My baby moved his things in today. I'm so happy. Nothing could be better. I know he loves me. Deep down inside I know we can have so much together. This man is so good to me, it's like a dream come true. If I'm dreaming, please don't wake me. Just let me sleep (just kidding). Talk to you tomorrow. Good night for now.

October 2, 1985

Dear Diary,

I am so mad. Guess what? Mark got suspended from his job, and check out why. They said he stole a roll of toilet paper. Now, how ridiculous is that? I told Mark not to worry about it—with his skills he could get any job he wants. Well, guess I'm through blowing off steam. Gotta go so I can meet Charlotte.

October 3, 1985

Dear Diary,

Mr. Chad got drunk and showed up today. He told me there was something about Mark he didn't like. We fussed for a long time. I don't like it when my brother and I argue. He really hurt my feelings and said some very mean and nasty things. Can you believe what he had the audacity to say to me? He said, in time I would see Mark for who he really is. Every breath in me wants to prove my brother wrong. What makes him think that there is something wrong with my boyfriend? I believe he is just jealous because he is so lonely himself, and you know how the story goes, misery loves company. Chad and his girlfriend, Lois, just recently broke up, and I know he must be hurting inside. But don't take it out on me. I didn't do it. And besides, he needs to get on with his life and stop feeling sorry for himself and dwelling on the past. Life goes on. You either live it or you die. Good night, Mrs. Diary.

October 4, 1985

Dear Diary,

My brother acts like nothing has happened. Even though he is still talking to me, it's very brief and straight to the point. It's eating away at me inside. I can't take it anymore. Guess I'll throw up the peace treaty. I give in. He's my buddy. Well, gotta go!

October 5, 1985

Dear Diary,

Today, I'm so excited Mark found another job; it pays good money, too. Boy, now I'm going to shop until I drop for real. I'm sooooooooooooo happy!!!

Good night, Mrs. Diary!

October 11, 1985

Dear Diary,

Today is my 25th birthday! I thank God for letting me live to see another year. I feel good about myself and my accomplishments. I'm at the point of purchasing the house we live in. I have a wonderful man in my life that is good to me. What more could I ask for? And let me not forget, an adorable seven-year-old son who is the light of my life. Right now my baby boy is staying with my Aunt Janice until I get settled. Wish my father could be here to share some of my happiness. I'm so happy, sometimes I feel as though I'm floating on a cloud. Well, Mark called and said he was taking me out on the town and had a surprise for me. Oh boy! I'm so excited. I hope it's a big, fat, juicy, diamond ring. That would be real, real nice. I have to have this man in my life. Good night, Mrs. Diary!

October 17, 1985

Dear Diary,

How could I have been so dumb? What in the world was I thinking about? No birth control, no nothing. I think I'm pregnant. Please don't let this be true. I thought I wanted another baby, but I just buried my second child less than six months ago. What is my family going to think? This cannot be happening. I have to tell Mark. Now is not the time to be having more kids. My future is starting to take shape and is looking brighter than ever before. I don't want to ruin it with such an unexpected surprise. What is this man going to think of me? Why did I not take better precautions? Guess I just got caught up in the moment. Pregnancy was the last thing on my mind. How could I have let this happen at a time in my life when I was finally so happy and at peace with myself? Little unsuspected surprises destroy relationships, and this one I'm not ready to give up. What am I going to do?

October 21, 1985

Dear Diary,

Today, I went to see my stepmother and confided that I suspected I was pregnant, I was not ready for another child, and I was unsure what I wanted to do. Of course, my stepmother was from the old school and believed if you made a baby, you took care of it. She told me in a nice, strong, stern tone that if I aborted this baby she would never speak to me again. To hear her speak those words sent piercing chills through my body. She and I were always very close, from the age of seventeen when she first came to meet me at the train station because my dad had to work. From the very beginning we were friends. Even though I admired and highly respected my stepmother always, I felt as though this was a decision that I and only I should have to make. Yes, you ask, so what did you do? I decided that I had no choice but to tell Mark and hope and pray that his reaction would be a pleasant one. Hope I'm making the right decision, will keep my fingers crossed. Good night, Mrs. Diary!

October 25, 1985

Dear Diary,

Guess what? Mark is going to give me $250.00 so I can go shopping. He says I earned it. Girl, he sure is good to me. I love him, just love him. I'm ready to shop until I drop. Girlfriend, I'm long, long overdue. I need a new hairdo, nails done, and the works. Also let's not forget the new outfits and shoes. When I go home, this brother is not going to know who I am. Have a good day, Mrs. Diary.

October 27, 1985

Dear Diary,

Today started out to be a beautiful day. I went shopping with my girlfriend. We had a ball. You know we had to hit every boutique on the avenue and bargain shop. We both had so much fun. It felt good to get out and, for once, not have to worry about how I'm going to pay my next bill. Like I said from the beginning, it started out to be a beautiful day. Hmmmm, if only I knew then what I do now. I would have been so much farther in the game. No wonder Mr. Mark wanted me out of the house to go shopping—now I know. Why? After being gone for about five hours, I couldn't wait to go home, only to return for a big surprise.

When I got home, I could hear faint sounds of laughter and partying coming from the kitchen. Instantly, I automatically assumed that a card game was going on. I could hear the voices of quite a few people, music flowing, everything so mellow. As I walked closer toward the kitchen, I could hear someone whispering, "Pass it to me." By this time, I knew something was going on in my house that was illegal. My heart raced the closer I got to the kitchen. Lo and behold the scene when I did stumble into the kitchen. Eight men and one lady all sitting around my kitchen table passing a cloud-filled, glass pipe back and forth to each other. I really was almost clueless about crack at this time, had never seen it, smoked it, smelled it, or anything, but always heard other people talk about it. So right away, I recognized some of the paraphernalia, especially the pipe. By the time it really hit me what was going on in my house, it was too late. I became like a raging, out-of-control bull that someone had thrown gasoline on. I turned over the table and started smashing vials of crack as they fell onto the floor and daring anybody to even look like they were mad. Everybody was so high they didn't even recognize who I was and offered me a hit of crack. Mark was so high, he told me to calm down and take a hit and I would be okay. Now you know he has really flipped out for real. The young lady that was sitting at the table smoking crack with them appeared to be very well dressed, attractive, and very businesslike, with her hair well-kept and maintained. But, as I got closer to her I could see the rings around her bloodshot eyes, making her look like a raccoon. Just by looking at her you could tell at one time or another she really had it going on. But today, she needed help.

Spinning around in the kitchen, trying to gather my thoughts, I couldn't help but think "this can't be happening." I thought to myself, *and now I'm pregnant with this man's child*. Any woman's worst nightmare was to be pregnant by a crack addict. Instantly, panic set in. If he is an addict, is it going to affect my unborn child? How long has he been getting high? I asked myself. All sorts of questions and panic-stricken fears of the worst consumed my every thought after hearing many, many horror stories of crack-addicted children (and just remember one thing, I had just lost a child six months earlier due to a sudden illness). In my heart, I truly wanted to believe that this is just an experiment for Mark and just another phase he is going through in his life.

Afterthoughts: Some women have a tendency to make an excuse for whatever they choose or don't want to believe, and we often lead ourselves down a narrow path of failed relationships that were already doomed from the very beginning when you first saw the man with the pipe in his hand. No, we have to pretend that we have the power within us to change what others won't change for themselves. Ladies, wake up, it's not going to happen. It will get worse before it gets any better. Trust me, and what I mean by this, is let go. Realize that in order to change, people have to have the will, desire, and determination within themselves to do so.

October 30, 1985

Dear Diary,

Here I am, four weeks pregnant and scared to death to even tell the baby's daddy. What kind of crap is that? At the same time, still in denial of facts smacking me right in my face. How much plainer could it get? I could hear the man getting out of the bed at 10:00 p.m. and walking back and forth, doors squeaking until 6:00 the next morning. Now it's time for him to get up and go to work. The alarm clock is going off, and he is talking about calling in. Now he wants to sleep all day. Well, this is just a passing phase; he'll be okay. (*Yeah, right.*) Who's stuck on stupid here? How long can he go on like this? It has been over three days, and I can see that his use is progressing, but I'm still in denial. This is my baby's daddy, and he is going to do the right thing. This is just a phase, and it will go away just as quickly as it appeared. Mark is too strong a man to let something like this get him down. Why am I worrying over something so minor? He'll never get hooked. I can't even imagine that happening to him *(not my baby's daddy)*. He is a hard worker, good provider, and a good man. I know that he's going to take good care of our baby and me. I won't go lacking for anything.

Afterthoughts: *Sisters out there, please don't fool yourself like I did. This one mistake took me down a long, winding road of ill fate, misconception, and deception filled with lies. Let's face it; it's starting to get a little ridiculous (especially when your man is talking about he's calling in, and you're busting your butt with two jobs).*

November 6, 1985

Dear Diary,

It's been a long time since I have had some quality time to just even sit down and write anything. I miss being able to do so. Since I've started this second job I barely have time to know my own name. I'm surprised my son even knows who I am. I'm gone to work before he goes to school, and when I return at night he is asleep. I still have not told Mark that I'm pregnant. For the time being, I can get away with it. I only weighed 128 pounds in the beginning and I lost weight before I ever gained, so the pregnancy isn't noticeable at all, even though I have been eating like an elephant. Time is ticking away and I need to do something fast. Good night, Mrs. Diary!

November 15, 1985

Dear Diary,

Today, I passed out at work. My supervisor took it upon her dumb self to call my house and leave a message on the answering machine telling my next of kin, Mark and my brother, that I was at the hospital. They suspected that I was pregnant. What happened to me spreading my own good fortune, if any? You cannot imagine how ecstatic Mark was. He came up to the hospital and hugged me, held my hand so gently, looked into my eyes and told me (the biggest, boldest lie ever) with all due sincerity that he was going to take care of me and our baby. Just to know he felt the same way I did about our little bun in the oven made me feel so special and loved. Once again I felt joy. That moment, I will always remember and cherish. We are both so young and both so in love. With every breath in my body, I want the two of us to be the best parents we possibly can. My goal is to purchase one house per year for a total of five years, pay off our debts, and retire early. We will just invest in properties, travel, and spend quality time with our families. We will live the kind of lifestyle others only dream of, but never dare to achieve.

November 19, 1985

Dear Diary,

Only one more week before Thanksgiving—can't wait! I think I want to go and visit my Aunt Stella in Brooklyn for the holidays. Why not? My Aunt Stella has always been the favorite aunt in the family. She's the one to tell it like it is. Everyone loves her, from the youngest to the oldest. I want her to meet the love of my life, and my son would enjoy being around my great aunt. It would give them quality time together to get to know one another. Great plan! Just hope I have some money. It's payday and Mark said they made a mistake on his check and underpaid him by $150.00. He's never lied to me before about his check, so why now? Good night, Mrs. Diary!

Afterthoughts: *Girlfriends out there that are going through this situation, please just turn around and stop in your tracks. Gain control. I believe in you and know you can do it. Don't allow something that should not have been anything from the beginning, especially when you see the handwriting on the wall, girlfriend. Gather your thoughts, pull yourself up by the bootstraps, and bail out. If you don't, you will only be setting yourself up for great disappointments, one after another. You will lose control over your own life, your dreams, and aspirations, and become a codependent for someone else. No, I'm not trying to be negative or unsupportive, just real with a real situation. Live your life to the fullest, not someone else's. If you can love yourself today, you can make the sun shine forever each and every day. For it is the light that shines within you that gives you that internal glow. Don't lose it!*

November 25, 1985

Dear Diary,

Thanksgiving is finally here, and I decided not to go to Brooklyn. Instead, I stayed home and cooked. Some of my friends came over and we really had a nice time. You know how it is on Thanksgiving—all the fellas gather around the tube for a game of football. Of course, the ladies do what they do best—sit around the kitchen table gossiping, or remember your oldest aunt reminding everybody about the time you were five years old and the neighborhood bully chased you home and whipped your tail in front of your door. (Yes, you know what I'm talking about).

Even though deep down inside I was hurting from Mark's actions,

I was determined not to show it. I felt if someone knew, it would make me so weak. For some reason, Mark seems paranoid. He can't keep still and is constantly walking back and forth, in and out. He must think that no one is paying any attention to him. Right now at this very moment, he is embarrassing me (does he know how foolish he is looking and making me look right about now?). Can you imagine the wrenching pain I felt every time in my heart, knowing that this man of so much intelligence and talent is letting himself go down the drain? The saddest part is the fact still remains that he is my baby's father. As little girls growing up, we all at one time or another imagined that some day we would grow up, fall in love, and have the fairy-tale wedding. We imagined that we would marry Prince Charming and live happily ever after.

Afterthoughts: *If at some point in reading this diary you feel as though this is (or is somewhat similar to) your situation, I pray that God will give you the strength and grant you the serenity to prevail and get out of the situation.*

January 1, 1986

Dear Diary,

We made it into another New Year. This is the first time in a month that I have had a chance to even take time out to write. The month of December was really hard. By the time Christmas came, I had my hands filled with working two jobs, not spending any time with my beautiful son. Terry is a very understanding and precious child who never asked me for much. I felt so guilty. Yesterday, while getting dressed for work, I went into my jewelry box to get my watch that I had for ten years (very beautiful, one-of-a-kind gold Seiko with crystal face), and it was gone. When I put my things away, I know exactly where I put them. Only one thought crossed my mind, and I tried with all honesty not to believe the slight possibility that maybe Mark took my watch and sold it. How could he? He knew how sentimental it was to me!

Afterthoughts: Sister, sister, crack addicts do not have any conscience or morals, and will steal from their own momma, daddy, sister, brother, grandma, granddad, and even the preacher if they could. Once your personal things start disappearing, you can rest assured that this is only the beginning stage of bigger things starting to disappear. Crack addicts target small things first because they are less noticeable. Then, as time goes on, they start scheming on how to get away without ever being discovered. When something in your heart told you from the very beginning he did it and that this was wrong, you still didn't listen. You so desperately wanted it not to be true. Sometimes, we are a hindrance to ourselves by not allowing our first intuition to guide us into the light.

January 5, 1986

Dear Diary,

I'm almost three months and counting. So far, I'm not really showing. I went to the doctor today, and she said everything is okay. Believe it or not, Mark went to the doctor with me. He seems to be coming around, and I think he has gotten over that spell where he wants to get high. It would be so nice if this is really a change and not just make believe. Today, we had the chance to listen to our baby's heartbeat. You talk about excitement; Mark was more ecstatic than I was. How could something that was supposed to be so joyous be so sad for me? This little, tiny life inside of me not only has Mark's blood flowing through his veins, but mine, too. I guess I'm still nervous and thinking about the possibilities of *what if*. What if he is still getting high on crack and this is a crack-addicted baby? Do you get the picture now? What was supposed to be one of the happiest times of my life was rapidly becoming more and more of an ongoing nightmare. Why? Because of all Mark's lies and deceit and me refusing to accept the truth for what it was worth even though little signs were slapping me in the face every day. At the moment, I still refuse to acknowledge it. I am too smart to be in a relationship with someone on crack. Good night, Mrs. Diary!

January 8, 1986

Dear Diary,

My son Terry is so thrilled that he may be having another little brother or sister. He helps me out any way he can. For Terry to be only seven right now, he is acting like he is nineteen or twenty. He's trying to open car doors for me, and he makes sure he has my hand when we tackle a flight of stairs (as if he is my little protector). It's so cute to see him make such a fuss over me when he does. From the moment I laid eyes on my first son, I knew that he was a special child, always very well mannered and polite and the joy of our family. My Aunt Theo thought the sun rose and set on Terry, even though she didn't think that when I conceived him at the tender age of seventeen. This really broke her heart. She had so many hopes and dreams for me. To her, I was her baby and she was forever so proud of me until that day I had to be the bearer of bad news, and she found out that I was pregnant by a married man. Vincent was his name, and he was twelve years older than I was and no one had the faintest idea that we were even seeing each other, much less having a baby. Everyone had perceived me to be this little, innocent prima donna. My dad had me so high up on a pedestal, you would have thought I walked on water. All he and my Aunt Theo ever bragged about was me going off to the best fashion merchandising college to be a top designer. Through me, my aunt was going to live her dream. Little did she know how soon this little angel was going to deceive her. In my mind, I knew that once this terrible secret came out it would be time to leave town. Which I did, just two weeks after graduation. You would have thought the world had come to an end. After I had Terry, he became the center of everyone's attention, from the youngest to the oldest. Adorable he was. His way of just simply smiling at you could melt your heart. Terry is the type of child every mother prays and hopes for. He is always willing to please me. I can tell he adores me as his mother and he feels the same from me. Good night, Mrs. Diary!

January 11, 1986

Dear Diary

Good news today! The realtor just called me to let me know that we should be closing on our soon-to-be brand new home within a few more days. I'm so excited, I can't stand myself right now. I can see my future starting to take shape, and I know that from this one good investment, many more good things will come. I'm only twenty-five years old and with the right backing, I can take this one investment and turn it into a dream come true, not only for Mark and me, but for my children. Leaving a heritage full of promise for your offspring is something every parent wishes for. Gotta go!

January 18, 1986

Dear Diary,

It is the day of the closing on our new home. I haven't had a lot of time to save much money, and I don't know exactly how much the closing cost is going to be. Mark says not to worry, that he has everything covered. If nothing else in this world goes right, please let this be the day that something goes right for me. At least, please let the deal for the house go through. All my life, I have dreamed of owning a home just like this. Thanks to John (the realtor)—he encouraged me and believed that I had a chance to purchase this home even when he knew I didn't have any credit or down payment and was pregnant, to say the least. He believed enough in me to devote his time and effort to trying to help me fulfill my dream of home ownership. Really, if the truth were known, it was through faith that I was able to get this house.

As I sat up straight in my chair, waiting to hear the lawyer give us the final fee for the closing cost, in my mind I was wondering if Mark had just one brown penny in his pocket. When I heard the lawyer say that the fee was going to be $500.00, I started praying, please Lord, don't let me get embarrassed today! I felt little tiny pellets of sweat pop out on my forehead. Before I knew it, I had goose bumps all over my body. It took everything in me just to maintain my composure and not jump out of my skin. If only they knew how hard I was praying. That day, I think I made more promises to God than I care to remember or could ever repay (I know I would go broke trying). Finally, the moment had arrived for the cashier's checks to be handed over to the attorney. I turned and looked at Mark: he was so cool, calm, and collected as he reached into his pocket and pulled out a white envelope containing the check. I was so happy I could have jumped on top of that table and just danced. In my mind, I was thinking finally we made it! The deal is sealed and now we are proud homeowners. It felt so good. That day was the beginning for all the other good things to follow. My mortgage was going to be $700.00 per month. To me that was a piece of cake, especially since it would be the three of us splitting the payment. My idea was since this was a three-family house, my tenants on the first floor would pay $500.00 per month, and I would rent the third floor to three boarders, which all together would equal up to about $1100.00 per month. Why not take the money from the rent we collected each month and put it in the bank and pay the mortgage out of our pocket? This way, in ten months, we would have enough money saved to put down on another house. My goal was to purchase a house every year for five years straight as investment properties, and by the time I reach thirty years old, we would be almost on easy street. Chad thought it was a great idea—so did Mark. We all vowed that this was the plan we were going to stick with. After leaving the attorney's office—with papers in hand, of course—we could not wait to get home to all the naysayers who said it couldn't be done for one reason or another. Some of their reasons were that I was too young, my dreams were too far-fetched, and I couldn't afford to buy a house. Boy, was I going to show them a thing or two! Of course, you know the first stop I had to make on my way home was to stop by the store to buy the biggest bottle of champagne I could afford to celebrate my new accomplishment. I couldn't wait to get on the phone so I could call all the naysayers to say it was a done deal, and invite them over so I could smile in their faces and just gloat. I had a ball that day.

Just the fact that I had made some improvement in my life means the world to me. I wish my dad could have been here to share this special moment with me. I miss him so much. My dad was always my inspiration and made me feel as though there was nothing in life so great I couldn't accomplish it. Before his untimely death, he made plans for us to purchase a home together, but he passed away a year before I returned to the States to settle down.

January 24, 1986

Dear Mrs. Diary,

I just came home from a long day's work; I'm so tired and I don't know how long I can last working two jobs. My body is so tired; instead of gaining weight, I think I'm losing it. My son has been so patient, waiting for me every night just for a hug and a kiss. He is such a sweet child. I want to give him the world, just like any other decent parent. Tomorrow is Mark's payday and so far, so good, as they say. I know he should have at least $250.00 to give me toward the bills. Everything is looking so bright. We can have the world at our feet. Right now, I feel as though there is nothing that we can't tackle together. Chad is constantly bringing me nice things from work (spoiling me rotten). Ever since we were kids, he has always taken care of me as if I was his little girl. You would have thought he was my father, even though he was only three years older than I am. He always made sure, when we were younger, that I had the best. The money Chad made was spent on me, buying me whatever toys I wanted. I remember the time when he saved all of his money so he could buy me an oil paint set, just because I said I wanted to be an artist. I really don't think he even knew how expensive it was going to be. Price never bothered him. At that time, I must have been about nine or ten years old. There was nothing that was too good for me. Yesterday, he brought me an Oriental hand-carved, wooden, mahogany-painted jewelry box. The kind you see in all those expensive catalogs like Spiegel's. This jewelry box must stand at least two feet. Just looking at it, I knew I couldn't have afforded to buy it for myself. It is so beautiful and unique, and I can't wait until my girlfriend, Charlotte, comes over so I can show it to her. I am so proud of this jewelry box. As I lie here across the bed, all I can think about is the beautiful jewelry my man is going to buy me so I can fill it. It has all kinds of neat compartments in it, a place to hang my chains, a ring drawer, and a bracelet holder. You name it, this jewelry box has it. It even plays beautiful music. Every day I come home, I will be looking forward to unwinding to the beautiful, serene sounds of the music coming from my new toy. Well, good night Mrs. Diary, hope to write more tomorrow!

January 25, 1986

Dear Diary,

Today was beautiful. I got a raise at my job and Mark came home and gave me the bill money just like he promised. Guess what? He is taking me on a shopping spree to buy some maternity clothes—he says it's about time for me to start looking like I'm the expectant mother of his child. I'm overwhelmed and flattered at the thought that he cares so much. Girl, I'm ready for a brand new look. Tomorrow, when I go to work, my co-workers are not even going to know who I am. For every outfit, I want a pair of shoes to match. Deep down inside I just know this baby is going to be a girl; at least, I pray it is. It would be nice to see a little me running around. I'm so happy—it's been such a long time since I have felt this way. I never knew what joy felt like until now. The sun is finally shining on me. What a good feeling. Nothing can stop me now. Have you ever felt like dancing on clouds? Well, just imagine, that's exactly how I feel right about now.

February 5, 1986

Dear Diary,

I just checked the mailbox, and I'm so happy now. It's tax time and I'm ready to file. Two days ago, I went to a car lot and spotted this 1982, tan, sandalwood color Audi 5000 that I wanted. The Audi has always been my dream car, ever since my tour of duty over in Germany when I was in the Army. I always promised myself that one day this was going to be my car. When I saw the car, something inside me was saying, "You have to have this. This is you! You have waited for this car for a very long time." The salesman walked outside with me to look at the car. I had no idea that he had the keys and was going to offer me a test drive. When he did, I was so nervous. It made me feel like a kid all over again. Do you remember what it felt like when you were a kid and your parents made you go to bed to get ready for Santa Claus? That's just how I felt. As the salesman opened the door and described the interior of the car and the features, the only thing I could picture in my mind was me in that car. It had dark brown, soft leather seats that swiveled, and racquet-pinion steering, and the sound system was out of this world. I was so busy daydreaming about the car that I never heard the man say, "This could be yours. How much do you have to put down on a car?" Shocked by his question, I was at a loss for words. It all happened so suddenly. Here I was, three months, almost four months pregnant, talking about buying a car—not just any car, but the car of my dreams. Never did it cross my mind that I had just purchased a house. Maybe I didn't give it any thought because among the three of us, meaning Mark, my brother, and myself, it would not be a problem if I wanted this new-found toy. Why not? I deserved it. After taking the car for a test spin around the block, in my heart, I knew that this car was meant just for me and me only. I had to have it. Oh, by the way, I forgot to tell you that it has a sunroof, too. When I drive this little baby down the block, all eyes are going to be on me. Mark has no idea how bad I want this car, and when I tell him I test-drove it, he is going to think I have lost my mind. Well, I guess he is in for a big surprise! Gotta have it. Good night, Mrs. Diary!

February 8, 1986

Dear Diary,

I told Mark about the car and that I test-drove it. He wants to go to see it, and speak with the salesman so he can find out how much money we need to put down on it and to see what it's going to take for me to get approved for a loan. I explained to Mark that I wanted this car more than anything else I have ever wanted, and that I wanted it in my name so I could establish more credit. He agreed. Oh boy! Was that a good feeling. My man backing me up and being everything any woman could want in a man. Only four more weeks and my taxes should be back. Every day I'm getting more and more excited about getting this dream car. The salesman finally gave me the information I needed so we could make a sound decision. He said considering that Mark makes more money than I do, he would have to be the co-signer. That was okay with me as long as I could have that smooth, slick, sporty-looking ride. Nothing else seems to matter. Good night, Mrs. Diary.

February 14, 1986

Dear Diary,

It's Valentine's Day, and my son greeted me at the door with all types of little sweet cards he made in school. Girlfriend, there should be a law against how much stuff kids can make and bring home. He had bags and bags of stuff he made for me. Terry even drew me a picture of a watermelon and told me that this is what I would look like in a few more months. We both had a good laugh at that one. Terry, sometimes, can be a little clown when he wants to. But he is so lovable and sweet; you can't help but adore him. Besides, who wouldn't? It's almost 8:00; maybe Mark had to work late. When he comes home, I know he is going to have a special surprise for me, and I can't wait, being that this will be our first Valentine's Day together. Every time I hear a door open or I hear someone coming up the stairs, I assume that it is him. Well, I guess I'll play my musical jewelry box and light a few candles so when he does come home and walks through that door, he will know it is all about him. My brother bought me a bunch of flowers, and not one but two boxes of candy. That was awfully sweet of him. He is just spoiling me rotten. Tell me you wouldn't love it? I'm wondering if I should tell him about my wish to purchase the car. Maybe I won't. I'll just wait until he sees me in it after I drive it off the car lot. Now, that would be a real shocker!

February 15, 1986

Dear Diary,

I'm so angry, hurt, and disappointed, to say the least. Mark didn't come home last night, and I have no idea where he could be. I was so upset and worried at work, I had one of my girlfriends bring me home early. My supervisor was so concerned—she knows that I'm pregnant and always tries to make sure that I'm okay. Now, my assistant supervisor, on the other hand, could care less. Her main concern is if the work is done and did you do some extra work before you left for the next day. Like, for instance, make sure all the coffee cups you didn't leave dirty are clean before you go home. You know she had some nerve. Slavery was over a long time ago. Besides, I was hired as an inventory account specialist, not the maid or butler. She made sure every day that those coffee cups were cleaned, if nothing else got done. She sort of reminded you of Sergeant Carter on *Gomer Pyle*. Her main thrill was to brown-nose up to the big bosses every day, as if they really cared about who did what. They were too busy arguing at each other in front of the whole office and could care less about anything she thought was important. Sometimes, it was like a comedy show just to go to work. If you really wanted a good laugh, wait until 10:00 a.m. and for sure, you knew it was time to pull out the peanuts and popcorn—the show was about to start. My two bosses hated each other but had been in business together for twelve years. One was nice and mellow, the other a very shrewd businessman who could not take no for an answer. It is all just too funny to think about at times.

The other day, one of the bosses walked into the other's office without knocking. You would have thought someone called the police. They argued so loud I thought the roof would come off the building. Everyone in the office stopped what they were doing and just stared at the door, waiting to see who would get thrown out first, Mr. Evans or Mr. Jowsky (my favorite). Nothing he did seemed wrong to me. He was the one who told my assistant supervisor to stop harassing us about cleaning those awful and filthy coffee cups which we didn't dirty in the first place, and that everyone should be responsible for their own. From that day on, he became the hero who saved us from the wicked witch of the East. Mr. Jowsky was a very soft-spoken, mellow man with a genuine heart who cared about his employees and valued their opinions. Mr. Evans, on the other hand, had no communication skills and did not trust an employee any farther than he could see them. How they became partners is a mystery to me. And if you knew them like I did, you would say the same thing. Together they made lots of money, and to me, that was the only thing they had in common.

It's about 11:00 a.m. and almost time for lunch, and I still haven't seen or heard from Mark. Where could he be? He has to know that I'm worried sick about him. If nothing else, he could be considerate enough to call my job to say that he is okay. I'm almost at the point of calling the police and checking all the hospitals to see if he is dead or alive. At this point, I don't know what to do. Deep down inside, I feel that he is okay, but I just want to hear his voice. "Dear Lord, I know that I'm mad and furious at this moment, but please let him be okay. After all, Mark is the father of my seed and I need him so badly in my life. I can't imagine life without him." As the saying goes, "No news is good news." At this time in my mind, I just want some peace. This is torture; not knowing the fate of your mate can kill you. In the back of my mind, I kept thinking, *what if he is still getting high*. But, it occurred to me that he had never stayed out all night long, and what high was worth it? No, it had to be something else. Nothing could stop this man from being with his woman and unborn child, especially not any drug. You must be crazy! What drug could be so important, or should I say *potent,* to take the place of love, assurance, and comfort?

Afterthoughts: *Someone should have smacked me upside my head with a wake-up stick and said, "Hello—is your brain computing or are you stuck on stupid?" When you are in love, nothing else seems to matter. You become sidetracked and only think one way. You want to believe that everything is all right and everyone is rooting for you when, in reality, you know that is not the way it is. You are in just plain old denial. So why not just face it?*

February 16, 1986

Dear Diary,

Here it is, two days later, and Mark still hasn't come home. There is no way I can go to work today and function like a normal human being. Now I'm really getting worried. My girlfriend, Charlotte, is the only one I feel that I can trust to tell about my situation. At least I know she will be understanding and not so judgmental. After calling her at work, she assured me that she would come by when she gets off. That would be some relief. At least I will have someone to hear me out (there's so much pain bottled up inside of me). It's even worse when you don't have anyone you feel you can trust to talk to without feeling like a complete idiot. Charlotte and I have been best friends for at least eight years or more. We cherish each other's friendship. For short, we always called her by her nickname, She-She. How she got that name still amazes me. She always presented herself as a very witty, charismatic, and just funny person, always joking and being the life of any party. If there is a story to be told, she would be the one to tell it. I couldn't wait for her to get off from work. The time could not go by fast enough until she would arrive. If nothing else, I knew that she could put a smile on my face, no matter what the situation. She just had that type of personality about herself. No matter how much rain there was in your life, she could make the sun shine. Everyone who knew her admired her for her charisma.

As the time ticked away, here it's almost 4:00 p.m. and just look at what the cat drug in. My, my, my, if it isn't Mr. Mark, wearing the same clothes he had on two days ago, looking as if he hasn't had any sleep in about a week. His eyes were all bloodshot and dilated, and his hair looked like it was just matted on his head like a Brillo pad. It was hard for me to even think that this was the man I fell head over heels in love with, and now just look at him. If I didn't know any better, I would have thought he was a homeless person. That's just how rough he looked. As I stood at the top of the stairs, just watching him climb those steps with this pitiful look on his face, I could not help but wonder what line he was going to use on me now—or what lie, I should say. By this time, I'm fuming. It didn't matter what he had to say in defense for himself. I was angry, pregnant, furious, hurt, and if you want to know the truth about it, just plain ole tired of being sick and tired. You know the feeling, as I'm sure you too have been there (you know who you are). *Must I call names?* As Mark reached the top of the stairs with his head hanging down, he couldn't even look me in my face. Even though I was feeling very angry, it was a relief just to know that he was alive and okay, at least. After all, this is my baby's daddy.

The look of disgust had to be all over my face, and he knew it. Each time I tried to open my mouth to speak, nothing came out. I was speechless. That's just how angry I was. My Aunt Theo used to tell me I was always like that when I was a little girl—get mad and not talk. I guess I felt as though that was my way of punishing the other person. Most of the time this worked. When I could finally get a word out, I asked Mark where he had been, since I had already tried patiently to wait for him to respond, to no avail, and there was no confession on his own. The only thing he could say, in a muffled voice, was that he was tired and needed to go to sleep. Nothing about, "Well, I was at a friend's, we partied too late, and I thought maybe you would be upset if I told you the truth." All he wants to do is go to sleep. I knew he had a problem for real. What happened to, "I'm going to work?" He probably forgot he had a job.

This is a real nightmare (*getting worse and worse by the minute*) and no one knows it better than me. Does he care, or is he just plain brain-dead about now? It has often been said that certain drugs can kill your brain cells. Why is it so hard to accept the fact that things aren't getting any better? Even a blind person could see this. But, I am too stubborn and ignorant to the fact that instead of it getting better it could get much, much worse. A little voice inside of me whispered *better get out now instead of later*. I'm at the point of just wanting out of this relationship—pregnancy, and just everything. But where will I go and who will I tell what is going on? Right now, I feel like a complete fool. How could I have been so blind to fall into a trap like this? As each moment ticks on, I'm beginning to wonder if I even want to be pregnant by this man. This was a mistake.

Afterthoughts: *Only if I had listened, I would have been all the bet-*
ter for it. If I can just reach out and touch one person and keep
them from going through what I did, it would all be worth it.

February 20, 1986

Dear Diary,

The days are going by so fast that I can hardly keep up. Before you
know it, it'll be time for us to pay our first mortgage. You know I'm
wondering if the money will be there. But, I guess that's something I
shouldn't really concern myself with now. Mark has sense, and I
know he isn't stupid enough to spend our mortgage money on
crack. Today was the first time I felt the baby move; it felt so strange
to know I had this little life inside me that I began to yearn for so
badly.

Afterthoughts: *Sister, sister, if you're thinking he won't spend your*
mortgage money, please think again. He will spend your money,
your momma's money, and anyone else's he can get his hands on.

February 24, 1986

Dear Diary,

Terry is at my every beck and call. Always right there, making sure
everything is okay with his mommy. I could not have been blessed
with a sweeter child. So far, I've managed to keep it a secret about
what has happened with Mark staying out. I'm so happy that my
brother is clueless. If he finds out, it will be like World War II on East
18th Street. I dare not tell anyone. It's killing me, keeping all this bottled up inside. But I have to. There is no one, and I mean no one, I
even want to tell—not even my best girlfriend, Charlotte, at this
point. "Dear Lord, please hear my prayer and let my baby be safe
from all this madness. It has to get better before it gets worse."

Before I returned home from Germany, I had always heard about
crack, but that was something that happened to other people and

would never happen to me. I was just too cool for that. The thought never crossed my mind. In reality, there were doctors, lawyers, politicians, policeman, and mailmen, even schoolteachers, getting high on this vicious, notorious drug. It excluded no one, not even grandma. It had no remorse, shame, or guilt and was timeless, just like a venomous snake waiting to strike at any moment so it could destroy all of your hopes and dreams, and even your soul. Just as I said, no one was excluded once the poison of crack seeped in, not even the preacher up in the pulpit on Sunday morning blaring out the sermon, seemingly so filled with the Holy Ghost.

Maybe if Mark and I go to counseling and get some help before it is too late, it will be okay. Right now, I don't know if it would matter to him. His moods are changing by the minute. One day he is okay, and at other times, he is very argumentative and demanding. Paydays have become a nightmare. When he comes home and gives me the money to pay bills, within fifteen minutes he is right back asking me to give it back to him to buy some foolishness such as this guy down the street is selling a VCR for $20.00 (I know we need one, don't want to pass up a good deal). At first I believed him and then, about ten minutes later, he would return without the merchandise and ask me for even more money this time. Like now, it's $50.00, and he is telling me the guy changed his mind; he wants more, as he has other people waiting to pay him a higher price than what he originally offered. Now he is playing on my intelligence and it works. From this point on, it's beginning to progress. As long as he continues to work and isn't blowing any real money, I'm okay. What the heck, it was only $70.00, and Mark deserves it; after all, he worked hard for this money. I have food in my house, clothes on my back, and a roof over my head. It won't be long before he realizes what he is doing.

He is a very, very clever man. So clever, in fact, he had already stolen my gold Seiko crystal-face, quartz watch and sold it to the lady down the street. How do I know this for a fact? Just a few days ago, I was coming home from the grocery store when I heard someone calling my name. As I turned around to look, it was Rosie. She was a very nice lady, or at least she appeared to be. I had only met her once before, through Mark. She was an older lady, in her mid-fifties, and always kept her hair very neat and well groomed, if I must say. Looking at her from a distance, she reminded me of my Aunt Theo. As I walked toward Rosie to see what she wanted, she signaled for me to come upstairs to the boarding house where she lived. Being pregnant, it took me just a little bit longer to move about and climb all those stairs. By the time I got to the top step, she greeted me with a smile and asked how far along I was. I told her I was four months and some weeks; she just chuckled as she laid her hand on my small, round belly. We talked for a moment or two before she invited me into her room. In my mind, I was starting to wonder what she wanted. After taking a deep pause, she looked at me with this mysterious puzzled look on her face; by the time she was about to speak, we heard a soft knock at the door. It was her neighbor from upstairs, coming to show off her new watch that she had just bought. When I took one look at that watch, it sent my blood boiling. It took everything in me to stay calm at this point. Tears welled up in my eyes, and I just couldn't contain myself any longer. I asked the woman where she purchased this beautiful, one-of-a-kind, original she was sporting. In reality, I really just wanted to rip it off her arm; it wasn't hers, it was mine. Deep down inside, no one could tell me any different. You know when something belongs to you, don't you? This woman really started to annoy me as she raved on and on about what a good bargain she had gotten, and that she had only paid $20.00 for it. I had that watch for about ten years, and it still looked brand new. At the time I purchased it, I remember it being worth $300.00. Now she gets to sport it for a measly $20.00, something that I worked so hard for and paid for with my hard-earned money. This was not happening.

Finally, I could not take it anymore. I asked her if she would take off the watch and look at the initials on the back. At first, I thought she would be perturbed by such a gesture, but she didn't say a word and removed the watch from her tiny wrist, turned it over, and looked at the initials on the back. I explained to her that this was my watch and asked her politely who sold it to her. She told me a tall, light-skinned fellow with very nice hair and, as a matter of fact, she said he was so handsome and such a gentlemen she couldn't forget a face like his. My teeth started gritting; I had to hold my tongue for fear of what might come out of my mouth. Sometimes it pays to think before you speak; in this case, it did. She was so nice about the whole situation and told me she only wanted the money she had spent for it. I felt that was only fair—no argument, just sisters sticking together and working it out. Turning a bad situation into something that could be resolved felt great. That day I was so grateful that I was able to get my watch back. Today was a pretty good day, after all. Good night, Mrs. Diary!

February 26, 1986

Dear Diary,

It's another day, and I have yet to tell Mark that I bought my watch back. I guess I'm too afraid if he knows, he might steal it again, and the next time I may not be so fortunate. It's really a shame to live like this. In my mind, I'm wondering what else I may be missing and too afraid to start looking around. The truth hurts, and who knows better than me? Deep in my heart, I can only wonder how long this can go on. Just sitting here, thinking about all the good times we used to have before crack came into my life—seems like it was so long ago. Will we ever get beyond this, and if so, when? At this point, I know we both need counseling. The last time I mentioned this to Mark, he told me he was not an addict and he could quit on his own. Everyone, regardless of age, color, or race, has the power within to change for the better. It has to be up to the individual to decide and then take action. *No action, no change.* Each day, I'm becoming more and more insecure and uncomfortable around my man for fear of the unknown. His actions and moods change from one moment to the next.

Afterthoughts: We as women have to empower ourselves with the awesome power of a greater being other than ourselves, and that is through our Creator which is God. Just remember, through Him all things are possible.

Afterthoughts: Remember this, if nothing else, FEAR will kill you. It is the fear that is within you that will take you to your very grave.

For it was through fear that I stayed in an abusive relationship with this man, believing and hoping that he would change, only to discover that as time went on, he only got worse. He became paranoid about any and everything and believed that everyone was watching and checking him out. Insecurity became his name, and jealousy his game. Before long, he started accusing me of seeing every man he thought wanted me. His imagination got more and more vivid each day. My job became my sanctuary away from this man, who had become a Beast Master. The more I tried to deal with his mood swings and give in to his abusive ways, the less I realized he was molding and shaping me for what he wanted out of his spouse, and that was someone intimidated enough to keep his little dark secret. Mark felt he could demand what he wanted from me because he knew how much I feared him. After all, how much could I do? I was almost five months pregnant and counting. If Mark said boo, I would jump out of my skin, and a window, if I was near it. I remember times when he was so high on crack it seemed as though horns were sticking out of his head. That gleam of urgency that I knew I would see in his eyes to fulfill that desire inside of him to get high gave off such a negative aura, you could feel it before he would even turn his key in the door. One payday, I remember trying to leave the house before he got home just so I wouldn't have to deal with the same stupid routine of him giving me money and then taking it back. The time had come when I could feel my stomach churning and chill bumps coming all over my body at the thought of what he would fuss and argue about that day. It was nothing for him to come home after a long days' work and strike up an argument for nothing, just because it was payday. Girlfriend, I hated it.

February 28, 1986

Dear Diary,

Finally the end of the month is here. Tomorrow, I will be collecting the rent money so I can pay our first mortgage. In my mind, I'm wondering why I am getting so excited. I guess it's the idea of feeling like this house is really ours and knowing that I'm taking care of my responsibility and obligation. The feeling of homeownership is one that should be taken with much pride, especially at the age of twenty-five.

My father would have been so proud of me. When he was alive, we did so much together, especially when I was pregnant with my first son. At first, he was disappointed to learn that I was pregnant at such an early age, but after he got over the initial shock, he became a girl's best friend. To see the two of us together with my little belly poked out was to see the picture of true happiness. Every day my dad came home from work, he would bring his baby girl a watermelon, sometimes two. My stepmom, Clara, would be so tickled and always asked the same question only to get the same response, "Did you bring me one today? You know I like watermelons, too," she would say with a chuckle. She was always such a gregarious person, willing to please you any way she could. Being around her and my stepsister, Joyce, was such a joy. Joyce was three years older than me and the only child. She acted liked she was my big sister, ordering me around, sending me to the store in 100-degree weather, just to get her an RC soda and some penny cookies (too cheap to buy a big bag, scared she might be losing out on one cookie) when she was pregnant. (One year before me.) I was thrilled to have a big sister; whatever she asked was never too much. I was thrilled just to see the glow on her face when she was pleased and also to know that whatever secret I would confide in her would be safe and sound. The bond we had together was so strong and special that nothing could come between us—I mean nothing! Joyce had the looks that any model would die for. Her shiny, jet black, long, curly hair and olive skin made her the center of attraction wherever she went. Men stared at her natural beauty, and even though she was pregnant and showing, it didn't stop men from approaching her and asking for her phone number and a chance to take her out on the town. Some men would even offer her money. The day I remembered the most was the day she asked me to walk downtown with her. I thought she was going to meet one of her men friends, but she told me she was going to treat me to pizza and that we were going to shop for the baby. Boy, I was so excited that day; I could not wait. In my mind, all I could think about was how good that greasy, juicy, cheesy pizza was going to be from Sal's Pizzeria.

As we turned the corner to Sal's, my mouth started watering. This Pizzeria had the best pizza in town. Everyone ate there. The smile on Joyce's face told me that her mouth was watering, too. She was trying so hard to be so cool, even though she knew before we stepped one foot inside this restaurant she didn't have a dime in her pocket. Little did I know, and in time I would soon find out. Especially after we both ate two large slices of pizza and drank a large tea and she started looking at me with those big brown eyes, like she saw the boogeyman. Naïve little me had no idea this girl, better known as my big sister, had pulled one over not only on the pizza parlor, but on me her little sister. She was supposed to be my protector, but I was soon about to discover she was penniless, and we both were getting ready to get thrown out and embarrassed by the owner after he repeatedly asked for the money and her reply was, "Oh, guess what? I must have lost my wallet on the way down here—my sister will pay you." Stunned at her reply, it sent shock waves through my body as she looked into the face of the owner with those big, sad puppy dog eyes, trying to appear so innocent. This girl was just plain full of it, if you asked me. Of course, you know the rest, or should I tell you? Needless to say, the owner threatened to call the cops and demanded that we pay. She apologized repeatedly, but it fell on deaf ears, for the owner had no mercy.

"Pregnant or not, you will be going to jail today," he replied. "Stealing is a crime," (even though she had already eaten up the evidence).

Her reply to him was, "Prove it. I dare you. Who's going to believe you?" she asked. "I'm six months pregnant—my baby was hungry, so I fed it," was her response. "Now if you will leave us alone, my sister and I will leave on our own." Believe me, she had some nerve and was not even big as a toothpick, to say the least. "The pizza wasn't that good anyway," she told the owner. This man turned beet red as he ran to the back and got the broom to chase us off. You should have seen the two of us scurrying to get out of there. Talk about embarrassing—*that* was embarrassing. Thinking back now, I don't know what was the funniest part—watching her tell this lie or wobbling down the street like a duck, trying to get away. Those were the days!

Even then, Joyce was always the one to encourage me to strive for greatness and excel at whatever I did. To her, nothing was too great for me to achieve. "Nothing ventured, nothing gained," she would say. "Life is a gamble."

When my second son (Boo) was critically ill and in the hospital, she gave her love and support every step of the way. At my baby boy's funeral she was my guardian angel, displaying her affection and comforting me any way she could. Some things you never forget, no matter whether good or bad.

The impact she had on my life during those early years helped prepare me to become the woman I am today. I could not relish the thought of ever telling her what I was now experiencing in my relationship. No one must ever know. This is one secret that I'll just take to the grave with me. How could I expect her to understand—her baby sister, the one she was starting to look up to, had a man strung out on crack cocaine. There were times when I would overhear her bragging to her friends about me and how I served in the military for three years and how I traveled, and how I did this and how I did that. You would have thought I was a millionaire, just to hear her talk about me. Joyce would always rave about the great potential she felt I possessed. Her conviction about it was so strong that I started to believe it. The more she hyped me up, the more faith I gained. Nothing was impossible and the sky was the limit. "Someday I see you accomplishing great things—I know you're going to make it big one day," she would often say. When I would ask her why she felt so strongly about it, her reply would be, "I just know." Well, gotta go!

March 1, 1986

Dear Diary,

Well, I guess today is the big day I have been waiting for. Now, on the other hand, I don't believe my new tenants are going to share my sentiments. Maybe I should wait until the fifth day of the month before I start trying to play Mrs. Landlord. This house is so huge—it's everything I have ever dreamed of. It's a three-family home and in a nice neighborhood. When the realtor first showed it to me, I knew that this was the one for me. The dark, shiny wooden floors and the bay windows stood out from everything else. In my mind, I was thinking that if I can't get this house, I don't want anything; that's just how bad I wanted it. My kitchen was nice and big. The floors were tile, of course, but I could live with that; after all, everything else was just the way I wanted. It had three bedrooms on the second floor, and the staircase was so dramatic, like a picture in a magazine. The winding mesmerized you from the top to the bottom. Also very steep, to say the least.

Even though this was an older house, it had a very warm and inviting spirit that seemed to reach out and take you by the hands as if to say "Please come in and embrace my charm." Every day, I daydreamed about furnishing it from top to bottom. This task would be something that would take time and money, something I had neither of at the moment.

Soon I would have to start getting prepared for my unborn child. Only four more months and this little bundle of joy inside of me would be ready to push his or her way into this world. Sounds like Mark running up the stairs. It is his payday, but this time he was sober and so overjoyed to see me. Now I'm beginning to wonder why he's being so nice. Has he sold something else of mine and I just don't know it yet? Or should I start looking around now to see if I can spot something missing? Whatever it is, he sure has piqued my curiosity. He's being too, too nice. It's unbelievable, but it feels so good not to see him angry and upset, especially on his payday. In my heart, I'm hoping that this will last and maybe, just maybe, we might have an opportunity to go out to dinner or do something fun for a change. That would be nice. It's been weeks on end, and this is such a sudden change in him. I want to believe that this is going to last forever. Terry is beckoning me to go to the store with him; he has a field trip tomorrow and I promised him I would buy him some goodies. Good night, Mrs. Diary.

March 2, 1986

Dear Diary,

Today is such a sad day. I have spent half of the day in a daze. Last night, after taking Terry to the store, I went back home and got ready for bed. About 3:30 this morning I woke up from a really bad dream. I had to pinch myself just to see if I was still alive. This dream was so vivid and real. It was like I was watching a movie, only to discover that a few hours later it would be for real. It was so weird the way the dream started out just like *déjà vu*. In this dream, a man appeared. I couldn't recognize who he was but he signaled for me to get up and go to the closet. As I approached the closet, he pointed toward my pocketbook and told me to open it and I did. My money was gone. Now mind you, this was in the dream. This dream was so real, I immediately woke up out of a deep sleep and ran to the closet, only to discover that this dream was for real and my money was in fact actually gone—all except my payroll check. I'll never forget that feeling of how my heart skipped a beat and my whole body shook all over. All the hard-earned money I had was for the mortgage. The only thing I could think to do was tear everything apart and search the closet floors in hopes that maybe it fell out onto the floor.

Not once did it ever cross my mind to wonder where Mark was. Here it was 3:30 in the morning, and he was nowhere to be found. Too many other things were on my mind that took precedence over where he could be. Right now, I could care less where he was. The only thing on my mind was where could this money be, and where was I going to get another $700.00 to pay my mortgage? Who was I going to tell that I had lost this money? How could I have been so careless? Mark is going to have a fit when he finds out. He may blow a little money to get high, but not money like this. Boy, was I in for a big surprise. For the rest of the morning, after tearing everything apart, checking every dresser drawer and looking under the mattress and other places that I knew I didn't put this money, I was finally exhausted, frustrated, and, to say the least, disgusted with myself. Where could this money be?

The last time I remembered seeing it was when I put my purse in the closet and went to the store with Terry and Mark to get snacks for

Terry's field trip. Now it's all coming back to me. When I went to the store, Mark opened the door for me and told me he had something to do real quick and would be right back, to go ahead and get what I wanted and he would pay for it. By the time I left the store, I had totally forgotten all about the fact that he had even left. My mind was on ordering Chinese food and going over Terry's homework before it got too late. Girlfriend, to be honest, that was the very last time I remember seeing my money and that's the truth, but I know Mark didn't take it. Hopefully, it will turn up somewhere in my room. Maybe I dropped it when I went to get some money to take Terry to the store and it's just lying around on the floor of my closet, probably right up under my nose. I'll find it when it's daylight. The thought never occurred to me that hey, it's 3:30 in the morning—your money is gone and so is your man. Now, is that a coincidence or what?

By this time, it seems as though reality would have set in, but I was too, too busy thinking of excuses why it couldn't be what was so desperately true, and that is, I had been robbed by the man that was sleeping in my bed. The very same man that supposedly loves me so much and is the father of our child. God, please give me the strength and serenity to go on. How much longer can I go on like this? All along I knew the truth and refused to believe it, making myself suffer needlessly like so many other women do every day. After realizing what had really happened to my money, I couldn't do anything but sit at the kitchen table and cry myself to sleep. The pain that ached in my body, no one must ever know. My heart is full, and my pride too strong to ever admit that I needed help and a way out of this terrible, terrible, non-ending, vicious relationship that would seemingly destroy me.

By the time I woke up, it was already 7:30 in the morning and my tenant from upstairs was knocking on the door. When I answered it, I had no idea how bad I looked. From the way my tenant Audra looked at me, I could tell that she knew something was wrong. Audra was about five feet, four inches tall and weighed about 100 pounds soaking wet. She had just moved to New Jersey from California to reconcile her marriage and had landed a good job with the telephone company. From the first day we met, we became very good friends and discovered that we both had so much in common. She enjoyed shopping and cooking, just like I did. Her children were between the ages of seven and eight years old (two beautiful girls) and were always so courteous and polite. We both enjoyed spending quality time with our families and doing fun things together every chance we could.

This particular morning when she came through that door and saw the look of hurt in my eyes and despair on my face, I could no longer hold what I felt inside. It was time to tell somebody what was going on, and today it was going to be her. She was always the type to mind her own business, very shy and timid. She was never the one to get into anyone else's business. I admired her for that. Audra would never cross that boundary to inquire, but this day I know I looked a little too rough for her not to be just the slightest bit curious as to what was going on. Her approach to me was to ask if everything was okay and if there was anything she could do for me. Shocked by her inquiry, I nodded my head to respond, too drained to say one word and embarrassed at what she might say after I exploded and told her everything. Fear gripped me, wondering if I should open up what would soon be a can of worms. Words flew out of my mouth so fast as if they were begging and pleading to come out.

It was a relief to know that I finally had someone I could talk to. Not just anybody, but to a friend, someone who shared my common interest. You see, her husband was a crack addict, too; little did I know it until that first day we started talking. Everything that looks good isn't always what it appears to be, and this was also her situation. When she pulled down her shirt and showed me the bruise marks on her body from being beaten by her husband, a man everyone thought the world of, I was stunned and my heart cried out for her. This woman, my friend, who smiled every day and pretended to be so happy, was just as miserable as I was, if not more. Here I was, going through a crisis, only to realize that I wasn't the only one. That day, we found strength in each other as we cried and embraced one another, each trying to convince the other that everything would be all right. She assured me that my mortgage would be paid on time if she had to work overtime to get the money so my brother would not find out what had happened, and so we would have a place to live. Before I knew it, she pulled out the pots and pans and started fixing breakfast, telling me I needed something to eat.

"You have got to get yourself together not only for you, but for Terry and that little life growing inside of you. No one is going to see you go without anything if I have anything to do with it," she said. "You're my heart and you were always here for me when no one else was. Even though you never knew the emotional and physical abuse I was going through, I love you and don't forget it. Oh, by the way, after we finish breakfast, get dressed—we're going downtown. It's time for a new hairdo, shoes, outfit, you name it—it's my treat," she told me.

This girl really knew how to pick a sister like me up out of the dumps, even in her own time of despair. Her willingness to help a sister out was just unbelievable, especially since we had only really known each other for such a short period of time. To be precise, only five months. We met around the same time I found out that I was pregnant. As we sat and ate breakfast, I felt so grateful that God had placed an angel like her in my life. Friends like her are hard to come by and should be cherished like rare jewels, because to me that's what she was.

After we finished breakfast, she washed the dishes and told me to go get dressed and be prepared to have nothing but fun and more fun. Of course, I rushed to get ready, as shopping was a hobby for me, and every opportunity that presented itself, I was right there waiting to take it. We both agreed to be ready around 10:00 o'clock so we could get to the salon early and spend the rest of the day shopping.

By the time we both were ready it was around 11:00 o'clock; nevertheless, the beat still went on. It felt good to be able to confide in someone that was much more than a confidante but a true-blue friend. I wouldn't have traded her for anything in the world. My hair looked so beautiful after it had been relaxed and cut into a nice style that suited my face. I looked like a totally different person, much different than that bloodshot-eyed woman she had seen earlier that morning.

After getting our hair adorned, it was off to the nearest boutique for the latest fashions. By this time, I'm thrilled. My little belly is finally starting to show, but not enough for me not to be able to find anything nice. Le Petite Fashions, downtown, had the perfect styles, and they came in many sizes. Their garments were soft and felt so good on your skin. The one I finally decided on was a very classy black scoop-neck dress with a slit in the back with an attached chiffon scarf. Just looking at this dress before I dared try it on made me feel like a million bucks. I could imagine myself out for an evening of fun at one of the most elegant spots in New York City, having the time of my life, and for once, kicking up my heels and letting my hair down, the little bit I do have. Not having to worrying about someone else's problems, just thinking about me and living and enjoying myself. For the moment, this is starting to feel good, and oh, by the way, I haven't even picked out my shoes yet. Now I know I'm really going to feel like I'm on cloud nine.

The shoe store was about four blocks down the street and on a Saturday, in the evening, downtown Paterson is packed as usual. It was almost like the people came out of the woodwork, and you were wondering how there could be so many people in this tiny town. Jones Shoes carried the best selection of designer name brands. This day I didn't care about the price; I only wanted to be treated and to feel special. Something I hadn't felt in a long time. Peering at the shoes in the window, I must have seen at least eight pairs that I liked. This is when I knew my girlfriend was going to have a time trying to help me select that special pair that would just look so elegant and divine on my little fat feet. Audra just shook her head as I smiled, nodded my head, and pointed to all the ones that I liked. She was thrilled to know that she made my day with her caring way and great sense of humor.

After finally arriving inside the store, I walked over to the clerk and pointed out several pairs that I wanted to try on. He looked at me as if I had lost my mind. I assured him that I was trying to save him time and that I was definitely going to buy a pair or two. After that confirmation, he was more than willing to assist me with my task and even offered me something to drink while I sat down with my little potbelly poking out. By the time I tried on the fourth pair, my mind was made up. I decided that no matter how many pairs I had tried on, only one pair caught my eye. They had a knob heel on them with a unique design on the front. When I tried them on, my feet felt so comfortable, I could just picture myself gliding across the floor, trying to do the electric slide.

Although I am pregnant, it doesn't mean that I have forgotten how to have fun. Today has been a long day, and I wish that it could last forever. The longer it lasts means that for the moment, I have escaped the unavoidable reality about my money and what's going to happen next. Audra, as sweet and understanding as she was, had no idea how she had rescued me today. I'm so blessed to have her in my life. I have no idea what I would have done today if it weren't for her. She has given me so much hope, even in her own emotional and physical pain. Never once today has she done anything but smile and spend her hard-earned money on me. It feels so good.

Tonight, she says we are going out somewhere nice and eat dinner and maybe go to a jazz club. In my mind, I'm wondering where she wants to go, because the town is so small there's only a handful of places. And if you're going out you need to be there before 10:00 p.m., especially on Saturday nights. Most weekends, the local clubs have a band or sometimes a comedian. This really is the last place I should be going, but to relieve some of the stress and anxiety, I needed it badly.

While riding the bus home, Audra and I talked and laughed. We even joked about our situation, vowed to do better, get out of it, and go on with our lives. This day, I had made up my mind that I was going to take control of my own destiny and that of my children. They deserved the best; after all, they didn't ask to come into this world. Why should they have to suffer? *Your life is all you have; you either sink or swim.* Right now, I need to be stroking for my life. If I don't do it now, I'll never get out from under this spell of madness that has consumed my whole being. My thoughts are no longer mine anymore. I'm being robbed, slowly but surely, every day. Robbed of my inner self, my pride, my dignity, and me, the person I am. I'm tired and my soul aches. The thought of taking control of my future is becoming more and more a yearning and burning desire. *I must, I must do this thing called "letting go."*

When the bus approached our stop, we both looked at each other as if to say, here we go again. Stepping off that bus with my fresh new hairdo and outfit and shoes in hand felt so wonderful. I spotted Terry about a block away as he started to run toward me with Audra's two little girls, looking so innocent. Of course, all mothers know that look . . . *where have you been? I see you have bags in your hands, and I know something is in there for me!* (They all three appeared to be saying this to one another.) You know the rest if you're a mother.

Nightfall could not come fast enough for me to get dressed and turn into the princess getting ready to be swept away to the ball for the first time. The time had arrived for us to get ready. In my mind, I began to wonder if or when Mr. Mark would show his face. It had already been at least twenty-four hours since I had last laid eyes on this brother. By this time, there was no doubt in my mind that he took my money. How was he planning on facing me, knowing he had stolen it? There wasn't anything he would be able to tell me differently. What was this man going to think when he came in and I, for once, was stepping out for a time on the town, looking like a princess? Right now, I could really care less, since there is nothing he can do to stop me. I'm my own person, and from this day forward, I refuse to give him any more control. Now is the time to start living. I have decided what is in the best interest of my children as well as myself.

Visions of the good time I was going to have danced around in my head and teased me while I got dressed. Audra came downstairs after she was dressed to show off her flattering new outfit with matching shoes, which made her look so sophisticated and simply adorable. Her hair was tapered into a nice coif style to frame her round, cute face and showed how beautiful her big, brown eyes were. She had eyelashes like Betty Boop from the cartoon, and a tiny, fit physique to match—enough to make any man take a second and a third look. By the time we were both ready to step out, my brother came in and asked if he could join us for the evening. Since he is my favorite brother—and a good dancer, I might add—I had no problem.

The club we chose was about three blocks from the house, and this particular night, it was packed. When we got inside, we were also joined by my godbrother Jeremy, who was a friend of the family. He was so shocked to see me out that he just stared as if he was in a daze. "Of course it is me," I said. "Yes, I'm out on the town for a nice time." I knew it would be a matter of seconds before he asked the expected question, "Where is Mark? Does he know you're out?" Inside I was screaming, *Who cares where Mark is! Don't ask me something so stupid. It's really none of your business,* I wanted to say. But for some reason or another, I was polite and responded with, "Oh, he's at home." And in my mind knowing all too well that I was lying, and that I hadn't seen the man in almost two days. I had no idea whether he was dead or alive. Without any warning, my brother Chad just popped up from nowhere and took me by the hand and guided me to the dance floor to do the Swing. We danced so perfectly together, as if we had been practicing all of our lives for this particular night. He twirled me around on the floor, and by this time, we had everyone in the club clapping and shouting for us. For a moment, I almost forgot who I was and that I was pregnant. I had so much energy; it made me feel alive, something I hadn't felt in such a long time. It felt good to dance and have fun. The only thing I drank was cranberry juice. *My girlfriend,* Audra made sure I took a break in between dances and rested while quenching my thirst. Her main concern was for me not to overdo it. It was so cute to see her make such a fuss over me.

The clubs in Paterson usually closed at 2:30 or 3:00 a.m. I danced and danced until my poor feet were tired, but my spirit could not rest until I was all danced out. I'm surprised I had soles on the bottom of my shoes. Well, what the heck? That's what I bought them for.

By 2:30, I was just getting cranked up when my girlfriend made a tempting suggestion, "Let's go get breakfast!" With that thought on my mind, food became primary and dancing secondary. I started thinking about the smell of bacon, sausage, cheesy eggs, and grits and how they were going to look on my plate with grated cheese on top of my grits and apple jelly on my toast. Now, that's talking! Audra knew, in order to get my attention, all she had to do was mention food. This is my one weakness, especially now since I'm pregnant. Everyone was surprised that I wasn't any bigger than I was because I always ate everything in sight, like a human garbage disposal.

We arrived at the diner down the street. It was known to have the best breakfast in town, and the prices were reasonable. When they fixed your plate at this greasy-spoon restaurant, you had a plate and a half, enough to feed two people (and that was me). This was just what I needed! It seemed as though the more I smelled that aroma of food from the kitchen, the little life inside of me kicked more and more as if to say, "Please feed me—I can't wait anymore!" Sometimes this baby would kick at the most awkward times, when I least expected it. Like 3:00 a.m. Now, why in the world would he or she even be awake? I would ask myself. This meant that I would toss and turn all night until this little booger would go to sleep. It's hard when you don't have control over the little life inside of you and can't turn it off when you want to. Overall, it was such a joy to know that this little life inside feels acknowledged and loved, spoiled rotten from the beginning before even seeing daylight.

When the food arrived at the table, my eyes told the story of what I was thinking at that very moment. The waitress could barely set the plate down; I couldn't wait to dig in. For a moment, I almost forgot my etiquette. All I could think about was food and how good it was going to taste once I got it into my watering mouth. Everything on the plate looked so delicious and cooked to perfection. "That's when you know a lot of love went into it," as my Aunt Theo used to say. "Judge your food by the way it looks and smells. If it smells good and looks good, it's great!" Boy, was she right!

After stuffing my face until I felt like I was going to pop, I no longer felt like the princess off to the ball. Instead, I felt like a bloated toad frog, stuck on a floating lily pad, just waiting for someone to come by, pick me up, and give me a ride home. Tonight was wonderful and well worth it. A chance to go out and just have fun all day and night did wonders for me and my girlfriend Audra. We both laughed so hard until tears were rolling down our faces as we joked and clowned about the people coming in and out of the restaurant, half twisted. Some of the women's wigs were just as drunk as they were and turned sideways on their heads. From the looks of it, nobody had informed them that their wigs were twisted, and they continued to try to flirt with the men sitting at their table. Now, this was so comical to us that Audra and I just fell out with nothing but laughter; the harder we laughed, the more we cried. There was no stopping us and no one else knew what we were laughing about, and that made it even funnier. Time went by so fast it was time to go home and get back to reality. Well, for now, good night, Mrs. Diary.

Afterthoughts: *Sometimes when you have problems, you want to think you're the only one, and how wrong we are!*

Afterthoughts: *It takes a bold brother to stand in your face and lie, and that's something a crack addict could do any day of the week. They have no pride or morals, lies come a dime a dozen. Mark had a convincing and charming way about him that made you want to believe him, even when you knew deep down inside he was lying. Sometimes love can make us do things that are just beyond us. We don't stop to think about it until it is a little too late. In my case, this was so true, many, many times over.*

March 3, 1986

Dear Diary,

It's another day, and morning has dawned. No Mark in sight. Maybe he left and won't be back. All I want him to do is call and let me know that he is all right. You cannot imagine how I feel. It's one thing to be pregnant, but pregnant and worried about where my man is, even though he has stolen our mortgage money and run off to get high on crack, is ridiculous. I'm still very concerned about his well-being. What is it about getting high that makes him spend all his money and stay away from home as if he is with another woman? Can anything be so good to keep you away from your lover, spouse, and partner for life—or your children? Most people that I knew who were on crack lost a lot of weight, their teeth started to decay, and sooner or later their cheeks were all sucked in and eyes bulging out of their heads, looking like zombies or the living dead. In reality, they were already dead, just still moving in the wrong direction. No one could have ever told me in a million years that I would be involved with someone like this, and that I would love someone so deeply as to take all of their abuse—verbally, mentally, physically, and, let's not forget, financially, to the point of accepting whatever they did just for the sake of trying to make it work. And at the same time, trying to maintain my sanity while all along I knew I was fooling myself.

Today marks the third day that Mark has been gone. I don't know how to feel. My brother has become suspicious and suspects something is going on, but he just hasn't put his finger on it. I pray that he won't. If he does, there's going to be a war. One thing for sure about my brother Chad is that he was always a very small-framed person, but he didn't take any slack from anyone regardless of height or weight. He didn't care; he wasn't backing down, no matter what. As a kid, he was the same way. All those years, and nothing changed about him. He's still just as crazy about his baby sister as he was when he was a child. My conscience began to bother me and guilt set in from my not telling my brother. I want to tell him the truth. I know what he is going to say: "I told you so!" We are so close. I have to tell him how I feel and what is going on. I'm going to need his support for my children and me. I'm five months pregnant—if I don't tell him now, later might be too late. " Please Lord, don't let this start a fire I can't put out. Let my brother be understanding and help me. I need his support so badly." Mark isn't a terrible person, just a little confused right now. By the time I have this baby, he will be so thrilled and excited that he will do what's right. I know he will; it's not like he has a choice in the matter. He's my baby's daddy, and I know that he is going to feel it in his heart to do the right thing. *Girlfriend, the only thing he is going to feel is his way to the next hit*. It may sound as if I'm being too harsh, cold, and bitter, but remember I'm telling you the truth. [As you begin to get into the heart and soul of this diary, you will understand where I'm coming from and be ready to board the new ship that's docking. That's the ship called *control*, taking what you want in life and demanding it. It's the way of life that you choose and the path that you take that sets your destiny. Don't let anyone, and I do mean anyone, detain you from your dreams.

(1) Dream big, not one day but every day; (2) When you wake up in the morning and your feet hit the floor, kneel down and give God thanks for waking you up and blessing you with another day; (3) Look into the mirror and tell yourself, "Today I'm okay, but tomorrow I'm going to be fantastic!"; (4) Keep your dream alive, more

vividly than ever; (5) Each day, start out by setting a small goal for yourself and write it down on paper, as you are more prone to try to accomplish it then; (6) Make sure you don't cheat yourself out of the life that is rightfully yours; (7) Count each and every day as a blessing and make each day count as if it were your last; (8) Remember you have the power to change, and through faith comes many blessings. They say when prayers go up, blessings come down. The more you pray and gain wisdom, insight, and faith, the more you can achieve. Do you know that God has a purpose and meaning for our lives? And wants us to inherit the riches of the land through our faith and belief in Him? My faith in God is giving me the strength to go on every day. I know that one day I'll be strong enough to break away from this cursed demon called crack cocaine. What can be on this man's mind? Doesn't he care at all that I'm worried sick, no matter how brave I'm trying to be with all the positive hoopla, hoopla. He is still my man and I love him unconditionally. Together we can get help for his addiction and he will stop getting high. First of all, nothing is ever going to change at all if you don't pray and leave it to a higher power. If it means walking away from house, car, furniture, material things, and just leaving them behind so you can have your sanity, it is well worth it. Better to walk away alive than to grow so tired that you're bitter and ready to retaliate because you feel you have been used, abused, and pushed to the edge. Before you let it escalate to that point, get out. It took me too long to learn the hard way, as you will find out later in the diary.]

Afterthoughts: *Crack addicts only have one thought on their minds, and that is where they are going to get their next hit and what they are going to have to steal or sell to get it. There is no limit. At one time I thought only poor people smoked crack until I started reading the newspaper headlines more often and reality set in. It was filled with stories of political figures, doctors, lawyers, teachers, stockbrokers, and other prominent people from all over the world, of different origins, color, and nationalities, all of whom at one time or another had held vital positions. It opened my eyes to the sad reality that this thing called crack cocaine was real and not something to just ignore and sweep under the rug. The poison was* *toxic and detrimental to anyone's health and well-being, regardless of whether you were a spouse or user. Your position in the relationship didn't matter. You see, it was just like you were an addict because you became someone else other than yourself. You lose your identity, dreams, and ambition for a better and brighter future, all for a puff of smoke you didn't even take. To be involved with someone getting high on crack and expecting them to change overnight is very seldom heard of. Run—run as fast as you can. That's the thought that occurred to me most, especially now that my money is gone. I said from the beginning, after the small things, bigger things will come. To think it is one thing, but to know it is another. Girlfriend, I know—remember, I lived it. Start thinking about yourself and what you want. Step up today and take your destiny back. Tomorrow may be too late.*

March 5, 1986

Dear Diary,

Another day has dawned and no sign of Mark. My nights are filled with loneliness and my eyes swelled with tears from soaking my pillow as I cried myself silently to sleep. Today, I'm going to tell my brother what is going on and handle his reaction the best way I can. Something has to give. What's the worst thing that can happen? He'll be upset, but he'll get over it. It seemed as though the phone would never ring. The more I wanted it to, the more it didn't ring at all. At one point, I just passed by the phone sitting on the nightstand and picked it up to see if it was still connected, knowing all along nothing was wrong with it. I wanted to believe so desperately in my mind that this was the case. Does this man ever intend to come home? Or did he run off with someone else? I don't know what to think, and to me he is just being ridiculous now. You know what? He wasn't the only one being ridiculous. I was, too, because I sat here and once again gave someone else control over my thoughts, my emotions, my dreams, my desires, my determination, and even my motivation because of their own selfish pleasure from getting high. Something I dare not equate, indulge, or entertain the thought of for myself. I was being passive and letting someone else cheat me out of what was rightfully mine—all my dreams, desires, and aspirations that I had carried around with me all my life. The ones you envision that you would fulfill someday and make a reality. No matter how rough the road seemed on the way to accomplish them, you were willing to go the distance.

Afterthoughts: *That's the way you were supposed to stay. Never stray away from your target; stay focused on what makes you happy, and strive for the better within you. No matter what the situation, if you keep a positive attitude, things will change. You will start to shine, and no matter what you're going through, you will have a natural glow about yourself and the comfort you feel in your spirit will take you to higher heights than you ever knew existed. Now what I'm going to tell you next is really going to make you think and search deeper inside yourself. Never try to change someone else. They have to want to change. Don't become a co-dependent for your spouse, or anyone else. Identify with one thing for sure, and that is if you give away your self-control to someone else it's going to take you a long time to win it back, if ever. The more you prolong agony, the more it will defeat you from every angle. If you cut it off before it gets started, the better your chances of coming out far ahead of the game and being the winner you are.*

March 6, 1986

Dear Diary,

Today is the fourth day since anyone has seen Mark. By now, I'm sure he knows I'm worried sick about him. At this point, I don't know what to think; there is nothing else left for me to do but to tell my brother, as I stated before. Knowing my brother, he already knows and just hasn't said anything to me about it. Any day now, my tax return should be in the mail, and that will help out for now. At least that would be some relief from the miserable situation that he has placed upon not only me, but also the house as a whole. If I lose my place to live, it not only affects me, but everyone else, too. This means that several other innocent people who are depending on me for a safe and comfortable place to live, a place they call home, will be in jeopardy, too. Deep inside, I long to know where my future lies if this continues. There is no future as long as this behavior is accepted, and nothing but more disappointment lies ahead. My mind is made up that this is the last straw, regardless of the fact that I'm pregnant with this man's child. What matters most now is that I must start taking control of my own life. Why not now? Today is better than any other day because it is now that you should do what is best for you. Don't procrastinate because tomorrow may be too late.

By 5:00 p.m., I could hear my brother coming up the stairs sounding just as chipper as ever, singing and humming to himself as if he is the happiest man in the world. I can hardly wait for him to reach the door so I can find out what all the commotion is about. As he walked through the door, I didn't even have to ask him. It was quite evident that someone had come into some money as he held up a brown envelope in his hand with a glow in his eyes and teased me with it, wanting me to guess whose it was. I knew it had to be mine or Mark's, being that we had both filed our taxes about the same time. When he asked me to guess whose it was, I replied it has to be mine. He said, "No. Guess what? It's Mark's. I know he disappeared a few days ago, so I'm giving you his check to hold on to. You see, Sis, you don't think I know what's going on with Mark, but you forget I'm the same brother that warned you about him from the beginning. Remember?" he asked as he looked at me with those deep brown eyes appearing to be so innocent and devilish at the same time. The only thing I could do was nod my head out of embarrassment and shame; how could I have made such a bad choice at this point in my life? My mind was at peace knowing that at least I could take this check of Mark's and deposit it into my bank account to pay our mortgage; after all, he owes it to me. After what he did, he should be glad I don't have him arrested and put behind bars. He has really lost it if he thinks he's going to come back in here and sleep in the same bed, eat from the same table, and act as though nothing has happened. Only a fool would think that, and in my book right now, that's exactly what I consider him to be. What was on his mind? How could anyone smoke up $700 worth of crack? I asked myself. To me that was just plain stupid and ridiculous. And ridiculous it was. Right now it may be for the best that he doesn't come back. My heart is becoming very numb. He's lucky if he can walk through that door without me leaping on his head like a mad dog right about now. Pregnant women have a temper when they get mad. So, to me, this brother better look out to make sure I don't pop him on the side of the head with one of those old frying pans like my grandma use to have. No matter how calm we are, there comes a time in our lives that we all have the thought to just haul off and hit something or someone to vent our anger. If it makes you feel better, just hit a pillow and take your anger and frustration out on it, rather than get real abusive and end up in a physical confrontation that could land you in jail, in the hospital, or even worse, the cemetery.

Mark is going to flip when he finds out I have his check and it is for $1,800.00. He will be a fool to think I'm going to give it to him to "crack" it up. This money is going into our bank account and if he refuses, I guess the only other choice I have is to press charges against him. That's too embarrassing and would create a bigger problem, one that I don't know whether I'm ready to deal with. Well, well, here it is 7:30 p.m., and as I stand out on the balcony trying to savor my thoughts, I can barely see a tall shadow of a man wearing a light-colored shirt walking toward my house and opening the gate. Shocked, I knew without any doubt in my mind that this was Mark. He doesn't see me standing on the balcony as he approaches the steps. I can see the hesitation in the way he walks, so slow, with his head hanging down as though someone is supposed to feel sorry for him. By the time he reaches the top step, I'm standing there mad as ever, but at the same time happy to see that he made it home alive once again. How many times is it going to take before this spell wears off? This time he didn't try to play me by telling me the same old line or saying nothing. Finally, he says to me that he is tired of getting high and wants to get some help, telling me how much he doesn't want to lose me and that he loves Terry and our unborn child. He would be willing to do anything if I will give him a chance to prove it to me, telling me that he feels like a fool and that I'm the best thing that has ever happened to him since bread and butter. *Girlfriend, girlfriend, this line became like a broken record for me, hearing it repeat itself over and over again.* If you have heard it once, why not spare yourself from hearing it twice? In order for someone to change, it doesn't take you to help him or her. It takes them to be willing enough to acknowledge their problem so that they can get help. You can want them to change until you turn blue in the face and the cows come home, but if they don't want it just as badly for themselves, it will never happen, *and please remember that!*

After listening to his begging, crying, and all the promises and confessions of his undying love for me, I just looked at him as if I was looking through the mirror of his soul. All I could see was a shell of a man, filled with guilt, shame, and confusion. I was too confused to know if he was even alive anymore or whether he was amongst the living-dead, better known as zombies. Of course, once again, I felt sorrow for him and together we both shed tears while hugging and confessing how much we missed each other. I knew this time would be different, because I knew I wasn't going to trust him anymore and that I had to take additional measures to protect myself and not let him know too much about our finances. [When you get to the point that you can no longer trust a person, and this is your spouse, then you know it's time to move on. Without trust, how can there be love? Trust is the foundation for all good things to come. Just remember that to hope for it in a desperate situation such as this is unrealistic. Keep things in perspective by being real with yourself, and prepare yourself for the better. Stay ahead of the game; don't give in to all those hopeless promises and dreams. For in reality, to the crack addict, dreams are all they will ever be. They have no sense of direction when it comes to reality and purpose and only see what is in front of them, and that is the next opportunity to get high. Nothing really matters to them anymore. As time goes on, they will get more and more outrageous and out of control, taking you for everything you have, your heart and soul included. As I said, nothing is excluded.] After talking for what must have seemed to be hours with Mark, I assured him that I would be there for him if he went into treatment, but I was not going to continue to let him torture us with his addiction. He agreed that he was going to do whatever he had to so he could stop smoking crack.

I felt better knowing that he had come home and was ready to start fresh with the thought of seeking some professional help. Something we both should have done from the beginning. I vowed to him that I would be in his corner to give him support and would not leave his side no matter what. Just the mere fact that he was, for once, admitting that he was an addict meant the world to me. This was something he had never admitted before and was a sign of a good start. Everyone has to start somewhere, and after all, he is my man and my unborn child's father. I need to stand by him and help him in anyway I can. Once he kicks this habit, we will be back on track before our child is born, and I know he is going to stay straight and fly right. The only thing I can say at this point is thank you, God, for opening his eyes and letting him finally see the light. Please, God, if you hear my prayers, let this be for real and not just a game or another trick to win sympathy or play on my intelligence. It would be so nice if he were finally coming around; after all, he is really a sweet and wonderful man when he is not getting high. Everyone knows this. Well, not everyone, but I know, and that's all that matters. He is still my man, and I know he can do it. Even though I believe he can, does *he* believe he can, is the question. No matter how much you believe in someone, they have to believe it for themselves because if they don't, it won't happen. Mark agreed to sign his check over to me so I could deposit it into the bank. He didn't put up an argument or anything. He was so calm about it and so positive, I couldn't believe this was the same man. The one who came home every day and fussed about anything just so he could have his way, run off, and get high with whatever little bit of money he did have or whatever he had stolen to get it. Mark's reaction to the whole situation was unbelievable. Please let this be for real—that's the only thing lingering in the back of my mind.

Afterthoughts: *Don't beat yourself up, just dust yourself off and keep on going. It's through our mistakes and failures that we learn how to overcome defeat. If you never get up and get back into the ring, you will never know if you stood a chance to win the fight, because you gave up before the bell even rang to begin the first round. Be bold, stand tall, and listen to that inner voice; and most of all, have much love and peace within you.*

March 8, 1986

Dear Diary,

Mark has signed himself into a drug rehab program, and it looks very promising. He says he'll have to take one day at a time. Each day, I know that it is going to be a struggle for him, being that he is such a young, intelligent man. I know that if he prays, God will give him the strength that he needs to succeed and defeat this demon called crack cocaine. Right now, my focus is on taking care of our home and making sure no one knows what's going on in our house. Whatever happens inside, no one must know. It's our problem and we will deal with it. The man is trying, and the last thing I need is the negative feedback from people on the outside trying to look in. This would only cause him to have a relapse and go into a deep depression, which would be a terrible thing right now.

March 19, 1986

Dear Diary,

It's been about two weeks since Mark signed himself into the drug rehabilitation program, and he seems to be doing pretty good. He comes home when he gets off from work, and for the first time in a long while, he came home on payday and didn't fuss and act up. This time, he didn't have a problem signing his check over to me. I knew he could do it all along and that through faith anything is possible. In my mind, I never gave up on him even though there were plenty of times I wanted to. The months are going by so fast, and I will soon be six months along in April. Before you know it, I'll be having this baby, which I'm hoping, by the way, is a girl. I only want one, just one, little me running around giving everyone a hard time. That would be too cute to see. My man is doing good and I'm so proud of him. There is nothing that I wouldn't do for him. He has proven that he is a real man and can take care of me and support our family. Everything I've ever wanted, I'm beginning to see I can have in him. Yes, we have had our setbacks, and yes, it was hard, but through it all we survived. It feels good! In a few more days, my taxes should be back and I can go pick up my little sporty toy car, if they still have it. Mark said he will co-sign for me and that he will help me make the car notes, even though it would be my car. I think that is awfully sweet of him. Good night, Mrs. Diary.

March 27, 1986

Dear Diary,

Tears are flowing down my face as I try to guide the pen across these pages. My heartaches and the memories of that tragic day almost one year ago when I lost my second son (Boo) are quickly approaching. This is going to be so hard, especially with me being pregnant on the anniversary date. It's been hard for me to go back to visit my son's grave without breaking down. He was so precious to me and had the biggest, brightest, sparkling eyes anyone could have ever seen. This baby smiled all the time, even when he was wet and needed to be fed. Most babies cried and were cranky when they wanted to eat. With him, he was so patient and sweet with the fattest, juiciest cheeks. A part of me is feeling so guilty inside because I don't know what happened to my son. All I know is that he was a healthy and happy baby when I took him to the doctor bright and early one Saturday morning. As he lay on his back, cooing with a big grin on his face and eyes shining, I teased and kissed him so softly while waiting for the nurse to first check his temperature and measure his little short, round body. After she finished what seemed to have taken forever, the doctor came in, examined him, and told me how much he weighed and that he appeared to be healthy. All his vital signs were fine and that he would be giving him his first shot for "DPT." He explained to me that this injection could cause an allergic reaction and may cause the baby to run a slight temperature. If that occurred, I was to take him to the hospital to be checked. When the doctor prepared the needle to give my baby his first shot, it took everything in me to hold back the tears, as I knew this tiny body that was a part of me would feel pain, and that sent chills through me. I cried as my newborn screamed with pain after being injected. It took me a few minutes to compose myself. For a moment I wanted to punch the doctor for making him cry. My baby cried so loudly and pitifully that other little patients that were waiting to see the doctor were holding on to their mothers' arms for dear life.

After returning home from our office visit, I watched my child closely as he slept to make sure he didn't run a fever. I constantly checked to see if any rashes had appeared on his body. Nothing! As I lay across the bed folding paperwork and stuffing envelopes with work I had brought home from the office, I heard someone calling me outside my window. When I pulled up the shade, it was my girl-friend Josephine's daughter signaling me to come downstairs to let her in. When I opened the door to let her in, she informed me that her mother had sent her to ask me if I would send the baby over so she could watch him. Even though I had only met her one week be-fore I had the baby, she became so attached to him and always wanted to keep him, from day one. I told her daughter that I had just come home from taking the baby to the doctor and that I just wanted to relax and monitor him for a few hours to make sure that he was okay. No matter what I said, she was persistent in her quest to fulfill her mother's desire to see this precious little baby boy. The only thing I could do was get up, get dressed, and wrap him up after he woke up and take him around the corner to see his Aunt Josephine. She was so attached to this baby. I met Josephine when I was nine months pregnant and standing in the unemployment line trying to sign up so I could receive what was rightfully mine, my unemploy-ment check, which was every bit of $181.00 after taxes for two weeks' pay. Back then, that's all I received after placing my life on the line for my country—how dare Uncle Sam treat me this way! Where was the real money I deserved? From the first day we met, Josephine and I hit it off and exchanged addresses. At that time in my life, I didn't know the real value of owning a telephone, but I was soon to learn. Approaching Josephine's house, I could see her peeking out of her window. She also lived on the third floor, and her stairs were much steeper than mine and very slippery, may I remind you. I couldn't get up the stairs fast enough for her to open the door and extend her arms for the little bundle of joy I was holding so tightly as if my life depended on it. Her smile told of the love and joy she felt in her heart to have this baby near her. Her kids were just as loving and sweet as she was and shared the same feelings, as it was apparent on their little smiling faces. This baby was bounced from arm to arm. After settling in, taking off my coat, and unwrapping the baby, I asked Josephine where her boyfriend Roger was. She looked at me and grinned as if to ask, "How should I know?" Roger was a kind brother who made you laugh and was the life of any party, even if he didn't know what he was talking about. He faked it to appear to be smarter than he actually was.

This particular evening, as my girlfriend and I sat around laughing and talking, we both played with the baby while he bounced up and down on his little fat legs. We joked about Roger and how he would make up stories out of the blue and tell them as if they'd really happened to him. Deep inside, he knew he was lying. He had a way of trying to use big words in the wrong sentence, messing it up, and thinking he had done something big. Josephine and I were falling out laughing so hard we didn't hear him coming up the stairs. When he staggered into the room, drunk and reeking with the fresh smell of alcohol all over his body, I thought my girlfriend was going to smack him silly. Instead she was nice and asked him not to get too close to the baby. This, of course, made him angry since he also loved this little boy and was always happy to see me when I brought him around. His first comment was so shocking that it took my girlfriend and me by surprise. The first thing that came out of his mouth, drunk as he appeared to be, was, "When are you going to take this baby to the doctor?" he asked. "This baby is sick. He is so sick, you can never imagine," he said as he slurred through his sentence, needing help to complete it.

Josephine sat up straight, and so did I. She replied, reassuring him that the baby was okay and that I had just taken him to the doctor. No matter what we said to assure him that everything was okay with my baby boy, he insisted that something was wrong. My girlfriend and I couldn't see it. "Boo" was laughing, cooing, and just showing out with no teeth in his mouth. I've always heard the saying, "Drunk mind, sober truth." To me, at this time, that meant nothing at all.

It wasn't until three days later when I awoke to get ready for work and to bathe and dress my baby that I would soon realize what Roger was saying would soon become reality. When I awoke and went to reach for my son, the spot where he lay was wet. With the light off, I couldn't see where all this water had come from. The spot where his tiny body lay resting was soaked; it was so wet that it appeared as though someone had taken a bucket of water and just dashed it on my baby. As I scrambled to reach the switch so I could click the light on, I almost fell out of the bed. The sight that I witnessed after I turned on that light, I would not soon forget, as it was the beginning of an unreal scene. What I thought was water was sweat from a fever that had invaded his body during the night. His pupils were dilated and foam was around his tiny little mouth where he'd had what appeared to have been a seizure. Shaking nervously and scared to death, I grabbed my baby and held him close to me as I screamed with all my might for someone to come to my rescue. My brother jumped out of his bed and came running into my room to find me just standing there holding an almost lifeless baby who was at the point of turning blue in my arms. I couldn't think. All I knew was that if we didn't get him to the hospital soon enough, he would surely die. If my brother hadn't been there for me at that moment, I don't know what I would have done. We did not have a phone; he had to run outside and flag down a taxi to rush my son to the hospital. Too afraid to take a chance on calling an ambulance for fear we might lose him, my heart raced as we got into the taxi to take him to the hospital. When we arrived at the hospital, a security guard I had known for years saw me come in and took the lifeless child out of my arms. He rushed him into the emergency room; by then his lips had already started turning blue. My body was numb with shock and disbelief. Just a few days earlier I had received a warning from a man who was so drunk that he was falling down. Why did I not take heed of his warning? He told us that the baby was sick, but no one, including me, the baby's mother, believed him. How could I have been so stupid? All anyone ever wanted to do to this little precious baby was to kiss him on his little rosy, fat cheeks.

If I can get past today, I know the sun will shine forever. The pain of losing a child is a feeling that can't be explained unless you, too, have been in my shoes. I guess the question I keep replaying over and over again in my mind is *why?* When my son died, no one had any answers for me. Not the doctor who watched and took care of him every day while he was in intensive care, not the nurses who made sure the intravenous tubes were attached and everything was working properly on all the machines to which he was connected. No one could give me an answer as to what was wrong with my son. Everyone seemed to walk around with rose-tinted glasses on. When they would see me coming they would act as though they were scurrying to get out of my way so I couldn't ask any questions about something they had no answer for in the first place. My patience grew thin and my spirit weary day after day as I slowly watched my child become a vegetable while asking the doctors day after restless day if my child was going to survive. Will he have brain damage? Has any portion of his brain died? "No, don't worry we are doing everything that we possibly can," they would assure me. "Go home and get some rest—you're wearing yourself thin," they would reply as if I was a child. Who did they think they were, with their fancy titles and non-caring attitudes? They acted as if my child was a toy or something that had no meaning. Maybe not to them, but to me this baby and my oldest son Terry were everything. This was going to be a very difficult anniversary for me. Today, I need Mark to be strong for me. Maybe we will have a chance to go out and eat dinner or go to the movies so we can rekindle our relationship and ease some of the pain I'm feeling about my loss. Deep down inside, I know that nothing is really going to work to soothe my pain other than time itself. After all, it has only been one year, so it is still fresh in my mind.

March 29, 1986

Dear Diary,

Today is beautiful, even though inside I feel so empty and alone. One year ago marks that dreaded day when two police officers rang my doorbell at 3:30 a.m. on a cool, brisk Sunday morning to tell me that it was urgent for me to call the hospital and that I would need someone to ride with me. In my mind I already knew that my beautiful, sweet baby boy had passed on. Each and every day prior to that dreaded moment, I had always kept hope that he would come out of the coma that he had been in for three weeks. This moment in my life was so painful and lonely. This baby that I had yearned for so badly with all my heart could no longer recognize his mother's scent, her touch, nor the sparkle in her eyes just to see him smile. It's so hard to think about sometimes. From the moment I walked through that hospital corridor and saw all the doctors and nurses gathered around waiting for me to arrive, I knew that my son had passed away. The look on some of the nurses' faces as they approached me, with tears welling in their eyes, to give me comfort and to let me know that their hearts were aching, too, for that sweet, innocent baby we all came to know as "Boo." One nurse could no longer contain herself; she broke down and sobbed so hard in front of everyone. You would have thought that it was her child. She expressed to me how much she came to love this baby, and that he was one of her favorite patients. She, too, was hoping that some magical force would intervene and propel him from his deep sleep.

I walked into the room and approached where they had laid his little body to rest before the long black Cadillac, called a hearse, would come to pick him up. I held his tiny, frail body in my arms for what would be the last time. I pulled up an old, solid pine rocking chair, the one like my grandmother used to have when I was a little girl. I held my baby ever so close to me as I rocked and sang to him his last lullaby as he was snuggled so tightly in a soft yellow blanket that felt so warm as it clung to him. The smile on his face was as though he saw angels and was just taking a nap.

Dr. Michaels came into the room and offered his support. He told me that he would be there for me and handed me one of his business cards so I could contact him anytime I needed someone to talk to. Never once in my entire life had I seen a doctor cry like he did. Most doctors never really showed emotions. The grief in his voice and genuine concern in his heart let me know that he was a man who cared. My whole world felt as though it was tumbling down and any minute I was going to pass out from all this heart-wrenching pain. People tell me that the first few years and holidays are the hardest, especially when you're around family and see other babies about the same age as yours would have been. Little did I know that I would be the one to experience this tragic fate at the early age of twenty-five.

When I returned home from the military, I was six months pregnant with my second child. Even though I was single and knew my family would not approve, I was grown and determined to do what made me happy. I always said that after twenty-five years, I didn't want any more kids and that two children would do, preferably two boys. Before my second son was born and I was just three months pregnant, I told my best girlfriend, Lanora, that I knew this baby I was carrying inside of me was going to be a boy and that he wasn't going to live long. When she asked me why I felt that way, I explained to her how badly I wanted this baby, and from childhood, I had always heard an old wives' saying that if you wanted something too badly, God would take it away from you. Of course my girlfriend Lanora assured me that this was just another old saying that really didn't mean anything. No matter what Lanora told me, whether it was the truth or not, it always made me feel better. She always knew how to say the right things to convince me when no one else could. She had a way of winning you over that was so charming. After I completed my tour in the military and came back to the States, Lanora and I kept in touch frequently by mail. We always found the time to write to each other. When I moved into another apartment, I regret that I lost her address and could no longer contact her. I miss her dearly and I often think about the good times we used to have and how much trouble we used to get into while we lived off post in our own two-bedroom apartment. It was very warm and cozy. Each room had its own charm with much class. Everyone who experienced the warmth in that house knew they were loved. Lanora was a Navajo Indian with short, black, curly hair that barely reached her shoulders; she stood about five feet tall and was born and raised in Phoenix, Arizona. She was the oldest of three children and the only girl. You could tell by her actions that she was accustomed to having her way, being that she was the only girl and her dad spoiled her all her life and gave her whatever she wanted when she wanted it. It was evident in the way she dressed and the jewelry she wore (and let's not forget the temper). At the age of twenty-four, she had already been in the military for six years, married for three, and ready for a divorce. She was a very outgoing and free-spirited person whom everybody just loved.

I remember the Saturday mornings when we would get up bright and early so we could catch the train and go to Frankfurt and shop. Those were the days; we would have so much fun. Money was never an object to her, and everyone around her knew it. If she didn't have enough to buy it, off she went to call her dad. Most times I would just simply look at her and shake my head as if to say, "When are you going to grow up and stop depending on your parents to take care of you?" Little could I say, due to the fact that she spent plenty of it on me, buying shoes and outfits just so she could shut me up and not have to hear me fuss.

We both got along great, being that we were both daddies' girls and were proud of it. There was nothing that could come in between our friendship. She was there when I received the tragic news that my father had passed away and consoled me and made me feel that everything would be all right. Friends like her don't pass through this lifetime too often. So when we get them, it's best to hold on and cherish every moment. The last time I wrote to her would be one of the saddest times in my life, and that's when my baby boy died. That letter was so sad; it still brings tears to my eyes just thinking about it. Some memories never die.

It was on a Tuesday when I received her letter in response to mine, and she told me how sorry she was to hear about my loss, and that she wished that she could have been there for me. We were making plans to meet each other in Texas. Her orders for her next duty station had come in and she would be arriving in just a few months, if only I knew where she would be stationed. Texas is a big state with more than four or five military bases. Where would I even start, was the question in the back of my mind.

It is so much easier to think about the good times rather than what is right in front of me, and that's the one-year anniversary of my son's death. I never knew that there could be a pain that hurt so deeply and continuously until it just left you numb and lifeless. Today is the first time in months that I have had a taste for alcohol. You see, after my son's death, I started drinking heavily to kill the pain and forget about the suffering I was going through. Every day when I got off from work, my first stop would be Tom's Liquor Store on the corner. I would purchase a pint of gin and slip it into my pocketbook so no one could see it, especially all the bums who hung out on the corner just waiting for a friendly, smiling face to come along so they could beg for a sip. To me that's all I had. This bottle gave me comfort; it didn't complain or talk back. No matter how much I drank or didn't drink, it never got mad at me. When I would hit the doorway, I couldn't wait to get upstairs so I could pull out that old, rusty mop bucket and fill it with soapy water, drag it into the kitchen, put me some Patti Labelle on, and pour what would be my first, but not last, drink as I mopped the kitchen floor over and over again until it had a white, dusty, filmy coating on it. If that floor could talk, I'm pretty sure it would have screamed out in pain from the bleach and Pine Sol I used to clean it with. You could smell the strong, stringent fumes all the way down the stairs. It was enough to knock a bull out. I'm surprised I didn't pass out from it myself. I guess I was too drunk and busy holding the mop handle as if it were a microphone, pretending that I was Patti and on top of the world, singing my heart out. Nothing else mattered to me. That was the only thing that soothed that aching pain deep down inside my heart.

Every morning I awoke to a nagging headache, better known as a hangover, and my alarm clock sounding off as if it was personally yelling at me to get up now and not a minute later. I drank so much the night before, the liquor had seeped into my pores and you could smell it on me. Little did I know about alcohol in those days. My thought was, just dress it up with a fresh shower, deodorant, some sweet-smelling perfume, beautiful clothes and, *BAM,* you're fine. Just like Puff the Magic Dragon. Boy, I was in for a rude awakening, one that I would never, ever forget. I went to work one day about one month after the death of my son, and my boss called me into his office to inform me that I was being laid off and that they no longer needed my service. Can you believe that? How cold of them to let me go when I needed this job so badly. At this time, I still had expenses to pay for my son's burial, and now I was going to be without a job. That meant no alcohol. Oh, the world is caving in! First my son, now this. When is it all going to stop? Inside, I was crying something that I could not do out loud for fear someone would hear me and offer me help. I wasn't ready to give up drinking. I enjoyed it. I convinced myself of this foolishness. Where was I going to get the money to supply my habit? I'll just get another job. No one was going to stop me from doing what I had to do, especially a crummy old job like this one anyway. God knew that I was on the brink of disaster and summoned His angels to shield me from all harm and protect me from self-destruction. After the loss of my son, I remember the pastor that preached his funeral asked me if I believed in God, and my reply was no, with anger in my voice.

"No, I do not believe in God. If there was such a God and He was so good, why did He take my son?" I asked. "How can I believe in a God who would do such a terrible thing?" I said as I broke down and sobbed uncontrollably. "Why my baby boy?" I screamed with many tears flowing down my pale face.

There was nothing or no one who could stop the tears or pull this dagger out of my heart. Who gave this mighty authority, God, permission to take something that was rightfully mine? My son was so precious; all he wanted was life. My stepsister Joyce was right there, as always, to wipe my tears and console me as she had done so many times before in the past. Except this time, it was for something totally different. It was the loss of something so precious and dear, everyone's heart ached. Even people that had never laid eyes on my son before and were friends of my late father were there to lend their support and witness the agony I was going through.

As I took one last view of my child's body, one of my old friends who had been there from day one when my son first got sick, came up to me. He wrapped his arms around me and told everyone in the congregation that he knew how I felt because this was his baby, too. From the moment I arrived home six months pregnant, Frank was always there for me. We had been friends for many years prior to me going into the military. There was nothing he wouldn't do for me. To me back then, he cared a little too much. His feelings for me were beyond friendship, even though I had expressed to him over and over again that I didn't share his sentiments, but it didn't matter. His thoughts were that if he wined and dined me enough, I would learn to love him. Tell me, how do you learn to love someone? He was a street hustler who knew how to survive in this cold, cold world. His tall, lean physique made him appear to be very strong and intelligent. But, when you walked down the block and saw a crowd gathered around shooting craps, rest assured he was amongst the group. Frank thrived on winning, and every time he did, he couldn't wait to share it with me. He took me to some of the finest and most exclusive restaurants in New York, to the theater, wherever I wanted to go. It didn't matter to him that I was pregnant and it wasn't his child; he was just happy to be with me. From the moment I gave birth to my son "Boo," he was attached. Never once did I lack for anything, no matter how much it cost.

The morning after I gave birth, Frank arrived at the hospital with an armful of bags, so many of the nurses had to help him bring them into my room. I was so shocked. This man didn't forget anything; he had six or seven outfits for the baby, bottles, a brush and comb set, baby oil, lotion, powder, you name it. And let's not forget blankets. He even bought me my all-time favorite mini-cheesecake with cherries on top, drenched in rich cherry syrup filling. As I dug deeper into the bag, I pulled out a box filled with chocolates and a card that said, "Congratulations!!! I Think You're a Wonderful Mother!" Oh, that made my day. While I lay resting with my head pressing into his body, he held my hand so gently with love. He sat on the edge of my bed waiting so anxiously for the nurse to bring this new, tiny, warm life into the room for him to lay eyes on for the first time. You should have seen his face light up when the nurse finally arrived. If you didn't know any better, you would have thought it was his baby by his reaction. All the nurses just smiled as they stood back and watched this man who was my friend cooing and awing over this baby as if it were a new toy. Just his actions put a smile on my face. In my heart I wanted to love him so badly, but in the back of my mind I couldn't dismiss the thought of who he really was and what he did for a living. He was a hustler, someone who would risk his life to survive, and any minute might be his last in a world of crime that would consume him. Fear gripped my soul at the thought of losing him as a friend. This was something that I would never want to imagine or even think about, for that matter. We were like a team; I just did not love him, but deep inside I wanted to. My stepmother would often say to me, "Cee, you need to give it some thought. This man is crazy about you and he loves this baby so much. Why not give him a chance?" For the life of me, I just couldn't do it. "Whom do you know that will do the things he does for you and the baby and never ask for anything in return?" she would ask.

Frank never bugged me or pressed me for anything physical. Just me being there was fine for him. His family even fell in love with this baby and took him in as if he were one of them. They treated me like royalty and were always very pleasant and polite when I was around. Everyone who saw us said how great we looked together. When he would come to my house, his first stop was the pantry to count how many cans of milk and baby food "Boo" had. Then it was off to my room to check to see if he still had a case of Pampers left. From day one, I think I only bought one box of Pampers for this baby; Frank supplied everything else. On snowy days when I couldn't get out of the house to go to the store, I could peer out of my third floor bedroom window and hear him calling my name for me to come downstairs so I could let him in. He made sure if nothing else that my baby and I were going to be okay. If he offered me money and I wouldn't take it, he would sneak and leave it on the ironing board in the other room where he knew I would find it. Sometimes he would leave me $200 or $300 of the money he had won gambling the night before. When I would fuss with him and try to give it back, he would only get upset and tell me that I was his princess and I deserved to be treated like one. He said that there was nothing I should want for. He wanted me to get my hair done, shop for new clothes, and pay for any expenses that I may have had for the baby. Money was something that he never made a fuss over. I myself should have felt honored to meet someone so gracious. Instead, all I felt was pure, unadulterated friendship, the kind every man wants from a woman, even though he also wants more. Well, I guess I'll stop here. I hear someone coming, so good night, Mrs. Diary.

March 30, 1986

Dear Diary,

I can't believe today is finally here. Today marks the one-year anniversary of my baby son's death. My mind is numb with much hurt, pain, and sorrow. I don't even think Mark has a clue as to how bad I'm really feeling. Last night he came home from work totally exhausted; I know he has a strenuous job, but for goodness' sake, can a sister get some acknowledgment? By the time he came home, even though I was feeling under the weather from my painful thoughts, I had already fixed dinner, run his bath water, and ironed clean clothes for him to put on just so he could relax. Even though I wanted him to take me out and just spend some quality time with me, I knew he was tired so I didn't mention it. It's been a long time since I've seen him this tired.

Lately he has been complaining about headaches and, in the middle of the night, he's been breaking out in cold sweats. Every time I mention the fact that maybe he needs to go to the doctor, he just shakes his head *no*. Men are so intimidated by that thought and can act like such babies. Right now he has been doing so good with his recovery program, and I'm so proud of him. I knew he could do it. He has really been trying hard, coming home every day reading his Bible and taking time with Terry and me. We went shopping and picked out some things for the baby.

My doctor says that this baby's due date will be July 20. I insisted that it will be July 18. Mark is getting excited and looking forward to the birth of our first child together. When I look at him I see such a handsome and loving man. How could this man have been such a monster just a few weeks ago? Well, right now that is beside the point and is in the past. All I can see is the brighter side, and that is what a wonderful future we are going to have. Everything is falling into place and for once it feels so good; it has been a long time since I've felt this good. If there is anything I pray for, it is that this feeling will last forever.

April 5, 1986

Dear Mrs. Diary,

Well, hello world! It's so wonderful to be alive. I'm so happy today—I went to my mailbox, and a little brown envelope was just sitting there waiting for me. My taxes have finally arrived. I can't wait for Mark to get home so we can go to the car dealer and pay the down payment on my dream car. This is the day I have been waiting for. I'm so excited I can't keep still. Have you ever been so excited you couldn't keep still or wanted something so badly that all you did was daydream about it every day? That's how I feel right now. When I was in the military, I couldn't decide whether I wanted to re-enlist or just get out. I was almost ready to re-enlist just so I could get the bonus money and buy me a sporty car just like the one I'm getting ready to buy now. The only difference is now I can really enjoy it at my own leisure, not Uncle Sam's. It feels so good. You have no idea. When Mark comes home and finds out I have the money for the down payment, he is going to be excited, too. All he wants is to see me happy. It's been a long time coming, and we both deserve it. I have to tell somebody about my happiness, and what better person than my buddy, Audra? When I told her, she just jumped up and down and screamed. Friends like her you can really appreciate. I told her that I couldn't wait until I had this baby so we could go shopping in New York. If you love clothes, New York and Newark were the places you wanted to go to buy clothes in every style, fashion, color, and design—and let's not forget the shoes. When I was a little girl, I used to daydream about becoming a world famous clothes designer and imagining people from all over the globe wearing my designs.

By this time tomorrow, if it's the Lord's will and everything goes right, I will be pulling up on the block in my sporty little new car. That's a feeling I have longed for. We all have desires and dreams. It's only when we take that step to make our dreams become a reality that makes us feel so proud of our accomplishments. Right now I have so much to be thankful for. God has truly blessed me. There were days, just a short time ago, when I never thought I would see daylight again and now things are finally, finally coming through for me. "Thank you, Lord, for answering my prayers."

It's almost four o'clock and time for Mark to be coming home any minute. By the time he gets here, I want to be dressed and ready to go. I've already called the car dealer, and he has all the paperwork ready for us to sign and then you know the rest—just hand over the keys. This is one day I'm hoping Mark will get off early and surprise me, but of course I know that's not going to happen. All this preparing, and I haven't even called him at work to tell him what was on my mind. Just too excited, I guess. Well, he will find out what's going on in enough time. In my mind, I'm trying to imagine the look on Terry's face when I tell him the good news. This, of course, will mean Mom, can we go here, Mom, can we go there? For him this spells relief. The thought of not having to wait on the corner to catch the bus and listen to other people's problems would be a relief. Like I said before, it's a brand new day on East 18th Street, one I'll never forget. Sometimes we can get so caught up in what we are thinking that we forget about the small things, such as dinner cooking—and now it's burning up while I sit here writing my heart out. Gotta go, Mrs. Diary.

April 6, 1986

Dear Diary,

Today is going to be one of the happiest days of my life. Yes, Mark came home yesterday but he was so tired. He said that his whole body ached with pain. I guess he was overdoing it at work and it made him sore. After all, the work he does on his job is very physically demanding. You have to be in shape to do the type of work he does. All the lifting and pulling Mark does, it is a wonder that he has time for anything else, especially a young and vibrant lady who demands his attention at all times. It does not matter if he is tired, aching, and he just can't stand my touch. At moments such as these, I still have needs, too. Lately, to be honest, he hasn't been in the mood for anything other than plenty of sleep, from the time he hits the door when he gets off from work until he wakes up the next morning. Mark doesn't even have the urge to say hello unless he is reminded. What in the world is going on inside his body? Maybe it is withdrawal from the addiction just kicking in. It's nothing I can't deal with, as long as he isn't getting high on crack. That drug made him stupid and me, too. Stupid for believing all the lies and alibis he told me and now that I know better, that makes me feel really stupid. But, today I can laugh because that was yesterday and yesterday is not today and that was the past. Who cares about yesterday? Not me.

That thought is slowly drifting from my memory. Never will I ever experience that again. Anyone who does, and lets it continue, is crazy. I looked at myself in the mirror with sheer conviction written all over my face, convincing myself that nothing could stop me now or change the way I feel about myself, my thoughts, and my man.

As I stood in front of the mirror I started imagining how Mark would come home from work and take me in his arms and rub my round belly with his warm, soft, gentle hands as if he was molding our child to perfection. Each motion of his hand, gliding ever so gently with care and ease, told of the affection he felt not only for me, but for our unborn baby. From staring into his dark brown, mysterious, but yet subtle eyes, you can tell he is a man of much love and compassion. The fire Mark created in my soul was burning out of control and needed to be approached with caution. This man knew how to make me feel, even when I didn't want to feel anything. Mark's charming and cunning ways made him a master in the making.

Here it is Tuesday afternoon as I sit here dressed and ready for Mark to step out of the shower so we can head off to the dealer to pick up my brand new toy. I couldn't wait to put on my beautiful pink dress with the big white stripes down the middle and my white pantyhose that were about a size too small and didn't go all the way up to my waist, so you know I had to fake it. My shoes are pink to match the dress, and, of course, you guessed it—I had to have my hair done. No one was going to catch me driving my brand new car with a raggedy hairdo. Oh no, not today or any other day. Bad hair days were going to be a thing of the past once those keys were passed over to me. The time seems to drag by, as I'm overanxious to get to the car dealership after waiting for a bus for what would be my last time. While waiting on the bus I kept replaying the scene in my mind where I would drive up the block in my slick automobile and all eyes would be on me and my baby. For a moment I almost left Mark out of my daydream as I gazed out of the window after boarding the bus, just staring into the silhouette of the cars surrounding the bus as we traveled down Route 4 to the car lot. The sooner we get there, the better, I thought to myself. My body and mind are exploding with anxiety, and nothing else can calm me except the feel of soft, buttery leather under me as I position my steering, adjust my mirrors, tilt my headrest, strap into my seat belt, and I slowly creep onto the highway, put this little baby in gear, and head straight toward my house. That would be my first destination, but not my last one. I would have to go see my girlfriend Charlotte, stepsister Joyce, and let's not forget Clara, my stepmom.

Mark reached for my hand as he pushed the buzzer for the next stop. I didn't dare attempt to stand up until the bus came to a complete stop. A few people have gotten injured by standing up when the bus came to a screeching halt. Today wasn't going to catch me like that. As the bus approached our stop and we stepped off, I felt a sigh of relief. It felt like God was watching over me and that today was my day for all good things to come. It was almost like Cinderella getting ready to go to the ball.

The car dealer I had spoken to over the past several weeks greeted us at the door with a radiant smile. I guess I would be smiling, too, if I knew you were buying a car and that was my living for me to feed my family. When it's like that, of course, you practice smiling even when you don't have to, just so when you do smile it looks so real no one but you will know that it's pouring rain on the inside like I used to. Boy, I'm so glad those days are gone. The car salesman's name was Darrell, and he looked much younger than his announced thirty-five years. He had smooth, pretty brown skin with one slight dimple on his right cheek and a deeper one on his left, almost as if it had been etched on perfectly. Looks can be deceiving at times but the look of truly genuine sincerity on his face let me know that he was a true gentleman and had my best interest as a customer at heart. You know how you can see through some people? Well, he was the type of guy that you could see his heart, how much he cared, and how much he appreciated others. Papers were scattered all across Darrell's desk as he reached for the stack that was so neatly held together with a paper clip. Those papers in his hand held my future dream car. A car that would soon be mine, no matter what. That car had my name written all over it. No one else was more right for it than me. It didn't matter that I was six, almost seven, months pregnant. So what? Dreams don't stop with pregnancy. If anything, you should be thinking about what's next. How can I do better? How can

I make my dreams a reality? At least if you think this way when you are small, everything else will fall into place when you become an adult. Boy, how wrong was I?

After going over and signing numerous pieces of paper for what seemed like an endless task, the moment had finally arrived for Darrell to hand over the car keys. It was like watching a dad let his son go off to college for the first time. When he placed those keys into my hands, you could hear my heart skip a beat. I thought for a moment that I was dreaming and needed to be pinched to wake up to come back to reality. Mark, of course, volunteered to drive home. His gesture made me feel comfortable and relaxed to know that now I had a real man, one who had just co-signed for his baby's mother to get the car of her dreams. Let me tell you, that is a wonderful feeling, one worthy of the praise. By the look in Mark's eyes as they sparkled with excitement and joy as he drove along the scenic route home, I could tell he felt the same way I did, which was happy!!! The smile on his face was worth a million dollars. It has been a long time since I have seen him this happy, glowing, and full of life. He is starting to put on weight and is beginning to look healthier. His skin tone is even and soft to the touch, just like the Ivory girl on the commercial. Looking at him, you would never have thought he had a drug addiction, something neither one of us were proud of, but were too happy to put behind us as though it had never happened. As the days went on after his recovery, we seldom mentioned his addiction. I think we were both afraid of all the hurt and pain it would remind us of. While riding along, the smile on his face and mine told of two people so deeply in love that they were struggling to hold on to whatever was left to make their relationship work.

East 18th Street would be our first stop, as we had planned. The day was nice and sunny. Of course, you know we had to go all out and have the sunroof peeking out just a little bit with the music slightly louder than the norm just so we could check out the speakers to make sure nothing was wrong. After all, it was equipped with the best sound system (Bose). The music was sounding awfully nice as we pulled up in front of my house with my car rims shining, as I watched to see how many nosy neighbors would actually come up, or stop in their tracks, to see who was getting out of this fancy car. I was so proud that I could hardly wait for everyone to know it was me with my pregnant self, and my baby's daddy. Look at us now. Mark got out first and came around the car to open my door so I could step out ever so proudly as if to say, "Look out world, this is only the beginning!"

My neighbors were nosy troublemakers who couldn't wait for you to do something wrong so they could slander your name. That's why I always kept to myself and only spoke to a few people, even though I knew just about everyone on the block. Some were pretty nice, and we got along well. That's because they knew how to mind their own business and didn't ask any questions. Those were the neighbors I liked the best. As the car door opened, I could see little, tiny feet on the other side and instantly knew that it had to be Terry. Bright-eyed and beaming with joy, he couldn't wait to throw his arms around my neck, kiss me, and, of course, ask the ultimate question, "Aren't we going for a ride?" And where, when, why—you know all the W's. This kid was like the Energizer Bunny all of a sudden. What else could I expect? This was my first real car and his, too. So to us it was like a toy made for us both to enjoy. No more boring days, wishing I could go here or there—just hop in the car and go. I hugged him tightly as I reassured him of all the promises I had made to him about us traveling and going places together once I got a car. When he hopped into the back seat, I couldn't help myself as I burst out with laughter at the silly look on his cute little face. I watched and instructed Terry on how to strap on his seat belt; then it was his time to take a spin around the corner, just the two of us. You would have thought the child had just seen Santa. Mark blew a kiss as we drove off and made me promise I wouldn't be gone too long. Of course, women will promise the world until they get out of sight, and that was me.

As soon as we turned the corner, I spotted my girlfriend, Audra, coming down the street. I blew the horn while slowing down so she could recognize that the kid with this new ride was her buddy, me! The look on her face told me that she was totally surprised even though I had given her fair warning days prior about my plans. She hopped in with a look of pure delight and shock. Audra was the type of friend that if she was really happy for you, it showed. I let her know from the moment that she got in and strapped on her seat belt that we were off to see my girlfriend Charlotte. The car drove so smoothly, it almost seemed to glide at one point. The seats were comfortable and the legroom was extra large.

My girlfriend Charlotte lives on the lower end of town. This is where the drug dealers with the nice cars like Mercedes, BMWs, Jaguars, and mouths and necks full of gold, hang out twenty-four hours a day, robbing not only adults, but our children, by poisoning them with deadly drugs like heroin, crack, PCP, and pee dope. Whatever they can get away with, peddling to fill their own greedy desire, driven by the lack of the almighty dollar. Nothing is excluded from their grasp. Drug dealers in that part of town care about no one. Most of the fancy cars they are driving, believe it or not, once belonged to someone prominent. Someone who wanted a hit so desperately they basically gave the ride away for a hit of crack. That sounds crazy, but it's true. Ask my girlfriend Danielle, she will tell you. Ask her what happened to her car. Her girlfriend's boyfriend borrowed her car to go cash his check one payday, and guess what? He never returned. When they found him, it was three days later in a crack house claiming that he had laid the keys down and someone rode off with the car. Yeah, right, believe that one if you want to. You will be next. Danielle was so upset; she told me it took everything in her to keep from beating the crap out of this man. She only had her car one week prior to this nasty incident. That shook her world upside down. At the time, she purchased the car from an auction; she never had a chance to put insurance on it before this idiot came along and stole her joy. It's been months since that incident but until this day, she is still riding the bus and walking when she can't afford the bus fare. I feel so bad for her and hope that from that experience she will learn not to loan her car out to anyone. Money is too hard to come by, especially when you're working and getting paid only $5.25 an hour. Tax time is like Christmas, and that is what she used to purchase her car. All that hard-earned money up in smoke, you might as well say. Smoke is what he did with the money he made from the sale of her car. They say he sold it for five hits, which, if I'm not mistaken, equals about one hundred dollars. That's so sad, I wish I had the money to help her. I would! We are all struggling and we all need to try to help each other.

As I pulled up to the curb in front of Charlotte's house, I saw her son playing outside and motioned for him to go upstairs to get his mother. While checking my rearview mirror, I could see one of our old girlfriends walking up the block with a bottle of wine in her hand. Diane used to be a very attractive young lady with a slender body and dark chocolate skin that glowed. As I said, used to be. Looking at her from the rearview mirror's display, nothing about her looked too good. Her skin was dark with what appeared to be blotches and her teeth had decayed and were falling out. Her hair looked like a permanent wig that hadn't been changed in days. The last time I had asked Charlotte about her, she told me Diane had started getting high and was strung out on crack, but I had no idea it was to this point. She looked so bad, I almost wanted to roll up my window and pretend I didn't know her just so I wouldn't have to come face-to-face with her and accept her for who she had become. It's sad when it gets to that point.

Charlotte finally stuck her head out of her third-floor window, trying to figure out who was in the car as I signaled for her to come downstairs. She yelled at me to step out of the car so she could see who I was, but I wouldn't so she had no choice but to come down. Once outside, shocked, she realized it was me and laughed out loud with joy. "Girl, you really did it this time," she said, looking at Audra and me. "One thing I have to do is give you credit, girlfriend," she said, as she climbed into the back seat for her spin around the block. "Cee, you really know how to live it up—look at you, new baby, new house, new car—what's next? Girl, you are my inspiration," she said.

We whirled around the block and down the street, cruising to sounds of the O'Jays and feeling the breeze of the cool, fresh air blowing through the window as we chilled with the sunroof slightly tilted. Everyone on the block knew Charlotte was in my car. It was so apparent, at each corner she would yell out and wave to everyone, even if she didn't know them. That didn't matter to her—it was just the fact that she was in a fancy car and wanted to be seen. She was a clown when she wanted to be. Arriving back in front of her house, she asked me when I got this new toy, and where did I get the money to afford such a luxury. The way she carried on, you would have thought it was a Rolls Royce. I told her I had saved my tax money and used it as my down payment. No matter what I told her, she refused to believe it, insisting that I must have hit the big numbers or something.

"One day, I hope to have it just like you," she said. "Girl, I don't know how you do it, but I'm proud of you. I hope to own my own home one day," she said. As she talked about the future, I assured her that I would encourage her all the way. Every dream has to start somewhere. Little did Charlotte know of all the frustration that I had experienced just a few months prior. If she had any idea of the hurt and pain I went through, she would not be saying this. Only Audra knew my deepest, darkest secret. Now that I'm doing well, who even cares to remember?

"It's almost 9:30 p.m., and I know Mark is getting worried sick," I said, "I guess I'll be heading home."

"Oh, you know Mark will understand if you stayed just a little bit longer," Charlotte replied. "He knows this is your debut," she laughed. "It's Burger King Day—have it your way!" she added.

"Yeah, right," I said as she opened the door to step out. "I'll try to catch you tomorrow once you get off work," I told her.

"Cee, now you know if I couldn't keep up with you before you got a car, what makes you think I will now?" she asked with a grin in her voice.

"Charlotte, you are just crazy." I began to laugh while Audra looked on as we clowned with each other. Charlotte came around to my side and greeted me with a big hug as we said good night for the hundredth time. "No matter what, I will see you tomorrow," I assured her.

"Girlfriend, you know Mark is going to have a fit when you get back," Audra exclaimed as she looked directly into my eyes. "You know he is worried sick about you—look how long we have been gone. Not to mention the fact that I haven't even been home yet from work. Pee Wee is going to have a fit, too. Lately, he has been tripping off of little things and it's getting worse by the minute. Well, I don't want to spoil your lovely day by spilling out my problems," she said.

"Audra, have you lost your mind? You should never, ever feel that way," I assured her. "Especially after you have seen what I went through with Mark, and you were right there for me. Don't ever be ashamed or afraid to talk to me. What are friends for?" I asked. "Girl, anything is possible and subject to change if you just believe and have faith," I told her.

From three blocks away, I could see every light on in my house and knew that one thing was for sure, everyone and their momma was waiting for me to pull up any minute. Mark must have heard the car and was standing on the balcony by the time I got out of the car. From the look on his face, I could tell that he was not a happy camper. Even though I knew he was a little upset, it didn't matter. As my girlfriend stated before, it was my debut, and after everything Mark took me through, he should be happy I came back.

The closer I got to the porch, the madder he appeared to be. By the time I reached the top step, he was standing there just as angry as ever, so mad that he had already turned another shade of red. If I didn't know any better, I would have thought he was the devil's brother. It had been a long time since I had seen Mark this angry. To me, he had no reason to be so angry; I was only gone for a few hours. Why was he so mad, I thought to myself, but dared not ask him. He didn't give me a chance to get in the door totally before he blared out, "What is wrong with you? Have you heard of something called a phone? Couldn't you call to let me know that you were all right and everything with the car was okay? That is my baby, too, that you are carrying. Don't let this car go to your head," he said with much anger deep in his voice. "I saw you park in front of the door, then you changed your mind and parked it around the corner," he said. "Why was that?" he asked. "Do you think I'm going to go on a crack binge, Cee, and run off with the car? That is what you're thinking, aren't you?" he asked with much hatred in his voice. If I didn't know any better, I would have sworn that he was high, but I know better. It's been over a month, and he is doing too good. So why go back? I know the devil is trying to trick me into thinking this negative thought, I said to myself. He went on and on for what seemed to be almost an hour nonstop. "If you keep looking out that window checking on that car, I'm going to take it, drive off and show you how it feels to just disappear for a few hours."

Finally, I had been silent too long and I was tired. I told Mark, "If that's what you want to do, then fine!!! Just leave me alone!" I would much rather be left alone than to have to hear him rant and rave on and on for endless hours over nothing. Little did I know this was his addiction kicking in, blaming me for everything, trying to make me feel guilty and sorry about something I did to make myself feel good. That was his way of playing on my empathy to have his way. But this time it wasn't going to work. To ignore him while he was having the temper tantrum of his life, I went into the kitchen and talked to Audra before she disappeared upstairs. Well, good night, Mrs. Diary!

April 7, 1986

Dear Diary,

While sitting in the kitchen talking and laughing with Audra last night, I didn't realize that I didn't have my pocketbook with me. By the time I did, it was too late. Mark had already snatched up my car keys and was gone. It didn't phase me in the least that he had taken the car. If this was going to cool him down, then so be it. I had no problem with that. After all, what was mine was his as long as he wasn't getting high. My eyes became heavy and sleep was creeping up on me by this time. Mark had been gone for about two hours. I figured he had enough time to cool off and would be back soon. Too tired to wait up, I went to bed, only to wake up the next morning with the birds chirping and singing on my windowsill. I did not realize that my man had not come home with my brand new car that I had only just purchased the day before. By the time I snapped into reality, my brother was knocking on my bedroom door to see if I was awake. He asked me about this new car that he had heard about, that his baby sister had just bought, and wanted me to take him for a spin. When I brought the car home, he was hanging out with some of his friends and didn't come home until the day after.

"Where is this new, fancy machine?" he asked with a big, bright smile. "You know what I'm talking about, sis—come on, tell me where it is. I know you are trying to surprise me," he said as I turned and looked at him. I finally realized what he was asking me as I was just coming to my senses out of a deep sleep. I had forgotten all about the fact that Mark had driven off with the car last night, and it never dawned on me that he had stayed out all night. In my mind, even though I knew the truth, I didn't want to believe the slightest thought that maybe he didn't come home.

As my brother stood in the doorway of my bedroom looking at the blank look on my face, he asked, "Well, sis, did you hear what I asked? Are you going to take me for a ride or what?" he asked again with a very puzzled look.

I'm pretty sure that the look on my face spoke a thousand words. For the first time in months, I was speechless. It took a few seconds for me to gather my thoughts. Before you knew it, out blurted the biggest lie from my mouth. "Mark has the car and he went to the store. He should be back shortly," I replied as I looked straight into my brother's eyes.

Chad just stood there looking at me as if he was surprised. "So Mark has the car and will be back shortly?" he asked with sarcasm in his voice.

"Yes, he will," I said with a bit of an attitude building in my tone.

"Well, sis, why are you getting upset with me for asking you something so simple? I only wanted to know, that's all," he replied as he walked away mumbling. "It's your life. If you let Mark use you, then that's on you. I have nothing to do with it. As long as he doesn't put his hands on you, we will be fine," he said.

"Where is all this coming from?" I asked. "Why do you always have to think of the worst? From day one, you never gave Mark a chance. Now he is really trying and you still just can't let up on him. I'm so sick and tired of your snide remarks. It seems as though the harder someone tries, you are right there to knock them down."

"Cee, I'm not trying to argue with you, and my only concern is that I want to see you happy. Don't you know that I love you?" he asked. "You and Terry are all I have," Chad said as he turned around and came back into my room to give me a hug. "Oh, by the way, I have a surprise for you if you want it," he said.

"What is it?" I asked.

"Close your eyes and I will be right back." I could hear the rattle of the bag as he approached my door, telling me to open my eyes. That moment brought back memories of when I was a little girl and my brother would often surprise me with all kinds of small gifts.

As Chad handed me the bag, I couldn't help but wonder what was inside it as I quickly stuck my hand inside to see what it was. "Whaah, this is gorgeous," I said as I handed it back to Chad to put around my neck. It was a gold pendant that had "#1 Mom" written on it. "Thanks, bro, you are the best brother anyone could have."

"By now, I know you must have that jewelry box filled with all kinds of trinkets and what-nots," he said.

"Yes, I do," I replied as I went into my closet to pull it out. "Boy, wait until I show you the bracelet and necklace Mark bought me. Some of the things he bought me I'm waiting to wear until after I have the baby. They are just too pretty to put on now. Remember that little music box I bought for my other son before he died? I have that and all my little trinkets that I bought from Germany in there. I have enough room in it to store all my little sentimental stuff. Chad, if you don't mind, will you come over here and remove these heavy suitcases out of my way so I can get my box out and show you my collection? You are going to be shocked. Some of the stuff I have collected came from Aunt Theo. She gave me my first Good Luck charm. Remember that time we went to Atlantic City and I held onto this little ceramic puppy? That was the one she gave me. The one that I didn't want anyone else to touch but me, especially after I won $350.00. Those were the days. We used to have so much fun, just the three of us—you, Daddy, and me," I said. "Only if we could turn back the hands of time, where would we be now?" I asked. "What's wrong with you, bro? Why is it taking you so long to remove the suitcase? I know they can't be that heavy, or did you lose all your strength from hanging out with your women friends?" I teased. "My closet is junky but if you move the second suitcase, my jewelry box should be sitting right behind it on the floor to your left. Disregard the clothes and shoes on the floor. It's a mess and I will get it cleaned up sooner or later, so please overlook it. Do you see the box?" I asked.

"No," he replied hesitantly.

"You have to see it—it's right there to your left. I know you can't be that blind, as big as that thing is," I said. The jewelry box was a big one, about two feet high and eighteen inches wide, making it almost impossible to miss unless you were blind. "Okay, brother dearest, if you will move the suitcases like I asked and let me get over there, I'll find it. Now I know my closet can't be that junky to where you can't find that big box."

"Well, sis, if you find it, you are good," he replied.

"If you move out of the way, I will. You are still in a trance or spell from last night," I laughed, "and couldn't find it if it was right there staring you straight in the face like it is." I continued to laugh and joke while I poked fun at him.

"Sis, I'm telling you, I don't see it. If you find it, I'll give you $50.00 right now just for proving me wrong." At that moment, I don't think my brother realized what he was saying. He was challenging me, and as broke as I was, the challenge was on.

"Just move your narrow butt out of my way and let me find it. When I find it, I don't want to hear any excuses as to why you can't pay me my money. Put up or shut up," I said with a big smile on my face. We always used to laugh and joke with each other when we were kids and often would challenge one another. Sometimes it seems as though we were still kids and never grew up. As my brother stepped aside and let me wobble up to the closet, I pulled everything out from the front to the back. I was just laughing and teasing him as I continued to search for my pride and joy. This jewelry box contained everything that held sentimental value to me. From the moment my brother had given it to me, I cherished it. I used to pull it out every day when I first got it, just so I could listen to the beautiful music that would serenade my soul, while I would lie back and relax. The serenity it gave me was so soothing and tranquil. While I searched for my prized possession, my brother sat there with his legs crossed and arms folded. He was looking at me as if to say, how long is it going to take her before she realizes it's not there? After searching and searching for what seemed like forever, I finally had to admit to not only myself, but my brother also, that it wasn't there. The expression on his face was one I will remember for as long as I live.

He stood up and came over to me and asked, "Is it possible you could have put it somewhere else?"

"No," I replied. "When I put my stuff up, I know exactly where I put it," I said with anger in my voice.

"Maybe Mark took it out and put it in the hallway closet," he said. At this point, I'm beginning to think that my brother is trying to be funny and is waiting for me to tell him what I really think happened to it. He must be nuts. If he thinks that I'm going to tell him that, he has to be out of his mind. Confessions like the one he wanted me to admit to could cause much drama and turmoil.

"Let's go and check the hallway closet—it could be there," my brother said. Just so he and I would have peace of mind, we both went to look for what had become the invisible jewelry box. When Chad opened the small, confined closet and did not see the box, I could see his blood boiling. "Sis, tell me the truth. What do you think happened to it?" he asked angrily. Even though my brother was a very thin and small-framed man, he was not afraid of anything or anyone. How well do I remember from all the times when we were children and he would go up against the biggest bully, never backing down, just to prove his manhood. Even if it meant getting his behind whipped, he didn't care. All that mattered to him was that he stood his ground. "You know that a box as big as it was could not just disappear without someone taking it out of here. Who else knew where it was?" he asked angrily. "Don't tell me you don't have any idea," he said. "Who else goes into your bedroom other than Mark and Terry?"

"No one that I can think of," I replied nervously. I could feel my body shaking and quivering at the thought or possibility that Mark may have taken it and sold it to some drug dealer.

"When was the last time you remember seeing it?" my brother asked.

"It was in there just the other day when I took it out to play my son's music box and reminisce. To be exact, it was on his death anniversary date. Remember when you came home and I was just sitting here in the dark? You asked me what was wrong? That was the last time I remember laying eyes on it."

"Girl, when are you going to wake up and smell the coffee? You know deep down inside that Mark took it, but will you admit it? Oh no, you are so busy trying to protect this man and keep his vicious little secret. I know he is smoking crack and so does everyone else."

"You don't know what you're talking about," I shouted. "You just don't want to see me happy," I yelled.

"Stop being a fool for this man. Here I am, your brother, living under the same roof. How dare you," Chad shouted, "keep secrets like this from me? There is no telling what else could be missing of yours or mine. Lately, I have been missing money, but because I had been drinking before I went to bed, I automatically assumed that it had dropped out of my pocket and I had lost it." As Chad continued to talk I tried to make myself believe that there was no way Mark would ever sell something so precious to me for a few measly pennies to get high.

"Now I know that I was right and don't need to evaluate this any further," he said. "I'll be waiting right here when Mr. Mark returns, if he returns at all. It wouldn't surprise me if he didn't come back anytime soon. That's just how bold he is, but you are too blind to see this. That man could care less about you or Terry. He is only concerned about his own selfish needs, and that is to support his filthy habit any way he can. You just don't want to admit it or understand it. When are you going to wake up and stop with all the excuses? Let him go, get rid of him. I'll help you raise my little nephew and the baby. You don't need this aggravation. Of course, you'd best believe that when he comes home I'm going to let him have it. Garbage is something you don't need, and it needs to be set out on the curb," he said angrily. "How dare he steal from you? Cee, you are my heart, and nobody, I mean nobody, is going to hurt you. Rosie, down the street, told me a few months ago that Mark had sold your watch and you came and bought it back from the lady he had sold it to. I wasn't going to say anything to you about it. I just let it go, waiting and hoping you would tell me. Sis, you know how I am. I try to mind my own business and give you your space with your relationship because I respect you. But, how can anyone hurt my sister like this, knowing that she is such a wonderful and beautiful person? You don't deserve this. He should have been gone a long time ago and, if I have my way about it today, he is out of here. I don't care what you say. There is no telling what else he is capable of. If he is stealing from his baby's momma, what else is he doing? You may be in denial and trying to hold on to make it work, but what you have to realize is that he is an addict. He could care less. I know you love this man, but he does not love himself. So, how can he possibly love you? Please think about Terry. While you're at work, what kind of influence does this man have on your child? Does he spend time with him? You know how Terry is. He is so humble and meek—he can be easily influenced. Is this the kind of man you want to raise my nephew and unborn niece or nephew? I'm not trying to make you upset or mad—the truth speaks for itself. Mr. Mark will be lucky if he gets to the top of the stairs before I knock him down. He needs to just get his stuff and go back where he came from. I'm going to knock his head off his body."

The more Chad talked, I could see the raging fire building up inside of him. This little man, better known as my brother, had a very bad temper. Once he got heated, there was no cooling him down. As he talked, I became a bucket of uneasy nerves for fear of what was going to happen. As hours passed, still no Mark in sight. By now it's 8:00 p.m. and getting late, even though it's still daylight outside. I could hear the doorbell ringing. Normally on Saturday evenings, my girlfriend Charlotte would come over with her kids, and Audra, with her two little girls, would come downstairs. We would all sit around, play cards, and listen to music until the wee hours in the morning. Since I couldn't go out partying, my enjoyment centered on cooking and entertaining at home. There was always plenty to eat, especially on Saturday night. This particular Saturday, I didn't feel up to entertaining anyone other than my bed, where I could lie and think about what my brother and I had talked about earlier. After all, what he had said to me was true. When was I going to wake up? What kind of future was I going to have with someone like Mark, who changed from one second to the next? It was ridiculous. How could I have once more let myself fall into believing him? Now here it is a day later, and he is gone. Not just gone but gone with my brand new car. Did he bother to call? No, of course not. I suppose he is off on one of his binges again. "Dear God, please give me the strength to let go and overcome the love I feel inside for this man who does not mean any good to my son, Terry, my unborn baby, or to me." As I prayed this prayer, I could feel the warm tears flowing down my face. This is so painful; it hurts so badly. "How could any man hurt a woman like this?" I asked myself. As I lay across my bed thinking, while I tossed and turned, I could feel the presence of someone watching me. It was my brother standing there at the foot of my bed holding his arms out for me so he could give me comfort. "I thank God for you," I said to him as he held and rocked me as I lay there crying.

I was always the one who felt that I had to be so strong not only for myself, but also for everyone else. The first time Chad had ever seen me cry in years was at my son's funeral. I always tried to hold up and be strong for everyone else. I felt it would make me seem weak to cry or express how I truly felt. Don't fool yourself. You're only human and can only tolerate so much. Everyone needs to be respected and feel loved. No one, I mean no one, should ever have to experience what I have been through and am still going through. This is pure hell. How could anyone subject themselves to this kind of disrespect, just for the sake of love? Love can be so powerful and at the same time so painful. I always thought that when I grew up and fell in love, it was going to be so wonderful. No pain, no deceit, just plain feelings of pleasure filled with happiness. Never in my wildest dreams could I have ever imagined the hurt and pain I would be experiencing at such an early age. When it gets to the point of hurting so bad that your whole body is numb, you should know it's time to go. Let go!!!! Not only to save yourself, but your soul and all those who love you.

A crack addict's only concern is his or her own pleasure and what they feel at that time, which is nothing. When they are on that roller coaster ride, you are, too. The only difference is that you didn't want to be, and he did. His actions become your problem. Here it is around 10:00 p.m., nothing all day long. This man that loved me so much has not even called to see if I even still existed on the face of the earth. What could he be thinking or feeling right about now? Was he thinking, or even feeling, what I was going through? He was on such a good path to recovery. What could have happened to make him relapse like this so suddenly and without warning? "Dear Lord, please do not let him get caught driving my car with drugs in it."

Right now as the clock ticks and it is getting later and later, my fears are worsening. Not only am I on pins and needles, so is Chad. It's been a few hours since the two of us said anything to each other for fear of what the other one may have been thinking. I don't know how to feel. Should I call the police, hospital, or what? This is crazy. How could this man just disappear without a trace and be so inconsiderate of others? I hate the thought of that demonic drug called crack cocaine and everything that it stands for. Which to me in my mind was only a life of living hell for anyone who subjected themselves to it. Sometimes in life it takes us, as humans, to stand up and fend for what we feel and know is right. We have to take control and stop giving someone else who is irresponsible the ability to lead us on an unforeseen journey into the darkness.

As time goes on, I can't help but stare at the clock and hope that any second the phone will ring and it will be Mark. Deep down inside I know he is not going to call, but he should know that the longer he stays away, the worse it's going to be. The later it gets, the more I worry. All day long, little Terry has been asking me what is wrong, where is the car? Are you still going to take my friend and me to the park? Let's not forget his biggest question, where is Mark? This kid had so much energy, he could never just ask me one question and wait to get a reply; instead he would ask about ten at once. How do you look a seven-year-old straight in his eyes and tell him a lie like I just did? I told him that Mark had to take the car to the shop and I wasn't sure what time he would be back. Of course, you should have seen the look of disappointment on Terry's face. Children have a way of making you feel guilty even when you have no reason to.

As I lay across the bed, tossing and turning, all I could think about was how happy I had been for the last few weeks, and how I felt like everything was going to be so beautiful. We were making plans to get married, discussing how we wanted our wedding to be and who would be my matron of honor and his best man. While I lay there reminiscing, I could hear someone coming up the stairs. The closer they got to the top of the stairs, I could feel my heart starting to skip a beat. Please, please, let this be Mark. Even though I really want it to be him, I don't want to face the consequences of what is going to happen if he and my brother start fighting and things get out of control. As I rolled over, facing the doorway, waiting for the unannounced visitor to appear, I could no longer wait and jumped up off the bed to see who it was. As I approached the dark, dimly lit hallway at the top of the stairs, I recognized my girlfriend Charlotte's boyfriend, Gregory.

"Hello, sis, how's everything going?" he asked while still climbing the stairs.

"I'm doing just fine," I replied.

"Charlotte told me you have a new car and you know she was bragging about how nice it is. She says that it has a sunroof and tilted seats. She even told me it made you feel like it was gliding." He chuckled with a grin on his face. Gregory was a very sweet and lovable guy when he wasn't drinking and acting foolish. He and Charlotte had been together for over ten years, and even though he had married someone else while they were still dating, Charlotte never gave up the hope that he would leave his wife and come back to her someday. I guess her wish came true because they are still together, even though it was a hard and rocky road, one I would never want to choose.

"Well, sis, what I really need is a favor," he said very shyly, almost as if he didn't want me to hear him.

"What kind of favor?" I asked.

"Can you give me a ride home? I just got off from work. The guy that was going to give me a ride home left early so that left me stuck. Please, please, say yes," he pleaded.

"Gregory, now you know you only have to ask me something once. I wouldn't have a problem giving you a ride if I had my car, but Mark went to the store and should be back shortly," I said.

"Sis, come on now, all I need is a ride home. I'll pay you."

"Gregory, did you hear anything I just said to you? Mark went to the store and should be back shortly," I repeated.

"What color is your car?" he asked, looking very serious.

"It's a golden tan color," I replied.

"How long has Mark been gone?" Gregory inquired.

"I guess maybe an hour."

"Well, sis, that's almost impossible."

"Why do you say that?" I asked. "My car isn't the only one that color and description," I added with a slight attitude.

"Because, if I'm not mistaken, I saw a car just like that parked down on Governor Street ever since earlier this morning when I was headed to work, and it hasn't moved yet. And from everything Charlotte has described to me about your sleek vehicle, this is your car. Come on, Cee, how many cars around here look as fancy as yours? Let's be for real," Gregory said, "and if it wasn't Mark, then what were you doing down there?"

[Governor Street and Patterson was where all the drug dealers and addicts hung out. People often got shot or killed there. It was nowhere to be caught, especially after midnight. Everyone in his or her right mind knew not to hang out there when it got dark. To put it better, Governor Street put the "G" in ghetto. My dad used to tell me stories about the times when, back in the early sixties, this particular street I'm talking about was once beautiful and some very prominent people used to live there. Now today I could never imagine that. When you turned onto Governor Street, you could smell the stench of garbage and see the paper trails of litter as it lined the walls of the curb. You could hear the commotion of whatever was going on, hoping and praying that you weren't going to be the next target to get robbed by a crack addict. Crack addicts all want the same thing, and that is to get high. This street, with the big "G," was one of the main reasons I decided to go into the military. After giving birth to my first child, Terry, and realizing how hard it was to find decent housing, I refused to move into government housing for fear of the worst in a city that was already ridden with crime. The only other alternative housing that was affordable for young people such as myself during this time in my life, was in the ghetto where rent was affordable but you could get stabbed or shot any minute. It was almost like living in a real, live combat zone, to tell the truth. After living in the 'hood for about two years, that was enough for me. I couldn't stand the thought of my child coming up in a poverty-stricken, drug-infested area. So that's when I decided to be all that I could be and join the Army for what would be a grueling three years. It didn't matter—I was determined to give my child a better life; after all he deserved it.]

As Gregory still stood there, waiting for an answer, my mind was blank, even though I already knew the answer, and was praying and hoping to myself that my man did not sell my car for a hit of crack. My eyes must have looked as if they were going to pop out of my head from the thought of what he was trying to insinuate or ask me. Did he already know that Mark was getting high? Was he trying to pick at me for information? Information that I wasn't going to reveal. Minutes seemed like hours as Gregory sat at the kitchen table watching me fix something to eat. I couldn't help but notice him sitting at the table, nodding his head uncomfortably.

"Well, sis, I guess I'll be going. I didn't want to leave so early, but it's getting late and I guess I'll have to prepare myself for this long walk home."

My insides were about to explode at any moment, and the tears continued to well in my eyes; suddenly I couldn't hold it in anymore and just broke down and started crying.

"What in the world is wrong with you, sis?" Gregory asked.

"I'm tired, tired of being a fool," I yelled at the top of my voice. "Why don't he just leave me alone and let me live my life without all those vicious lies—right now, I just wish he was dead. Gregory, I can't take it anymore—this is it." The more I cried, the louder I got, until by now everyone in the house heard me, even my tenants on the third floor.

"Sis, come over here, calm down, everything is going to be all right. Why don't you come home and spend the night with me and Charlotte and the kids?" he asked.

"If I do that, I will still be worried about my car and where this idiot could be. Why is he making my life a living hell? Why me? Gregory, I've been through enough—I don't even know why you are playing dumb on me. You already know that Mark is getting high, so why are you playing on my intelligence like this? From the moment you came and asked about the car, you already knew didn't you?"

"Yes, I did," he replied, "but it was not up to me to tell you this. Some things you keep to yourself, and I'm not one for telling anyone's business. Get a bag and pack some of your things along with Terry's, and you both come over," he insisted. "Girl, if you don't, you're going to sit here and go crazy with thinking about it," he insisted.

"Is Mark trying to drive me crazy or what, Gregory?" I asked. "He knows that I'm almost seven months pregnant and he could care less. The only thing on his mind right now is getting high."

"How long has he been getting high?" Gregory asked.

"Do you want a lie or the truth?" I asked.

"Tell me the truth—you know I don't play games with something like this," he said.

"To be honest, I don't even know."

"What do you mean, you don't know?" he asked, looking sort of confused.

"Just like I said, I don't know. All I do know is that one day I came home from shopping a few months ago, and he and some of his friends, including one female, were sitting around my table having a good time party at my expense. Please don't make me relive that moment or I may just go into labor early just thinking about it and how mad I was."

"Does your brother know?" Gregory asked.

"Yes, he does, and believe me, he is not too pleased about it at all."

"Cee, get your things and let's go, because you know if he comes home tonight and Chad sees him, there's going to be a big fight, and that's the last thing you need right now. Why haven't you told Charlotte what's going on? You know she would have been right here to support you. Pride is the last thing you need to be concerned with right now. Do you know how many people are in their graves because of pride?"

"Gregory, the last thing I need right now is for you to start preaching to me. I'm already feeling like a fool and don't need the lecture right now."

"Okay, sis. I'm going to grant your request and shut up only under one circumstance, and that is if you say you're coming home with me."

"I give in, Gregory," I said. "I'll go with you. Now are you satisfied?" I asked with a chuckle in my voice.

"I'll be right back," he said. "I'm going to get us a ride from one of my friends down the street."

"Please hurry," I pleaded as he walked away.

[One thing about Gregory, he was always around when I needed a shoulder to cry on. Whenever he and Charlotte were having problems, I was the one he would come running to, as if I could do something about their situation, like I had a magic wand. Some of the things they would fuss or argue about were so silly, but to them it was like they were in World War II. On average, the two of them were usually pretty cool together.]

When he arrived back and yelled up the stairway for me to come on, I was ready and so was little Terry. I knew my baby boy was concerned; by the look in his eyes, I just knew he was going to ask me what was wrong at any moment. The fear of him realizing what was going on and dying to ask me was like a question mark on his face. It's one thing when you worry, but when your child starts to worry, that is just a little bit too much and creates an even bigger problem for all concerned. Deep in the back of my mind I know that sooner or later I'm going to have to sit Terry down and tell him the truth, and that is something no parent wants to deal with, but sooner or later it will have to come to pass whether you want it to or not. It is only fair to the child, for after all, he is a part of your life, and nothing, but nothing, can change that. How do you tell a seven-year-old that his mother's man is on crack? That's something that should not have to be discussed, because it should not be going on in the first place. No parent, child, or anyone should ever have to deal with this situation. Terry has always been a very bright child, and even though I think he knows what's going on in my life, just the thought of telling him the truth made me feel like a loser. What parent do you know who wants to appear to be a loser in front of their kid? No one, and I do mean no one. Sometimes as parents we have a way of sugar-coating things in our lives to make them appear to be so perfect and "peachy keen," which actually hurts a child more than the truth. Telling the truth is always supposed to be the best answer, but in my case I felt like an idiot getting ready to walk head-on in front of a firing squad. I could feel Terry holding onto my dress as we walked down the street to get into Gregory's friend's car.

"Boy, you sure are out there—how many months are you?" Gregory's friend asked as I struggled to get into the front seat.

"I'm almost seven months."

"Do you know whether it's a boy or girl yet?"

"No, I'm hoping and praying that it is a little girl," I replied with a grin on my face.

"What does your husband want, or does it matter to him?" Now out of all times, why did he even have to go there with this dumb question? For in my mind that's what it was. Did he already know who my man was and was playing me for stupid, too, so he could have a good laugh? Girlfriend, when one person outside of your household finds out your man is on the big "C," better known as crack, you feel like the whole world knows.

"Which question do you want me to answer first?" I asked. "Are you always this nosy? And where do you live, and how many children do you have?" I asked as I watched him scramble for an answer.

"Oh, by the way, my name is Leon. I'm Gregory's cousin—nice to meet you," he said. "And is this your little young man sitting back there in the back seat so quietly?"

"Leon, that is your name, right? Do you always ask so many questions?"

"Well, to be frank, yes," he said with much laughter in his voice.

"I owe you an apology," I said to him.

"Apology for what?" he asked.

"I was just being rude, and I'm sorry if I hurt your feelings, but I'm not in the best of moods this evening, and I shouldn't have been so snappy with you."

"How many pregnant women do you know that aren't snappy?" he asked, laughing out loud. He laughed so hard I thought for a moment he was going to lose control of the car and hit the truck in front of us. I have to admit the guy had a great sense of humor, and even got me to laugh. Before arriving at Charlotte's, Gregory asked if there was anything I needed from the store.

"No," I replied. "I'm just tired and sleepy—all I want to do right now is go to bed and get a good night's sleep."

"Sis, I forgot to tell you that I spoke with your brother before we left and told him if he had any word from Mark to please come by the house and let us know. I hope that was okay with you, and I'm sorry I didn't mention it to you earlier. You were already upset, and I didn't want to make it any worse by mentioning his name."

"Gregory, at this point my only concern is if I still have a car and what if he gets stopped and they find drugs in the car? Then what?

This means I lose everything. I'm trying so hard and no one, and I do mean no one, deserves this living hell."

"Sis, everything will be all right once you get some rest and, like I said, your brother Chad will get in touch with us if he hears anything. Now go in there and talk to Charlotte."

For some reason, Terry was sticking to me like glue as if he was afraid I would disappear out of his sight. I assured him that everything was okay. He looked at me with a sadness in his eyes and told me how much he loved me and that he knew something was wrong and begged me to tell him what it was. Being that I had Terry at such an early age, it made me feel like he was my little brother instead of my son, and I felt almost obligated to tell him the truth, but something just would not let me do it. I reassured him that everything was fine, and that Mommy was a little tired and she and the baby just needed some rest. Terry held my hand, and when we reached the door to my girlfriend's third-floor apartment, he ran to open the door and announced that we were officially there. He was always such a gentleman. I hope this baby I'm carrying has all of his big brother's traits, regardless of whether it is a boy or girl. Now, that would be a true blessing. Charlotte came out of her bedroom looking shocked as ever to see me.

"What brings you here so late on a Saturday night?" she asked, happy to see me. Before I could answer her question, Gregory walked in. "Oh, you must have given him a ride home," she said.

"No," I replied.

She was so busy chitter-chattering, she never gave me a chance to answer her first question, so I played like I had forgotten it for fear of opening up a can of worms. As the time rolled on, she pulled out a game called Trouble—that was her favorite, and sometimes we would get caught up playing it for hours. Charlotte was a pro and played it all the time, so she knew how to pop the dice and make it roll in her favor. No one stood a chance to win against her. I guess if I played it day in and day out, I would be an expert, too. I knew that sooner or later my time was limited. In my mind I already knew that dreaded moment would come when I would have to tell her the truth and all hell would break loose.

"Cee, I thought you were coming by earlier today so we could go shopping or just browse around. I was mad and bored to death, just sitting here waiting for you to come. I told you once you got that car you were going to forget all about me. Now here it is almost 11:00 o'clock at night, and you come walking in just when everything is closed. But, guess what? I know exactly what we can do," she said excitedly. "We can go to New York down near the waterfront and look at the skyline and Gregory can watch the kids."

Charlotte was a lot of fun and very spontaneous, just like I was. We always did things on the spur of the moment. "Even though the thought is a good one, Charlotte, I'm tired and just want to go to sleep," I said to her.

"Cee, I know you didn't come all the way down here to my house to go to sleep. When have you ever been sleepy at this time of night on Saturday, especially since you know we always get together and do things on this day," she questioned with a disappointed look on her face. "I'll drive," she insisted, "and you can sleep. We will stop by one of the hot dog stands and I'll buy you one of those juicy sausage dogs you like and get you a lemonade and you'll be set. Come on, Cee," she pleaded.

"Charlotte, slow down. Maybe tomorrow we can go, and then we can take the kids."

"Take the kids?" she laughed. "Girl, right now all I want to do is run away from the kids is more like it," she hollered with laughter. "This could be our girls' night out—we can even stop back by your house on our way to New York and pick up Audra so we can have some real fun. You know she would be ready to jump at this opportunity. Please, please, Cee," she begged.

[My girlfriend knew how to beg when she really wanted to have her way. Only, if she knew what was really going on right now in my mind, I'm sure she would understand, but at the same time I knew she would be madder than ten bulls. Charlotte was known all over Main Street for her bad temper, and anyone who knew her, knew not to get her started because once she was, it was hard to calm her down. Believe me, the sister got mad respect from the junkies, to the winos, and anyone else who knew her. It was funny to watch some of the winos, sitting on the stoop sipping on their wine with the bottle turned up to their heads, and all of a sudden just drop the whole bottle once they would spot her coming down the street. Sometimes that was their first and only drink for the day which they bought with money they hustled. Jake was my favorite wino. You could tell at one time or another that he was a very well educated and well respected man by the way he carried himself; even though he was a wino, he was a neat one, always so courteous and polite, and willing to sing for whatever change you could spare. I called him the dignified wino, always singing and wearing a derby hat; no matter if the weather was a hundred degrees or not, he had it on along with his plaid pants. To me it seemed as if he got stuck in the sixties or seventies and was just as happy as a bug in a rug.]

"Cee, do you hear anything I'm saying to you right now? Why is it so hard for you to say 'Yes, Charlotte, let's go'?" she asked. "You're just standing here looking like you're in a trance. What's wrong with you?" she asked. "You were always the one so ready to jump before— what is wrong now that you don't want to go? You never let anything stop you before when you would come by my house and go hop on any bus going to New York," she said. "Now you have a car and you're hesitating? Are you afraid someone is going to steal your car? Or you think your car is too good to drive to New York, or better yet you don't trust my driving?"

"Charlotte, you are asking too many questions at one time." I had to ask her to slow down before I gave her a ticket. "Let me answer your first question. Yes, I would love to go to New York."

"Well, what is the problem?"

"For starters," I said, "I don't have my car with me."

"What do you mean, you don't have your car with you?"

"Mark has it," I replied.

"Well, how did you get to my house?" she asked.

"With Gregory and his cousin Leon. Please do me a favor and sit down. Charlotte, I have something to tell you."

"Cee, this better be good," she said. I could tell by the look on her face she was not prepared for what I was about to say. "I'm waiting," she said impatiently.

"Well, girlfriend, to be honest, Mark left with my car last night, and I haven't seen or heard from him since," I said.

"Are you joking?" she asked, a look of much curiosity lurking in her eyes.

"No, I'm not joking," I said to her.

"Has he lost his mind? Or did the two of you have an argument?"

"No, not really, he was a little upset because I left yesterday and went over to your house and stayed longer than he thought I should have. But, it wasn't reason enough for him to be gone for almost two days and not call home at all. Charlotte, we have been friends for a long time and have shared so much together. There is so much I have to tell you—I just don't know where to begin."

"Start at the beginning, and don't leave anything out," she said as she poured herself a glass of beer.

"I don't know if you're ready for what I have to say," I told her.

"You don't know what to say?" she asked. "Tell me something," she said, "because I know whatever it is, it isn't going to be good. So just tell me," she insisted. "We have been friends too long, and through thick and thin. No matter what it is, Cee, I'm always going to be your friend and love you the same, so don't be afraid to tell me."

"This is something I should have told you months ago. Mark is getting high."

"Girl, that is nothing to be ashamed of. Everybody does something," she said. "I drink my beer—so what? As long as I pay my bills, take care of my children, and go to work, it is nobody else's business what I do," she said boldly. "Let the man have a life—so he drinks a little, or smokes some pot, and who doesn't?" she asked.

"No, you don't understand," I said.

"What do you mean, I don't understand? There is nothing wrong with it," she stated.

"Charlotte, do I have to spell it out for you?" My lips trembled as I told her in a muffled tone, "Mark is smoking crack and I don't know where he is with my car." Once those words rolled off my lips I knew by the expression on her face that she was not pleased at all and that the war was getting ready to be declared any minute now.

"He really has lost his mind? she said. "Who does he think he is? How long has he been getting high? And where do you think he could be now?" she asked.

"Charlotte, I have no idea."

"Are you sure he is smoking crack?" Charlotte asked.

"Yes, I'm sure," I replied.

"How do you know, Cee?" Charlotte asked.

"How about, I came home a few months ago and caught him and some of his friends sitting around the kitchen table getting high."

"You have got to be kidding me?" she said in an angry tone. "This fool is asking for a real beat down," she said. "Tell me this, has he stolen anything from you?"

"Yes, he has, Charlotte—watch, money, and now my expensive jewelry box my brother gave me."

"Oh no, not that gorgeous, hand-carved jewelry box. Girl, tell me this is not happening and that you're just making this up," she said.

"It's very real," I told her.

"Cee, why haven't you come to me before now? What took you so long? Girl, come here, I promise you everything is going to be all right. Does your brother know that Mark is getting high?"

"Yes, he does."

"And what does he think about the situation?"

"To be honest, right now he wants to rip Mark's head off and kick him out of the house."

"What about Terry? Does he know what's going on?"

"No, he doesn't, and I don't want to tell him right now," I replied. "Would you tell your child something like this?" I asked her.

"Of course not," she replied. "That was foolish of me to ask you something like that in the first place. Please forgive me, Cee. Right now I'm so shocked I don't know what to say," she said as she looked at me with a look of hurt on her face. "Mark is going to pay for this," she said. "He knows that you're pregnant and don't need this aggravation—how could he be so cruel? This is not the time to be getting high. You just bought a new home, car, and just when everything is supposed to be getting better for you, he is out acting stupid and getting high."

Little did Charlotte know, instead of her making it better she was only making it worse. The more she talked about it, the worse I felt as a person. Didn't she know how this was making me feel, that it was tearing me up inside? Some good *she* was at a time like this! Now, here I was, sitting here wishing that I hadn't opened my big mouth, but this was my best friend. Someone that no matter what, I was supposed to be able to talk to about anything. Even though I knew she didn't mean any harm, right now she wasn't helping my situation by rambling on and on about things I already knew.

Finally, I couldn't take it anymore and threw my hands up and yelled, "Please stop, just stop! I can't take it anymore! I know you're my friend and you only want the best for me, but right now it does not help with you going on and on about this and that—what's right and what's wrong. All I want this man to do is bring my car back—can you understand that?" I asked coldly. "Why is all this happening to me?" I screamed. "I feel like I'm being punished, no matter what I do good, something bad is lurking around the corner waiting to happen to me."

By this time we were both so loud that our kids heard us and came running into the kitchen to see what was going on. Terry ran and jumped into my lap and hugged me as he watched the tears flowing down my face.

"I hate Mark," Terry said, as he, too, started to cry. "He's always making you cry, and he is mean to you. I wish he would go away—he's a bad man. I don't want to see my mommy cry," he said as he continued to cry and hug me. "Ma, please don't cry—I'll take care of you," Terry said so strongly as he wiped the tears from my eyes with his little dirty hands. This child had a magical way of making me feel better, no matter what. Instead of continuing to cry, I couldn't help but smile through all my tears, for this child was just downright funny, even when he was trying to be so serious at a time like this.

"What's so funny Ma?" Terry asked as I broke out into laughter, thinking about what he had said earlier. Now how was this little seven-year-old boy going to take care of me when I was his mother and supposed to be taking care of him? His gesture was just too sweet and thoughtful. At the time I wished I had a tape recorder so I could remind him of this whenever he gets into mischief. Children say some of the sweetest things sometimes. I told him that everything was going to be fine and to go back into the room and play.

"Mommy, I don't want to leave you because you might start crying again," he said, so seriously.

"I'm going to be all right," I assured him as I kissed him on his cheek and whispered that I loved him into his ear. He jumped off my lap and hugged my girlfriend and thanked her for being there for me. Charlotte apologized to me for not being considerate of my feelings as she rambled on about Mark.

"Girl, you don't owe me anything," I told her as she hugged me.

"Cee, I'll always be here for you," she exclaimed. "Will you please forgive me? No one but you knows what you're going through, and it isn't anyone else's business. Does Audra know?"

"Yes, she does," I said.

"How long has she known about this?"

"It's been quite sometime," I answered.

"I'm just so sorry you are going through this," she said. "Right now I'm so angry at Mark—here he has everyone thinking he is such a nice guy and wishing they had someone like him. I guess that goes to show you everything that appears to be good isn't like that all the time. What can I do to help you?" Charlotte asked.

"At the moment, the only thing I need you to do is pray for me that God will give me strength and that my baby will be healthy and strong. I know everything else will be all right. You know my baby Terry is going to take care of me." Charlotte looked at me as we both embraced with laughter.

"Girl, you know that's too cute," she replied. "Have you tried to get Mark some help?"

"Yes—when I first found out he was getting high, that was my first suggestion, and he pretended that he didn't need any help because it wasn't affecting him. It wasn't until after he stole $700 of the mortgage money and ran off for several days that he realized he needed help and signed himself into an outpatient drug rehab after he returned. He stayed clean, so I thought, for about a month until this incident with the car."

"Maybe he just got angry, Cee, and is waiting to cool off before he comes back," Charlotte said.

"Are you stuck on stupid or what?" I asked her. "This man has been gone for two days—did you hear anything I said? Or are you still in a daze from hearing about the situation? What if Gregory ran off for two days and came back and told you some lame excuse, like he just needed to cool off. Now answer me, would you buy it?"

"Now, you know the answer, Cee, so don't play crazy."

"That's all I wanted to know," I said to her. "Well, you should understand how I feel and where I'm coming from. What makes me any different than you? We are both women with the same emotions, but this time I know it is hard for you to understand how I feel, because you are not dealing with a man who smokes crack, and that is a world of difference."

"Has he ever hit you?" she asked.

"No, he hasn't, but there were times when he would come screaming and yelling, demanding money so he could buy crack, and would get so mad when I wouldn't give it to him until, if I didn't know better, I thought that he was going to."

"Where is Terry when Mark is acting up?"

"Most of the time he is outside playing with his friends or in the other room with the door shut, looking at TV."

"If you need a place to stay until you get this situation under control, please don't hesitate to let me know. All you have to do is say the word," she said. "Remember, I'm here for you. But, when I see Mark, he has to answer to me. After all of this, I know you must be tired, so let's go to bed. I'll get some covers for you and Terry so you can sleep comfortably. Don't worry, everything will be fine."

Her comforting words, no matter how reassuring they sounded, let me know I was headed for trouble if I continued my relationship with this man. I loved him so much and wanted so badly for our relationship to work, as became more and more evident in everything that I was doing. "Nothing, and I do mean nothing could have ever prepared me for what I am going through," I said. "Staying up late at night, barely sleeping, wondering if Mark was coming home, or if he was somewhere dead. Charlotte, right now I'm numb and almost to the point to where I wish he were dead."

"Girl, don't say that," she said.

"Well, at least I wouldn't be going through this," I said to her. "I want my life back. When is that going to happen?" I asked her coldly.

"Cee, I know you do. You are a strong black woman, and I know you have been through a lot, but there is nothing that you can't do—I believe that wholeheartedly," she said. "No one can convince me otherwise. You are the best. I admire you for your strength and often have said to myself that I wish someday I could be like you," Charlotte said.

"Are you nuts?" I asked with much laughter.

"No, I'm for real," she said. "Now let's go to bed and hope and pray that tomorrow Mark will be back with your car and everything will be fine," she said as she turned off the light and said good night. Guess I'll go to sleep and write more tomorrow, Mrs. Diary.

April 8, 1986

Dear Diary,

Last night I didn't really sleep well; I tossed and turned all night, wondering if Mark was okay and if anything had happened to my car. This morning I awoke to a loud noise; before I could get my composure, so I could respond to someone actually knocking on the door, I could hear my girlfriend's boyfriend Gregory yelling out loud, "Who is it?" Their bedroom was all the way in the front of their house, and the kitchen was the closest to the door. Even though I could barely make out the response of the person knocking, I jumped up and told Gregory I would get it. He told me to lie back down and get some rest. As I listened to Gregory dragging his feet in his bedroom slippers lazily across the floor, I began to wonder if it was my brother—or, better yet, Mark—coming to get me. But, here it was almost 8:30 in the morning—why would someone be knocking on their door this early? Don't they know it's the weekend, and that everyone should be resting? While I lay there thinking, not able to go back to sleep, I heard Gregory call my name and tell whoever it was that I was asleep, but he would wake me up. Upon hearing those words, I anxiously jumped up and almost tripped trying to scramble to the door to see who it was that was looking for me. When I reached the kitchen doorway, I saw my brother standing there.

"Good morning," I said as I hugged him and asked what he was doing up so early and what made him come to see me. Before Chad could answer, I looked up and saw Mark standing over by the door, looking all tired and worn out.

"I came to make sure Mark brought you your car. I'm so mad right now that I don't know what to do," my brother stated. "It's taking everything in me not to beat the crap out of him. Mark, give my sister her car keys and tell her where you've been," my brother demanded. "Tell her the truth, or I will," he ordered.

As I said before, my brother was one you didn't want to make mad. At that moment I was so relieved that Mark and my car were both okay that my anger almost disappeared. All I wanted was for everything to be okay. Listen to how stupid that sounds. I had to really ask myself, *Cee, are you willing to let this man get away with this again? Look at how you have suffered and yet you are feeling sorry for him, as if nothing ever happened. Get a grip and stop tripping. He needs his behind beat.* And if that were going to happen there surely would be a long line of people waiting to give him his first licks.

"Chad, let's go outside and give your sister and Mark some time to talk," Gregory insisted. As they passed Mark on their way to the door, I could feel the tension heating up.

"Mark, so where have you been? And I want the truth—no lies," I asked angrily. "What's wrong? The cat got your tongue?" I asked. "Don't make me do something I may regret."

"Cee, you already know, so why are you asking me this dumb question?" he replied.

By this time, I had lost it and ran up to him to slap his face. Before I could reach him, Charlotte came into the kitchen and stopped me. She was also mad and demanded that Mark leave her house until things cool down. Well, cooling down they weren't. Sooner or later I knew I had to go home, and that is where turmoil would surely be awaiting me.

I stared out of the window and watched as he walked down the street, passing my brother and Gregory. For a moment there, I thought they were going to jump on him and really hurt him. (From the motions they were making, I could tell that they were arguing and getting ready to fight. Some other men were outside and broke them apart. That's the only thing that saved Mark's tail from a good whipping. Now, whether that was good or bad, I would soon find out.)

When my brother and Gregory cooled off, they both came upstairs and talked to me while Charlotte started cooking breakfast. No one mentioned what had happened for fear of my reaction, and if the truth be known, I was happy they didn't bring up the thought of this horrible scum of the earth. To me, at this minute, that's what I was thinking. How dare he say to me that what I was asking him was dumb? This man is insane and really needs someone to teach him a lesson. One day he will get it, and when he does, I hope I'm right there watching.

Charlotte was a great cook and could cook her butt off when she wanted to, as was attested as we all sat there and ate like we hadn't eaten in weeks. To see us eating, you would have thought we were starving. The kids could hardly wait for seconds. Terry ate so many pancakes I thought his little stomach was going to pop. For a moment there, he almost looked like the Pillsbury doughboy. The more I watched how he stuffed his face, the more I wanted to laugh at how funny he looked. This moment was so relaxing and peaceful, knowing that I had my car back and that I was surrounded by friends who cared not only for me, but my child also.

After we finished breakfast, it was time for me to pack our things and get ready for the short ride home with Terry and my brother. The ride I dreaded, not knowing what to expect when I returned to my so-called castle. Chad was angry, even though he had no words to express himself at that moment. When we reached my car, I told my brother he could drive, thinking that this would erase some of the anger I knew he was feeling at the moment. He jumped at the opportunity, grinning from ear to ear.

"Now sis, you know Mark is going to have a fit when he sees me driving your car."

"Who cares about what Mr. Mark thinks? He is lucky he got to walk away without a scratch," I said as Chad turned the corner, gently cruising along the riverside as we talked and laughed and made up songs to sing with Terry. It felt good to see a smile on my child's face. This little boy means the world to me. And to see him happy made me glow amidst everything else that was going on around us.

"Sis, I must say, this is a smooth-riding car—I wouldn't mind having one just like it," my brother said. "I have to give you credit, girl. You sure know how to pick them. Hopefully you will let me borrow it sometimes."

"Chad, you know I don't have a problem with that. You can borrow almost anything I have, as long as you're not drinking. And I do hope you know what I mean."

No sooner did we reach the block where we live than we spotted my godbrother Jeremy walking toward our house. I told my brother to blow the horn and pull over so we could give him a ride. When Chad blew the horn, Jeremy turned around to see who it was but kept on walking. At that moment we realized that he didn't recognize that it was us, so I told my brother to pull over and call to him. After realizing it was us, Jeremy came across the street. His mouth was open in shock as he checked out the ride and the people in it.

"Now, okay guys, whose car did you steal?" he asked jokingly.

"It's mine," my brother replied.

"Now, I know that is a big joke," he said as he laughed out loud. "All kidding aside, whose car is it?"

"It's mine, Jeremy," I replied.

"All right, sis, I'm proud of you. This is really nice."

"Get in," I demanded as he stood there admiring the car and listening to the radio as the Bose speakers sounded off quite nicely. "Classy Lady—is what I'm going to call you from now on?" he stated.

We pulled off and glided around the corner for a spin while the breeze gently blew into the car with the sunroof tilted halfway.

"Girl, this car is smooth. I don't know what to say about you. For a pregnant sister, you have it going on," Jeremy said. "First the house, and now the car. I surely would like to know what is next. I dare not ask how you're doing it," he said.

"Well, for starters, how about my own company?" I said, trying to be modest.

"Are you serious?" he asked, laughing out loud. "Cee, where do you get this drive? I mean, energy? You are so young and yet so ambitious. Girl, if you aren't just like your daddy, Jimmy Lee. If he could see you now, he would be so proud of you. I know he would, because I am."

Little did he know about what else was going on in my life, and I dared not tell him. The ride was very relaxing and soothing for a while, until we passed by Mark, walking down the street looking like a lost soul.

"Hey, stop the car," Jeremy said as we passed Mark by.

"Stop for what?" I asked.

"Didn't you see Mark back there?" Jeremy asked. By this time we were already about two blocks away.

"Yes, I did," I said as my brother continued to drive.

"Aren't you going to give him a ride?"

"A ride where?" I asked. "He's done all the riding he is going to do in my car."

"Cee, why are you being so cold? Don't you want to stop and give the brother a ride?"

"Jeremy, I appreciate your concern, but please don't go there with me. Right now I'm not in the mood to be bothered with Mark, and the less we talk about him or I hear his name, the better off we will all be."

"Okay, baby girl, I guess I'll back off of that conversation," he said.

I could tell he was curious and wanted to ask more questions about what was going on, but dared not because of what my reaction might be. Everyone knew that I could be very blunt and direct when I needed to be, but why couldn't I be that way with Mark? He's the one I should have been straight to the point with, and just maybe I wouldn't be going through the changes that I am going through. It was my own stupidity and lack of knowledge about that dreaded drug called crack cocaine that kept me blinded. Love sometimes can make you or break you, and breaking me it was, for I was blinded by it for many months. Not only was I suffering, but also my child and everyone else who came into contact with me and knew what was going on. It put a strain on them as well. There comes a time in our lives when we have to say enough is enough and move on to bigger and better. Why was this so hard for me to do? It wasn't so much the love I had for this man as it was a challenge for me to prove that anyone could change if you believed in them enough.

"Cee, I'm not trying to start anything," Jeremy said, "but don't you think that Mark is going to be mad when you get home and he knows that you purposely didn't stop to give him a ride?"

"Well, Jeremy, he should have thought about that before he took off and went for a joy ride and stayed gone for two days," I said.

"Say what? Please repeat that again. Let me be sure I heard you correctly," Jeremy asked as he sat straight up in his seat with his ears perked.

"You heard me right," I said as I repeated it, but before I could finish my sentence, my brother took over, adding that he had to make Mark bring my car to me at Charlotte's house, and how he and Gregory wanted to beat the daylights out of him for aggravating and disrespecting me like he did.

"You mean to tell me he was gone two days?" Jeremy asked. "Where in the world was he at? And did you give him permission to drive your car? Because now he has to answer to me." Jeremy was a big, husky guy that you didn't want to make angry, not even just a little bit. He didn't play at all. "Now, I can't wait to get to your house," he said, "I think it's time for me and Mr. Mark to have a good talk. I'm not going to let him dog you out like that. I thought the brother was cool and about something. How long has he been doing this?"

"I would really prefer not to talk about it," I said as I threw my head back into the headrest, tired from the thought of what I would be faced with when I returned home. No one could imagine the fear that was lurking inside of me, even though I was putting up this brave facade in front of everyone. Like I was so bad and mighty. All I was doing was trying to muster the strength to be brave in front of my brother and friend. Inside I was trembling with fear, just thinking about what the Beast Master was going to say or do once everyone was gone, and I would be left alone with no one to call on when he would start his reign of terror. This man was a fiendish monster when crack cocaine set in. No one, and I do mean no one, knew better than me what it was like. Fear gripped my body as we pulled up in front of my house. Of course, Terry was overjoyed to be home again so he could play with his friends and ride his bike.

"Ma, can I go play with my friends?" he asked excitedly as the car came to a complete stop.

"Sure you can, and remember—don't leave off the block," I said as he jumped out of the car and ran to catch his little friend named Buddy down the street.

The three of us stared at each other as we stepped out of the car. I heard Jeremy taking a deep sigh as if to say, okay, let's get ready to rumble.

"All right fellas, I know the both of you are angry and the last thing I need right now is for the two of you to go into the house and pick a fight with Mark. What you both need to do is remember that this is my problem and I will deal with it. Please promise me, Chad that you won't start, if nothing else. Please make me that promise, right now," I pleaded sadly.

My brother hated to see me upset about anything and made me a promise that he would try to be sane about the situation. My next task was to get Jeremy to also agree to the same—now, that was a challenge in itself. This brother told me straight out that he was not going to agree to something so profound.

"I'm telling you now, sis," Jeremy said, "Mark needs to be handled and I'm going to be the one to take care of him for you. Whether you know it or not, I've already heard some things that I want to talk to him about anyway."

"Some things like what?" I asked.

"Don't worry about it," he said.

"How dare you tell me not to worry," I said as he kept on walking like he didn't hear a word. From the way he was walking, I could tell trouble was only a few seconds away. My heart started fluttering, and I could feel my body trembling for the fear of the unknown. I begged Jeremy one more time before we reached the stairs. "Please Jeremy, please, not today. I'm the one who has to deal with him when everyone is gone," I pleaded.

"After today, you won't have to worry about dealing with him anymore," Jeremy said as he climbed the stairs with the look of fire in his eyes and anger in his heart.

The look on this man's face told the whole story; when he reached the top step, there was Mark just standing there waiting, as if to say "bring it on." Why did he have to be there at all, was the question in my mind. Didn't this man have enough common sense to leave, run, or whatever? Jeremy was not one to back down from anyone, and I know that if I were a man and he approached me, I would probably still be running for fear of my life. But today, this was not the case.

As I walked in behind Jeremy, Mark called me into the bedroom so he could talk to me and ask me why we drove by him earlier. I looked at him and replied, "Because I felt like it. I don't owe you anything," I yelled. "Who do you think you are? And what makes you feel that you can get away with this?"

"Look, you are my woman and nobody, I mean nobody, can change that," he said in a hateful voice. "You may think that you are safe now that you have your little bodyguards around, but how long is that going to last? I know exactly why you brought Jeremy over," he stated. "You think I'm afraid of him and your brother, but I'm telling you now," he said, "I don't care how big he is. He can fall just like the rest. When I get through cutting him up—and your brother—then what are you going to do Ms. Prissy? I wish your brother would think about doing something to me—they will find him in a body bag, and you can tell him I said so."

At that moment I was so afraid, I didn't know what to do. I didn't know whether to scream for help or just fake like I had fainted or what. This man was scaring the living daylights out of me. I could feel my heart skipping a beat and my blood pressure rising.

"Cee, are you okay in there?" I heard my brother ask.

"She's fine," Mark replied. "No one's hurting your sister," he yelled as he looked at me with those piercing, evil eyes that told me he was high on crack at this very minute. "You better tell your brother and Jeremy that you are okay," he said as he pulled me closer to him. I could feel the heat from his body as he stroked my face with his hand, looking deep into my eyes as if to say, *I love you, but I will kill you,* in the same breath. Once again, I could hear my brother calling out for me to stick my head outside my bedroom door so he would know that I was okay.

"Mark, please let me tell my brother I'm okay and that we will work this out—please?" I begged.

"You don't have to tell anyone anything," he said, "but me. First of all, I want to know right now—do you love me, and if you do, you will tell them both to leave and let us work out our problems. If you don't, you will be sorry." By now, at this moment, I'm scared to death and started to cry. This man had no empathy and insisted that I shut up immediately. I could hear my brother and Jeremy mumbling on the other side of the door.

"Mark, let my sister out of the room," my brother demanded.

"Make her come out," Mark yelled back.

By this time Jeremy became very angry and knocked on the door, telling Mark that if he doesn't let me come out he's going to come in and, "I don't think you're going to like it if I do," he said. All of a sudden, without warning, Mark opens the door and tells Jeremy and my brother that I'm fine. My brother calls me out and sees that I've been crying.

"Come over here, sis," my brother demands.

"No, come over here," Mark insists.

My brother takes me by my arm at the same time Mark snatches me by my other arm. Now I'm like Raggedy Ann; the tugging match begins, and I'm being yanked back and forth until I'm almost dizzy. Don't they know I'm pregnant? They continue for a second or two until my brother hauls off and hits Mark hard with his fist until he falls to the floor, daring him to get up. "Is that the best you have to give?" Mark asks, as he slowly rose up from the floor and returned the blow, hitting my brother dead in the eye. Before you know it, they are in a full-blown brawl! By this time, Jeremy is really mad and angrily picks Mark up and body-slams him into the wall. I'm scared stiff; I couldn't move; I didn't know what to do first, call the police or an ambulance.

My poor brother had no idea that his eye was busted wide open with blood dripping everywhere. When he realized his eye had been busted, instead of him wanting to go to the hospital, he wanted to continue fighting Mark, as if that was going to solve the problem. I had to beg him to go to the emergency room. His eye was a horrible sight to see. All I could do at that moment was cry; I guess you could say I was a big crybaby, and I agree a hundred percent. A big crybaby I was; when you are pregnant you become very emotional about everything. In this case, I had every reason to cry; look at what was happening to me. My man was on crack, stealing everything in sight.

Now my brother was going to have to go to the hospital and get stitches, all because I didn't know when to get out of this tired relationship with a man who had no goal in life but crack cocaine. It was all my fault, as was evident while I drove my brother to the hospital with a blood-soaked towel wrapped around his head. One of my worst fears at that moment was, what if he loses his sight in that eye? It would all be my fault. How could I live with that? I asked myself as guilt set in.

"Cee, Mark is going to pay for this—you wait until I get home. I'm going to take him out," my brother said. "If Jeremy hasn't done it already," he added. Why did my brother have to remind me that Jeremy was still at the house, and there was a good chance or possibility that he and Mark could be at it right now as we speak?

"I have enough on my mind with worrying about my brother without having to worry about that, too. Chad, please let's talk about something else," I said.

As I drove along the highway, speeding all the way, I couldn't help but think about what my family was going to think once they found out what had happened to my brother's eye—not to mention the fact that my mother was beaten blind just eight years prior to this incident. If my mother knew what I was going through, and that her son was on his way to the emergency room because my man busted his eye, she would be on the first thing smoking to see her baby boy. One thing I can say about my mom is that even though she is totally blind, she never let it stop her from doing whatever she wanted or going wherever she pleased. My mother was a very beautiful person, in spirit and in looks; it brings tears to my eyes even now to think how some cruel person could have been so mean as to take her sight. Her skin was a pretty, tawny, light tan and her hair was coal black and felt very silky to the touch. I remembered as a little girl how she used to get all dressed up to go out and she would smell so good as she would lie beside me and my baby brother Chad and read us a fairy tale before she would depart for an evening of wining and dining. This woman had much class, as was evident in everything she wore; even her walk was sophisticated. At least when she left the house, that's what I remember; now, when she returned home, that was a horse of a different color. By the time she would reach home, her wig was twisted and there were three or four holes in her stockings from dancing so hard in her bare feet. I never knew, I guess, what put those holes there and was too afraid to ask, especially after she had a few drinks. Before she had a drink, she was the sweetest person in the world, but after she had too much of the firewater you knew it, and so did everyone else. She was part Indian and would go on the warpath, and if you had good sense you got out of her way. No matter what, she was my mom and I still loved her.

When my brothers and I found out that my parents were going to separate, I was only twelve years old and as children, this really made us so sad and filled with anger; I resented my mother for years and often felt that it was all her fault, never giving her a chance to tell her side of the story. I could see no wrong that my father was doing and could only find fault in her for drinking and partying. To me, this was the only thing that stood in between them. Deep inside I knew there had to be more to it than that, but I didn't want to admit it and only wanted to see one side of the story. Favoring my father all the way. It wasn't until after my mother's horrible fate, losing her eyesight, that I tried to come to grips with reality and what I was feeling. From the moment I walked up onto the porch after school one day and saw my mother sitting there in the swing, with her face beaten so badly that I didn't even recognize her, I began to feel so much hurt and pain. Can you believe that I didn't know who my mother was? I know that may sound unreal, but this woman who gave birth to me and brought me into the world I did not recognize as my mother. Instead I thought she was some ill-fated woman who was just passing through and my aunt felt sorry for her and was just letting her sit there on the front porch to get some rest while maybe she fixed her something to eat. As I walked onto the porch, I spoke to the lady and went on into the house and straight to the kitchen where I could smell nothing but good food cooking.

"Aunt Theo, who is that lady on the front porch?" I asked. I sniffed from pot to pot to see what was on the menu for dinner.

My aunt looked at me with tears in her eyes. Now, this was a major shock here. All these years I had never seen my aunt cry. She was always too strong, and often she told me that crying was for other people, as she would tell it. To watch tears fall from her eyes, I knew it was something bad. Not this woman of steel; I always felt like she was the female version of Moses.

"Auntie, are you okay?" I asked. "Who is that woman?"

Choking up, she could barely speak; finally she whispered in a low, painful voice as tears streamed down her face, "Cee, that is your mother," she sobbed.

"My who?" In my mind I just knew this couldn't be true; my mother, looking like that? This has got to be a joke, as I wanted so badly to believe. This woman that was said to be my mother looked like someone off the street (as horrible as that sounds, it was true).

"Well, if that's true, where is my baby sister?" I asked.

"She's hiding under the table, still in shock."

"In shock from what?"

"Please, Cee, don't ask me any more questions—just go and give your mother a hug and let her know that you love her," she said.

"Okay, but are you sure that is my mother sitting out there?"

"Just do what I asked," she yelled.

"Peanut, where are you?" I called out. "Peanut" was the name my father had given my little sister when she was two; at the time this terrible and brutal incident happened to my mother, she was five years old. What a horrible thing for a kid to witness at such an early age.

Peanut was my father's pride and joy, even though he and my mother weren't together when she had my baby sister, he adored this little girl and every summer would go over to New York and take her back to Jersey and keep her for three to four weeks at a time. My little sister was so tiny and fragile, almost like a porcelain doll, so pretty and only made to look at. I could hear her breathing and moving up under the table and told her if she came out I would take her to the store and buy her some ice cream. Before I could finish my sentence, there she was, peeking from underneath the tablecloth, asking me in a soft voice, "You're taking me for some ice cream?" I grabbed my little sister and took her into my arms and kissed and hugged her ever so gently while whispering to her that everything was going to be all right, and that I was going to protect her from all harm and danger and never again would anyone hurt her or our mother again.

Finally, I mustered up enough courage to go outside and sit in the swing on the porch with my mother and hugged her, telling her how much I loved her. Her face was so badly swollen and disfigured that it was a blackish, purplish color; her eyes were drawn shut from the pressure of the swelling, and her once-beautiful lips were busted. You could still see little, tiny lines of blood where her lips were split. It was a pitiful sight, and deep inside I wanted to cry so badly, but I knew I had to be strong for her and my baby sister. I wanted to ask her how she let this happen to her. Was she in an accident or did someone do this to her? How do you even bring yourself to the point of asking your mom something like this? It's harder than you could ever imagine.

As I sat there beside her, swinging back and forth, trying to strike up a conversation, my mind was blank. I was too busy looking at her face and how disfigured it was. And wanting so badly to believe that this was a terrible dream that would soon end. After sitting there for a while, she finally asked me what her face looked like, and she made me promise to tell her the truth; that was one of the hardest things I have ever had to do in my life. Listen to me—this was my mother, the woman that gave birth to me and brought me into the world; now it was up to me to tell her what she looked like.

"Cee, I know I look horrible, don't I?" she asked.

At that moment, if she could have seen the expression on my face, there would have been no need for her to ask that question. I would have given myself away. My mother was a gorgeous-looking woman who had much wisdom and knowledge; how could she let something like this happen? As we sat there swinging and conversing, I could tell, even though my mother was hurting emotionally, she still wanted to tell me what had happened. I didn't want to push her into talking about anything that she didn't feel comfortable about. I knew it would just be a matter of time before she would tell me. And she did; by the expression on her face and the sound of her voice, I knew she was in much pain—physically and emotionally. You're talking about a woman who looked like a living doll, not one day, but every day. Now, how can you stand there before her and tell her how bad she really looks?

"Please, Cee, tell me the truth—I can take it," she says. "What color is my face?"

"Ma, please don't do this to me," I begged.

"Baby, I need to know—Cee, please tell me the truth." By the sound in her voice I knew she was getting ready to cry, and so was I. "All day long I have been asking Theo to tell me, and she wouldn't. The only thing she would tell me is that it's going to be all right. How can it be all right if I don't even know how I look?" she cried.

As she broke down, I cried with her. I told her that everything was going to be okay and that maybe within a few days the swelling would be gone down enough for her eyes to open up a little. She asked me if I thought she looked like a monster; this hurt me so badly, just as it is hurting me now to write this.

"No, Mom, you don't look like a monster—you look like my mom, and I love you regardless of what you look like on the outside. It's the inside that counts." That day, I'll remember for as long as I live. "Ma, if you don't mind me asking, how did this happen to you?"

"Well, baby, to make a long story short, my boyfriend had been drinking and we got into an awful argument and one thing lead to another, and before I knew it he was hitting me in the head with a porcelain teacup."

"Why, Ma? Why? Did you know this man was a woman-beater before you got involved with him?"

"No, I didn't," she replied. "I thought he was a nice guy until this happened."

"So what you're telling me is that this man was a Dr. Jekyll and Mr. Hyde kind of guy?"

"Yes, baby, sometimes you don't know until it's too late. I never knew I was beaten so badly until your uncle was coming through from Rochester, New York, and stopped by to see me. He found me lying in a puddle of blood and rushed me to the hospital and made me pack my things up and come with him here."

"You mean to tell me you could have been dead if no one had found you in time?" I asked.

"Maybe," she said, still crying and sniffling at the same time.

"Oh, Ma, I'm so sorry this happened to you. I wish I knew who this monster was—I would strangle him myself. Does Dad know this happened to you?"

"No, he doesn't, and please promise me you won't tell him" she pleaded.

"Ma, now you're asking me to do the impossible," I said.

Even though my parents had been separated at the time for six years, I could see no reason not to tell him what had happened, but as the days went on I understood. The doctor told my Aunt Theo to bring my mother back for her second visit after the swelling went down so they could check to see if any damage had been done to the nerves around her eyes. Two weeks had gone by, and the swelling was slowly disappearing. The color started to come back to her skin but her eyes were still not open and looked as if they were glued shut. In my heart I feared the worst. Before she was due for her next visit, I prayed that she would be spared her sight. I knew my mother was afraid and that she, too, feared the worst. It wasn't until her second visit that she found out for sure that she would be totally blind and that there wasn't any surgery that they could perform to bring her eyesight back. At the time my mother lost her sight, she was so young, only forty-two years old. That one moment in time changed her life forever.

Deep down inside, my heart went out to her, for I could not feel her pain but only imagine it. That's when I made up my mind that I would never, ever let a man put his hands on me. The thought of a man putting his hands on me terrified me to no end. How could someone be so cruel as to beat on a woman and leave her for dead? Someone, that is; my mother, at that. A woman so genuinely pure and innocent, and now she must face living in darkness for the rest of her life, a sad fate that she had no control over. The only thing she ever wanted was love and respect, something that she and every other woman deserved—not just because she was a woman, but first and foremost, a human being. I know if my dad knew, it would break his heart. My parents had a great relationship, even though they had been apart for six years; they acted like best friends, always understanding and caring about each other's needs. My parents were both raised in the South and were instilled with deep Christian values and morals. Dad always told my mother that he would never give her a divorce, and if she wanted one, she would have to file for it herself. I remember the times when they used to sit out on the porch and laugh and joke about the idea of Mom wanting a divorce so she could move on with her life. His reply was the same each time. He would say to my mom, "Ida, when I took my vow for better or worse, in sickness and health, and until death do us part, I meant it." And you know what? That's exactly what he meant until the day she filed. He was a real man, and I must say that I will honor and cherish him always, for in my heart he was a hero, one to be hailed for being the wonderful, loving human being that he was. If only there were more men like him, the world would be all the better for it.

From the day we received the shocking news that my mom would be blind forever, everyone's life changed. In my mind the fear of a man hitting me sent chilling thoughts through my body; it was a long-lasting nightmare that would remain with me always. After accepting her tragic fate, she stood strong and continued to strive hard to empower herself by going to school for the blind and learning all she could so she could survive. This meant starting all over again, like a baby trying to learn how to walk. I admired her strength and courage; not only did it help her to develop into the dynamite person she learned to become, but it also helped us, her family and loved ones around her, to accept the things we could not change and let God take care of the rest. It was faith that kept her strong and gave her the will to come to grips with her condition. Believe me, it was a hard lesson. In the beginning it was very hard for her, because at first she could only see shadows and was so afraid, until one day she could not see anything at all but the darkness that loomed around her. Little did she know that we her family would become her new-found eyes. She was always very independent, and I knew it hurt her to feel as though she was a burden. That she could never be, because she was our mother, the love of our lives. No matter what.

As I patiently sat in the emergency room waiting for the doctor to X-ray my brother's eye, I couldn't help but worry about what the outcome was going to be. I dared not tell my brother what I was thinking, knowing that in his mind he probably had the same thoughts as I did regarding his eyesight. He always had very beautiful brown eyes that seemed to sparkle in the light, making you wonder if they were hazel-colored at times. People used to always tease us and would often ask if we were really sister and brother because of this. This sometimes made him very angry. Here he was, in the emergency room, all because of me. My fault for being so stupid, dealing with a man I should have left from the start of something so bad. If I had listened to my brother, I wouldn't be sitting here, looking and feeling so stupid and guilty right now. If I could turn back the hands of time, I would.

After waiting for almost two hours, the doctor finally called me in to give me the prognosis, telling me that he had to have fifteen stitches and would need to have more X-rays within a few more days to determine whether he would have permanent scar tissue damage from his injury. Before the doctor could finish telling me the information, my brother walked in on the tail end of the conversation with a bandage over his eye. For a moment, if I didn't know any better, I would have thought he was the new reincarnation of the mummy. My baby brother—here he was, only twenty-nine years old, and facing almost the same fate as my mom, but only one eye instead of two. This is a nightmare, one that would never be forgotten.

If this man, my so-called lover, could do this horrible thing to my brother and become so angry and violent at the drop of a hat, what would he eventually do to me? That question played over and over in my head. The violence he displayed that day made me realize that he was not fit to be the man that I could spend the rest of my life with— or anyone else, for that matter. One thing I need to come to terms with is that sooner or later it is going to get worse and that if I am going to get out of this terrible thing called a relationship with him, I need to do it now, today, not tomorrow. For tomorrow may be too late. I could tell by looking at my brother that he was hurt and in much pain, physically and emotionally. His pride, and spirit, were broken. And from his expression, I could tell that he was also very disappointed in me, his baby sister.

Our ride home to the house of horror where it all began was a long one, filled with much solitude and silence for fear of what the other might say. The last thing I wanted was an argument with him that would estrange us. This day would be the beginning of all old things to change and new things to begin. What I needed was strength to move on and the courage to do it. But how am I going to break away from this man that has become the Beast Master? When in desperate situations, we sometimes make even more mistakes, like making the person that is making our life so miserable feel that it is our fault that they have become so messed up in the first place.

As we circled the block where we live to find a parking space, my brother turned to look at me as if to say, what are you going to do now? My face was flustered with much confusion, hurt, and pain for what I knew he had to be feeling. I could feel the eyes of people staring as we both stepped out of the car and walked toward the house where we lived. What would I say? How was my brother going to respond or act when approached by these nosy individuals who were not concerned for one moment about how he felt or what had happened to him, but only wanted to satisfy their own sick curiosity.

Who would be the first to muster the courage to approach us and ask what happened to Chad's eye but Nosy Nadine. Wasn't it apparent by the huge, protruding bandage wrapped around his head that something traumatic had happened to him, or was she blind? The insensitivity she displayed with her ignorance was not to be tolerated by me or my brother this day. It angered me to the point of being very snappy and rude with her. My response to her stupid question made her realize quickly, without further ado, that I was a very angry, agitated woman and that regardless of my pregnant condition, I was not going to tolerate her ignorance this day. It didn't matter to me that half the block was related to her. I didn't care and told her if she opened her mouth to ask one more question, she would regret it for the rest of her life. This day she had the right string, but the wrong yo-yo, as my Uncle June Bug used to say. Nothing made me angrier than a nosy, noncaring person who had no respect for anyone else, not even themselves, than to show so little concern for others.

The walk to my house seemed to drag for a moment, and the anticipation of what was going to happen next left my mind reeling. Terry was peeking out the window, and I knew by his motions that he was running to the door to greet me and my brother. Chad was Terry's favorite uncle and always spent time with him; he was there when I went to work so he could help Terry with his homework and make sure his clothes were ready for school. The genuine love he displayed for my brother showed when the door swung open and this little body was standing there with open arms ready to show so much love and affection.

"Uncle Chad, are you all right?" Terry asked.

"Yes, baby, I'm fine," my brother replied with much shame and hurt on his face. If I didn't know any better I would have thought that I saw one tear flowing from his beautiful brown eye, the one that he could barely see out of.

"This is all my fault," I said as I walked up the stairs, feeling self-pity and worn out and exhausted from the pain I felt inside.

My Grandmother Letha would have been so disappointed and angered. Here I was, only twenty-six years old, and living a life filled with so much confusion and hell, if I must put it bluntly. There comes a time in our lives when we must all take responsibility for our actions, whether right or wrong. Just the mere fact of standing up and admitting your fault sometimes helps, especially in my situation. It was only my situation because I became too blind to the circumstances surrounding my life, circumstances that I should have known better than to get involved in were slowly draining me of my life, energy, and self-respect. "Where is the monster?" I asked myself under my breath, thinking that no one heard me, no one other than my godbrother Jeremy, who I didn't know was still there waiting for us to return so he could find out if everything was all right with my brother.

"Cee, I'm so sorry this happened," he said as he embraced me with much love. "Chad, is there anything I can do for you?" he asked, as my brother held his head in shame, feeling less than a man. "Well, for starters I need both of you to sit down and hear what I have to say," Jeremy insisted. "Mark is gone. I made him leave—now my suggestion is for you to go and take out a restraining order against him so he can't come back," he said. "First of all, you don't know what's going to happen if he comes back. He is not a very happy camper right now and will try anything to get back in. So Cee, please take care of this matter tomorrow, because if he puts his hands on you or Chad one more time, I won't be responsible or held liable for what I might do. This man has lost his mind, and never once has he apologized or seemed like he even really cared about what happened today. He told me that it was your entire fault, and that if you hadn't ignored him when we drove by, none of this would have happened. Mark went on and on about how big your head has gotten since you bought that car and how you think you're almighty now, you and your brother. If I didn't know any better, Cee, I would have thought that he was on more than just crack. Mark's rash behavior leads me to suspect that something else is going on. Watch your back, and don't let him back in. Don't make me have to put this miserable soul of a punk out of his pain. If I hear he has stolen one more thing from you or put his hands on you, he will have to dance to this drummer's beat, and I'm more than certain he won't like it, not one bit. But, I'm going to enjoy beating him down, just like he did my best friend, your brother. I love both of you and always promised your father that I would look after you. How do you think your father would feel if he knew I let something like this happen to you and your brother? Girl, it is time to wake up. You better smell the coffee now and start thinking about you and your family and this baby you're carrying. Cee, I'm telling you this because I don't want anything to happen to you or the kids. From this day on, you need to think about you. Don't let this slimeball control your future, something that he won't have if he continues to live the lie that he is. I need you to be strong, and Chad, please do not add salt to injury by trying to be Superman to the rescue. If he shows up, just call me. I'm only a few blocks away. Do the both of you hear me?" Jeremy asked with much concern.

Just thinking about the things he said makes me feel like a real fool, a loser. Why should anyone even consider caring about someone who doesn't care enough about their own life or future? This is how I feel. Self-pity never works and will only send you into a tailspin of depression. Time is something that is quickly slipping away, and soon it will be time for me to give birth and bring another life into this world. A little life that I am clueless about. Is this baby going to be addicted, and if so, what will be his or her chance of surviving such a terrible fate? Well, good night, Mrs. Diary.

Afterthoughts: *Sisters out there, listen. This is not enough, for the person has to want to change for themselves more than you or anybody else wants them to. Remember, you don't have the power to* *change anyone but yourself. You know if it's a struggle for you to change, what makes you think that you are so great and mighty that you have the God-given ability to foster that for someone else? Please think about it.*

April 9, 1986

Dear Diary,

Here it is, another day, one that I thought I wasn't going to live to see because of what happened and the pain and hurt I felt inside for my brother. I must have slept really hard, because I didn't even hear the phone ringing this morning, but when I went to check the answering machine it had ten new messages flashing in bright red neon. My biggest fear was pushing that little button to see who called, hoping that it wasn't the Beast Master. Sooner or later I know I won't have any choice but to play my messages back once I regroup and gather my thoughts. Sleeping alone felt so good I had almost forgotten what it felt like.

Right now, the only thing I want is a big bowl of peaches with cottage cheese—and to check on my brother and make sure he is okay. I love him so much, and I'm so sorry this happened to him. The doctor said for the next few days he will be in constant pain due to the fifteen stitches he has over his eye—he gave him a prescription for some painkillers. They must have really worked well, because it is almost 9:30 a.m. and he is still sleeping, so I know they had to work. Chad was always up bright and early, regardless of whether he had to work or not. He made it a habit to get up early and didn't believe in sleeping late. This is a habit he inherited as a kid, and it was hard for him to break. While fixing myself something to eat in the kitchen, I could barely hear the phone ringing and by the time I reached my bedroom to answer, it had already stopped. Whoever was calling didn't let it ring long enough; oh well, maybe it was a wrong number, I thought to myself as I returned to the kitchen to finish doing what I had started, and that was to consume everything that I could as if I hadn't eaten in days. I could feel the baby kicking rapidly like it was saying, "Please feed me—it's time to eat."

The smile on my face was evidence of how good I felt to no longer have this man named Mark in my presence. Even though it took a bad situation to happen for him to be gone, it sure felt good. So good, in fact, that I was singing until the telephone rang again for the second time. Now I have made up my mind that I'm not going to answer it. I'm tired of running back and forth, and by the time I get there it will stop. Well, Mr. Telephone, you won't get answered this morning, I thought to myself as I finished my last spoon of peaches filled with cottage cheese. "Um, how delicious."

As I sat in the kitchen relishing my newfound freedom from the Beast Master, I could hear someone talking. At first I thought it was the automatic alarm clock that would often come on with music, but the more I listened, it sounded like the answering machine. By the time I reached the doorway of my bedroom, all I could make out was a brief part of a message left by a Dr. Chou at Barnett Hospital, requesting that I give him a call and that it was very urgent. Fear gripped my soul as I tried to prepare myself for the worst, thinking that maybe this doctor had already re-examined my brother's X-ray and was getting ready to give us the bad news on what he had discovered.

It took me a few minutes to get myself together so I could return his call. I closed my door so I could have a little bit more privacy and finally gathered the courage needed to make that dreaded phone call. "Hello, my name is Cee Davis, and may I please speak with Dr. Chou?" I asked. The party on the other line must have asked me fifty questions before putting me on hold and then connecting me with the doctor. At this point I'm a nervous wreck, trying to hope for the best and at the same time preparing myself for the worst. This was going to be so hard, but I had to do it for my brother's sake. For I knew he would have done it for me.

"Hello, Mrs. Davis, this is Dr. Chou," the other voice on the end of the phone responded. "How are you this morning?"

"If you must know the truth, Doctor, I'm miserable right about now. Please don't beat around the bush—tell me the truth about my brother Chad's condition," I said.

"Your brother who?" he asked, surprised.

"My brother Chad," I said.

"I have no patient by that name," he replied.

Shocked, I looked at the phone as if I had seen a ghost. "Well, Doctor, what is the purpose of your call?"

"Last night a young man by the name of Mark walked into the emergency room and said he needed to be treated for a wound to his right hand. After examining him, we discovered that he had a nasty bite injury that caused infection, and if gangrene sets in, we will have to amputate his hand."

"Are you serious?" I asked. "This is a joke, right? Did Mark put you up to this stupid trick? Who are you really?" I inquired suspiciously. "I have never heard of anything so stupid," I said, laughing hysterically. "Now, Doctor, or 'whoever you are,' will you please tell Mark that this is not working and he needs help, because this is a sick joke and you're sick for going along with a fool. Now, if you will please hang up this phone, I have no more time for this foolishness. And also, since you are such a good friend of his, please tell him if he shows his face around here he will be arrested. He is no longer wanted or needed here. If you care about him at all and you're such a good friend, please relay this message, Mr. Doctor." I laughed so hard until I cried. To me this was downright funny. "Poor little baby has a bite mark—yeah right! Get real, buddy, and please don't call my house," I said as I hung the phone up.

Mark has some nerve. Isn't that a trip? The audacity this man has is just beyond me at this point. How dare he get one of his drug-infested, get-high partners to call me and pretend that they are a doctor to get my attention. Mark must really think that I'm "Boo-boo the fool." He really has *some* nerve. I'm so tickled this morning, I can hardly stand up, and tears are rolling down my face as I sit here hysterically laughing and thinking about how stupid Mark was to think I was going to fall for something so silly as to think he is in the hospital from a simple bite on the hand. Who does he think I am? I think he's been smoking a little too much of that crack and it has cooked his brain. If I laugh any harder, my brother is going to wake up. But, I just had to write this; it is too funny not to capture on paper. For him to have someone call my house and tell me something so ridiculous is just beyond me, and now I definitely know he needs some help.

Sister, sister, if the truth be known, this man needed help from the very beginning; you remember when.

While I sat back down and tried to finish my third cup of coffee, I wanted so desperately to pretend that I did not hear the phone and that eventually it would stop ringing. The more I sat there thinking my thoughts, this nagging phone kept ringing, first ringing twice, then three and four times. Whoever it was, they were persistent in their quest to get my attention. Maybe it is Mark, trying to play another kiddy joke, and who has time? His jokes had already cost me plenty of money, and right now was not the time for his bad sense of humor. How could this man let me believe for weeks on end that he was sober and clean, and most of all, that he was really striving for the same things in life as I was. I started feeling more confident that he would eventually become the man I always dreamed of having in my life.

What drug could be so good to a man that it would make him sell his soul to the devil and steal from his baby's momma? Never in this lifetime did I ever imagine that I would be competing with a drug called crack cocaine. This drug acted like another woman, so to speak (keeping my man out all night long just so he could chase after that first hit). I overheard someone talking in a public restroom one time about how everyone that was smoking crack was trying to get that same feeling they had the first time they hit the pipe. From what everyone tells me and everything I have read, it's a noted fact that the high from crack only lasts for about three seconds. Now, how true this is I'll never know, because if I have to smoke crack to find out, I guess I will never know.

"Terry, is that you? Please answer the phone for Mommy," I said, as I could hear him dragging his feet down the hall to the kitchen in his black plastic bedroom slippers. This little boy was as bright as the sun glowing on fresh morning dew; he smiled all the time. I must admit I really was surprised to see a smile on his face, especially after yesterday. Maybe he forgot or it hasn't dawned on him yet that maybe, just maybe, he is happy Mark is gone. It may be terrible to think this way. But, to be honest, I'm starting to enjoy the fact that he is gone, too, and I have no regrets, even though my brother could have lost his eye, all because of me and my not-so-wise choices. Right now, I only want my child to be happy. My mind is made up and I'm going to sit Terry down and tell him the truth about what's going on in my life. After all, he needs to know the truth. It's not fair for me to keep him in the dark.

Every mother wants the best for her child. To me, Terry was my best friend and guardian angel. Sometimes he seems more like my brother than my son. He is so mature and bright for his age. Even though he was only five when my dad died, he promised he was going to take care of me. I remembered the first time he overheard me and Mark having an argument. How he ran to me after Mark left and fell at my feet and wrapped his little arms around my legs and cried out so loudly with pain as he professed in front of all my friends how much he loved his momma and that he would die for me. This little boy, my best friend and confidant, was professing his love for his mother to the world. To me that was so special and moving, it put tears in everyone's eyes. When you see your child like this, you can't help but wonder to yourself, now, what kind of fool am I to allow someone like Mark to take control over me and my children's future? We all have done some foolish things in our lives, but there comes a time when we have to let go. And what I mean is to *let go*.

"Momma, the phone is for you."

"Who is it?" I asked.

"It's some doctor."

Immediately I jump up from the table and waddle down the hall to find out who it was. "Hello, who I'm I speaking to?" I asked. "This is Dr. Chou at Barnett Hospital and I'm calling on behalf of Mark Davis; is this his wife?" the voice on the other end of the phone asked. "No, I'm not his wife, and why are you calling me again? Didn't I make myself clear the first time?" I inquired. "As I told you earlier, please don't call my house with this childish nonsense. Now, who are you really?" I asked. "Ma'am, I don't know what it's going to take for you to believe that I am who I said I am. The only reason for my call, ma'am, is to inform you that Mr. Mark Davis has been admitted to the hospital, and he wanted me to call you and let you know. He also asked me to see if you would bring him some clean underclothes and his aftershave, cologne, toothbrush—you know, the regular stuff everyone needs when they are in here."

"Are you sure you have the right number?"

I was not about to be played like Boo-boo the Fool once again. This time if Mark was playing a game, the trick was going to be on him and not me. For this time I was not going to fall into his trap. Nothing he could say to me would ever make me believe him again, no matter how hard he may try. I would be a fool to take him back under any circumstances; regardless, if this man on the other end of the phone was for real or not, I had to stand up and be strong and recognize who I was. My ancestors, especially the women on both sides of my parents, were very strong-willed, determined, and down-right proud. Now I'm looking in the mirror, trying to see if I see any of those traits in myself. Looking back and reminiscing about when I was a child, I always saw my grandmother as the strongest woman in the world, at least to me—this is what I thought. And to be like her would be an honor. There were days I used to wonder if my grand-mother was really this strong or was she putting on a facade? Nothing seemed to bother her, no matter what the situation. She never let anything get the best of her, and if it did, her children and grand-children didn't see it.

"Ma'am, this is very serious, and if you need proof of what I'm telling you, please hang up and call back to the following number— 555-742-5021—and ask for room 326. That is the room Mr. Mark Davis is in. And please ask any of the nurses on staff for verification that I am who I say I am."

By the time this man finished talking and rambling on, I was left speechless. Here I was, just sitting here, thinking about how much I didn't miss this man and enjoying the thought of him not being here. Now Mark is really in the hospital. Oh, my God, what can actually be wrong? Is this another one of his tricks? If this man can go to this ex-treme, he has got to be out of his mind for real, and a person like this is not only crazy, but also very dangerous. The only way I'm going to find out is to call, and right now I'm not sure if that may be the right thing to do (I thought to myself). How can a bite on his hand get so infected that it puts him into the hospital? This is too weird and sounds like something off one of those science fiction movies you see on TV. This sounds serious, but maybe I need to leave this one alone, and not even follow up by calling him. Who wants to hear that sad, pitiful voice telling me that he is sorry, and he won't do it again, for the millionth time. Well, Mr. Mark, it is time out for Boo-boo the Fool. "No more tricks on me," I said to myself as I lifted up the phone hook to call the hospital so I could check this story that seems to be a make-believe lie.

"Good evening, this is Jenny at Barnett Hospital," the voice on the other side of the phone said as she answered the phone cheerfully. "May I help you?"

"Yes," I answered, "could you please check to see if you have a patient by the name of Mark Davis?" I asked, (hoping in the back of my mind that her response was going to be no).

"Yes, we do," she replied. "Would you like to be connected to his room, Ms.?"

"Oh no, that's all right," I responded. "Before you hang up can you please tell me his condition and if he is okay?"

"If you can hold on for one moment I'll pull his chart and check," she responded. After a few moments, she said, "Ma'am, Mr. Davis has a bite wound on his right hand that became infected and now gangrene has set in—he may have to have surgery."

"Surgery—is it that serious?" I asked, my mind still reeling from the shock.

What in the world could have happened to this man since the last time I saw him, which was twenty-four hours before now? I have to call him and at least find out what happened. After all, he is still my unborn child's father, and no matter how I try to be hard and cold, it is just not me and how I really feel. This man and I once were so deeply in love and shared such a passion that others only dreamed about. There was a time in our lives that we could never have imagined hurting one another, much less being apart. Right now, he has turned my whole world upside down. For once again, he had won my trust, my love, and my faith in him as a man, that he would become everything that I could have ever hoped, dreamed, or dare imagine. Once again, empty promises filled the air so thick it was almost impossible to breathe and feel alive. One thing I can definitely say about crack is that it doesn't discriminate at all, regardless of color, race, age, or gender. It treats everyone who gives it a try the same by getting its victim so hooked on those tiny little white rocks of powder that they are crawling around on the floor thinking that every white speck or particle is crack. Looking stupid, so to speak— it's a shame. And here I am, an adult, and should know better than to let a man like Mark take control over my life when he couldn't even control his own.

Now is not the time for me to feel sorry for myself, but if anything, to move on and forget the past and start preparing for my unborn child. I so desperately want the best for my children, and with the help of God, I know he will give me strength just as he has done so many times before. Every moment I feel this little life inside of me kicking, I want so badly to feel joy; sometimes I do, and at others I feel so sad. My darkest fear is thinking the thought that maybe something may be wrong with my baby. There are times when this thought doesn't even cross my mind until Mark does something stupid, such as being missing in action for a few days at a time or starting an unnecessary argument like the ones he would initiate on payday just so he could ask for his money back to get high. The more I stand here and think about all the hurt and pain this man has caused me, the more I hope he stays where he is. So what if he has an infection from a bite wound—who cares? After all, look what he did to my brother; he was right-out cold and vicious when he hauled off for no reason and punched my brother in the eye. He was just plain downright mean, if the truth be known. For months I didn't want to face that fact. This man named Mark was just downright callous and ruthless when he couldn't get what he wanted. And here I was, not making the situation any better by hiding the truth. The more I hid the truth, the more it gave him power to control my way of thinking and who I was becoming. Molding and shaping me to become the person he wanted me to be (a codependent).

As long as we hide their nasty little secrets, we are just as guilty of the crime as they are. Sometimes he would have me so petrified I dared not tell anyone, for fear of what he would do if he found out. If he said "boo" to me, I would almost jump out of my skin; this is just how frightened I had become of him before he started going to treatment to get help. His eyes were so glassy and demonic-looking and his tone would change completely, as if he were someone else, especially when I refused to give him the money to get high. It started getting to the point to where I was so afraid to keep money on me I started giving it to my son Terry, explaining to him how important it was for him to conceal my secret and that Mommy needed him to hide this money so they could have money to go shopping and have fun in New York. Being that he was so young at the time, the idea of him and his mother sharing such a special secret made the bond between the two of us inseparable. There would be times when I would have collected over $700 for rent and would have to sneak and give it to Terry before Mark would come home. Each time I entrusted my son with a large sum of money that was so essential for our well-being, I reinforced everything I had told him the first time, sitting him down at the street corner diner while watching him scoop up his favorite ice cream piled high with Cool Whip and cherries. I knew in order for this little boy, my son, to keep my secret safe, I had to instill into him the importance of trust, integrity, and the honor in keeping a promise. One that must never be broken. While staring at me with his big, shiny, bright eyes, I couldn't help but smile at him and wink my eye as I always did when we both agreed on something. He was so determined that he was going to take care of his momma. This little boy was no longer to be considered a child, but a young adult, soon to become a man at such an early age. To Terry it was almost like an adventure keeping his mother's treasure, which held all her secrets that only he knew. Many days when I would go to work I couldn't wait to rush home to check and see whether he still had all the money. At work I was a nervous and pregnant wreck, wondering if one day I was going to come home and this little boy was going to tell me that he lost some or all of the money. My whole life was at stake, depending on my son. And I knew he knew it. Even though he dared not ask. It's been about a month so far since I have started entrusting Terry with my secret, which was to keep my money and find a safe and secure place to hide it. This child of mine had become obsessed with the thought of making me feel confident in him and strived every chance he got to prove to me that he was more than a little boy but a little man indeed.

Even though at the time I had never mentioned to him what was really going on between Mark and me, I felt in my heart that he sensed something, but he just didn't know what it was. I could tell by the way he clung to me every time Mark was around that it was something, but I didn't know what it was. From the very beginning when he first met Mark, he always held back and I often wondered why. For Terry was a very humble—fun-loving child that got along with everyone. To be plain honest, he was a very sweet and friendly child. He has shown me that even though he is only seven years old, he is very mature and worthy to be trusted. How could anyone resist loving a child like that? It almost started to feel like my child, as young as he was, had become my father, brother, son, and confidant, all rolled up into one tidy package. And I felt good knowing that at least I could trust someone. Even though the little person I trusted was so young, my confidence and ability to trust him grew more and more.

But, in the back of my mind I couldn't help but think about what would happen if my son lost this money. I knew that the one dreaded day would come when I would be returning home from a long day's work and my child would come running to me so he could confess that something had happened to the money, and how sorry he was. No matter how positive I thought or how much faith I had in my child, the fact still remained that accidents do happen and Terry was still a kid, even though he was trying hard to fill an old man's shoes by pleasing his momma and showing her that he was dependable, reliable, and that she could trust him no matter what.

It's getting late—guess me and baby will take a nap. Write more later, Mrs. Diary.

April 10, 1986

Dear Diary,

My hands are itching to pick up this phone and call the hospital to find out how Mark is doing. But I know if I do, one thing is going to lead to another. The longer I can go without contact with him, the better off I'll be. If I didn't know any better, I would say that I was an addict for love going through withdrawal from not seeing this man; it's been two days and I'm beginning to long for his touch; every time this baby kicks inside my round stomach, I think of him. Within two more weeks I'll be seven months and getting so much closer to my due date. This pregnancy really has taken a toll on me, but I have come to love and want this baby growing inside of me. No matter how hard the road seems or how tough it may get, I still love my unborn baby. When I pass by the mirror and see the outline of my funny-shaped, watermelon-round belly, I can't help but laugh and think about the times when Mark and I would be lying in bed together, laughing out loud at the silliest things and trying to imagine what we were going to be like when we grew old together. He used to always say, you're not in love unless you can imagine getting old and gray together. To him that was the epitome of love. As stupid as it may sound, I can't lie to myself—I really do love this man. Why is it so hard for him to get himself together and do the right thing? And why is it so hard for me to get over him? Sometimes I wonder if I wasn't pregnant how much easier would it be to get over him? I guess that's one question I may never be able to answer, for it is too late. "Please dear Lord, let this be a little girl, for I fear if it is a boy that he will be just like his father." And right now that is a terrible thought. Yes, this is a bad thing to think, and yes, I wish I could change it, but that's almost impossible. My mind is made up. I'm going to call and find out how his test results turned out and just say hello. What harm can that do? This is one time like no other that I will have to be strong and maintain my new way of thinking, which is the mere fact of not letting Mark get to my weak side and know exactly how I feel. Over the phone I feel that I stand a better chance of not subjecting myself to the acting routine he would put on every time he messed up awfully bad. I must admit the man was good. If I didn't see him face-to-face, it would make a big difference. Once I saw him, I knew he was going to melt my heart, and that was something I didn't want nor could I afford. For now I had to not only look out for my own well-being, but that of my beautiful children whom God saw fit to bless me with. The only way I know if I'm making the right decision or not is if I pray and ask God what I should do. And whichever way he leads me is the road I'll take when deciding what to do about Mark. This way I know

I'm not wrong. Baby starting to kick harder—guess I'll write more to-morrow. Good night, Mrs. Diary.

April 12, 1986

Dear Diary,

It's been about three days since I found out that Mark was in the hospital. Boy, I have to say it's been a rough three days trying to keep from calling him. Each day that goes by and I don't talk to him gives me more strength to continue to stand strong on my own. When the phone rings the first thing I do is let the answering machine pick up, so I can check to see who it is and hope and pray it's not Mark. This morning, for some reason or another, I'm hoping that he will call; I need to hear his voice. Just because he and I are no longer together does not mean we can't be friends. In the Bible it says that we are supposed to forgive and forget. Besides, I don't want to block my blessing if I don't. My mind is made up. Today I'm going to put my pride and hurt aside and call him; at least I'll know for myself that he is okay. Then my mind will be at ease. Now, here I was, kidding my-self again, trying to make believe that I could just talk to this man over the phone and hear his voice and everything was going to be just fine. I knew better from the beginning, but did it anyway. After picking up the phone and making the first call, I knew that it would not be my last. From the first moment I heard his voice, my heart dropped and all that mattered to me was if he was okay. If my granny were alive, she would have smacked me upside the head for being so stupid. And who in their right mind would have blamed her?

By 8:00 p.m. that same evening, Mark and I had already spoken on the phone about four times. Each time we spoke to each other, the conversation became more intense, until we both were at the point of surrender and longing and wishing for one another. We both were so wrapped up and engaged in conversation that I forgot to ask him what had really happened to his hand. By the time I remembered to ask, it was almost time for him to be released from the hospital. The doctor said that he should be ready to go home in a day or two. He had been treated for the infection to his right hand with antibiotics and should be well enough to go home if he continued to progress. To me this was good news; to my brother I knew it spelled disaster and would be like starting a blazing fire all over again. More than anything, I needed this man to come clean with me and tell me what happened to his hand, first of all, and then he would have to bow down and apologize to my brother for doing what he did. If nothing else, he owed not only my brother an apology, but me, Jeremy, my son Terry, and everyone else he had acted a fool in front of.

The day before it was time for Mark to be released from the hospital, he called the house and asked to speak to my brother. It was early on a Sunday morning and we were both getting ready for church. When the phone rang and I answered and the party on the other end was asking for my brother Chad and I realized it was Mark, I could feel the heat coming on; someone was going to be on fire, and it wasn't going to be me. For a moment, if I didn't know better, I would have thought my brother was going to have an anxiety attack and blow up when he found out it was Mark. I knew if I told him in advance, before he picked up that receiver, he was not going to respond—and if he did, it wasn't going to be pretty. And that I would be to blame once again for a disaster. The look on my brother's face when he recognized Mark's voice wasn't a pleasant one—it was filled with much anger and dismay.

"Why are you calling me?" my brother screamed. "Don't you have anything better to do than to bother me and my sister? When are you going to get it through your thick skull that my sister doesn't need you in her life anymore? And that she is better off without you?" Chad yelled in a loud and very angry voice. "What kind of monster are you, Mark?" my brother asked. "You thought that by hitting me in the eye it would prove that you were a man, but it only proves one thing— you're a coward. I know you have been pushing my sister around, even though she won't tell me. I just know it, and when I see you again it's going to be just the two of us, just you and me," my brother said as he angrily slammed the phone down. "Have you lost your mind?" he asked, yelling and screaming while throwing his hands up in the air. "I'm curious as to why you, my sister, of all people, would be so stupid that you would give me the phone to talk to an animal like Mark. I want to know, here and now!" my brother said coldly.

"What did you tell this man for him to feel like he can do whatever he wants to you, me, and everybody else, and continue to walk around as if nothing happened? Tell, me Cee. Where does this man get the gall to say anything at all to me? How can this ruthless coward be so bold as to ask or tell me he needs to see me and that it is very important that I come to the hospital tomorrow? No one can convince me that this man is not insane, and that he does not have rocks in his head. He has smoked so much crack that he is beginning to think everyone is like you, and so gullible to believe him," Chad said as he stormed out of the room, continuing to fuss, pounding his left fist in his right hand in much distress.

To tell the truth, I don't know what distressed him the most: the fact that he thought that I was going to be gullible enough to take Mark back, or the feeling of how much he now despised this man for scarring him for life. My brother knew that after the stitches were removed, that he would have a mark on his body for life, something he didn't have a choice in. Some things in life you have to accept, and this happens to be one of those things. I only hope and pray that one day my brother will not use this to hold a grudge over me. Even though he is trying hard to show me that he is not, inside my heart and soul I know better. Yes, my brother still loves me, but I can't fault him for feeling the way he does about Mark or his crazy, forgiving sister that has forgiven her crack-addicted lover for the one-hundredth time. Never once did I think about the impact my emotions and stress were going to have on my unborn child, being that most of the time my life was a pure mess. After fussing and mumbling for what seemed to be hours, my brother finally came over to hug me and apologize for acting up and snapping about Mark.

"Sis, I know that you love this man and that you would like for it to work out, but I also know that you are going to do what's best for you and the children. In your mind, I know you can't help thinking about Mark and hoping and praying that he will change, but you must know that it takes him wanting to change himself. Sis, I don't hate him," my brother said. "I'm just angry that he has taken you for granted so many times and stolen from you, and right now in my mind, I don't want to think this and I know that you won't tell me the truth, but I really do believe that this man hit you or at least attempted to put his hands on you. And if I knew that for sure, I would break him in half and you know it. Girl, I love you," my brother said as he stood there looking at me, piercing my soul with that serious look of his. He always had a way of getting next to me and winning my love. I dared not tell him how I really felt and that I'm missing Mark. He would think that I was crazy and probably that I, too, was smoking crack. How can you look someone straight in their eyes and tell them you love them, knowing how much hurt and pain you have caused them? And this was exactly how I felt about my brother.

Here it was, only one more day and Mark would be released from the hospital. I couldn't help but wonder where he was going to go and what he was going to do. Who would take care of him? And how would he survive? All these questions were like a merry-go-round in my head and were beginning to give me a headache. What would my son think if I took this man back? No woman wants her child to think less of her and lose respect. Most sons adored their mothers, and I was honored to know mine really adored me. It was a blessing and such a wonderful feeling—so wonderful, in fact, that I didn't want to risk losing it. But, at the same time I wasn't willing to take the risk for fear of losing the man I love. Regardless of how stupid this sounded, I had twenty-four hours to come to a final decision. Something that I was going to have to live with. A choice that could ruin my relationship with my brother, son, and, of course, destroy the respect of all my friends who cared.

The only person that I could turn to for advice would be Audra, for I knew she would understand and not be so judgmental. She knew all my secrets and always listened to me, no matter how ridiculous I may have sounded at times. It's getting late and I need some rest. Right now I want to pray and just leave everything in God's hands. Maybe tomorrow I'll get a chance to talk with her.

Good night, Mrs. Diary.

April 13, 1986

Dear Diary,

Here it is, 5:30 a.m., bright and early. I can't sleep anymore and woke up with the thought of Mark on my mind. This is the day he will be released from the hospital. Hopefully he will have somewhere to go and won't come knocking on my door. That's the last thing I need.

The harder I tried to go back to sleep, the more I couldn't and felt restless. I could feel the pressure of bags starting to form up under my eyes and my body was drained, thinking about what was going to happen to Mark and where he was going to go. This was a grown man who'd made his own bed hard, yet I felt pity for him. Crack cocaine has destroyed so many people's lives (not to mention what it was doing to mine). Everytime I turned on the TV, there were more and more horror stories about crack—children stealing, then robbing and killing their parents; husbands killing wives; dope dealers killing crack addicts for robbing them; women prostituting their bodies for this demonic drug and eventually transmitting STDs to their lovers; and, of course, last but not least, babies born addicted to crack. The list just goes on and on of what happens when someone gets hooked on crack cocaine. It's gotten to the point where I don't even want to look at the news for fear that one day I may just see myself. In my mind, I was wondering what the headline would read: "Woman Beaten to Death by Crack-addicted Spouse." This was a scary thought, one I never wanted to ever even think could possibly happen to me. But I knew if Mark continued down that path of self-destruction, it could very well happen. When you start thinking these thoughts in your mind, it's time to let go and let God handle it. For me, I wanted to handle everything. The thought of defeat and me not having control over the way this man thought and what he did boggled my mind and became an obsession. How many times was it going to take for me to realize the truth, which was that this man did not have what it took to love me because he did not love himself. What was it going to take for me to realize this and start the transition to a better life for not only me, but also my family? While I lazily lay in bed bombarding my mind with thoughts of what the future may or may not hold for me, time was ticking away.

When I was restless, this little life inside of me kicked and kicked furiously for what seemed to be attention. How could this baby be so demanding and hadn't yet entered the world? It was funny watching my stomach move as if someone was having a boxing match on the inside of my fat, round body. When the baby kicked like this, I knew it was time to be fed. My only craving was for peaches and cottage cheese. I could eat them morning, noon, and night; it didn't make a difference. I loved this stuff; it put a smile on my face and warmed my soul. In my heart, I was hoping that the phone would ring and that it would be Mark, calling to say he was okay. The urge to hear his voice engulfed my thoughts with much emotion. This man was like no other. He seemed to have the power that could control my every emotion. His wish was my command. My only hope is that I will hear from him soon. Good night, Mrs. Diary.

April 18, 1986

Dear Diary,

It's such a beautiful day. I took Terry to the park, and he played and played. I could tell he was so happy to have my full attention. By the time we left the park, he looked like a dirt doll. It made me feel so happy to see a smile on his face. Audra's two little girls were also delighted to be out of the house and playing with their buddy, Terry. I knew that by the time they reached the house, they were going to be drained and ready for nothing other than their beds. The pleasure of Audra's company made my day so wonderful. We both think so much alike and like the same things. Even though we had a nice time at the park, I could tell there was something on her mind and was waiting patiently for her to tell me what it was. Whatever it was, I knew it would be something serious. While relaxing in the park, bathing in the sun and talking, I couldn't help but notice how preoccupied she was at times, often staring off into space with such a serious expression on her face. Each time I conjured up the nerve to ask her what was wrong, one of the kids would come over and ask a question or need someone to push them in the swing. In my mind, I knew it would just be a matter of time before she would tell me what was going on.

As we took the long ride home, the kids fell asleep in the back seat. The smiles on their happy little faces told us that they were pleased. And we both felt happy for it. The closer we got to the house, Audra seemed restless as she sighed more than once. By this time, I could no longer ignore the urge inside of me to ask her what was wrong. As I turned the corner to the street we lived on, I politely asked her if there was anything she wanted to talk about. With a slight smile on her face and hesitation in her voice, she finally broke her silence.

"As a matter of fact there is something I would like to talk to you about. Cee, I love you and you know this—it's been bothering me for some time now. May I ask you a question without you getting mad or upset?"

"Sure," I replied.

"For the life of me, Cee, how could you take Mark back after all he has done to you and your brother? This man put you, your family, and friends through hell. How could you find it in your heart to forgive him and continue on as if nothing has happened when you know it's just a matter of time before he pulls another stunt? I worry about you, Terry, and that baby you're carrying," she said.

"There were so many nights when you didn't know that I could hear the two of you arguing," she went on. "Sometimes I wanted to call the police or someone to come and help you. I heard him threaten you and I knew you were afraid of him. But then, who am I to talk when I have subjected myself to being abused by my own husband? I felt more afraid for you because you're pregnant, and you know how Mark is when he gets into a rage. Cee, please promise me that you will be careful. I know you feel compassion for this man and this is your unborn child's father, but don't trust him. He may appear like everything is okay now and that he is going to try to do better. We both know the truth. Before, I never judged him and always gave him the benefit of the doubt because I would want someone to do that for me, but when you see a person taking advantage of someone as beautiful and kind as you are, it makes you sad and hurt to know that they are going through this. Whatever happens, I'm always going to be there for you. Right now you need to be there for yourself and your children, Cee," Audra said as she expressed much concern with nothing but genuine love. "Girl, it's time for you to start thinking about yourself. I know you're feeling guilty about what Mark did to your brother and about what your brother did to him that placed him in the hospital for a week. Thinking about it right now is just downright funny. Your brother must have the bite of Dracula, to have bitten this man on the hand so hard that it caused infection to set in, and he had to be admitted to the hospital. Now tell me that's not something from *The Twilight Zone?*" she said as she laughed. "When I first heard that, Cee, I thought it was a joke until Mark showed me the papers he received from the hospital. I laughed and laughed until Pee Wee had to tell me to shut up. This was so funny to me. When you told me about the day that you and your brother went to pick Mark up from the hospital, and the doctor saw your brother's eye all bandaged up, and Mark's hands, and put two and two together, and said to all of you, 'Well, I guess no one needs to ask what happened—it's plain to see.' The doctor's remarks were funny. Especially when he asked your brother what his teeth were made of. For him to have caused so much infection to this man's hand, girl, this made me hysterical. How could a brother cause so much injury to someone just from one bite? He must have pretended that Mark was a piece of tough steak, and he hadn't eaten in days. Tell me something, how is everything between you and Mark now? Is he treating you okay and are you happy? Do you think he is for real this time? And how does Terry feel about the two of you being together again?"

"Well, for starters, Mark and I have decided that we are going to get our lives right and start going to church every Sunday. I don't expect things to change overnight, but at least it is a start, and right now he is trying. For the past week or so, he has brought home all of his pay, and he is continuing to go to his substance abuse support meetings every day."

"Are you sure he is really going?" she asked.

"Yes, he is," I replied. By this time I had started to get annoyed, and I know it didn't matter to her and she told me so.

"This is one time I don't care if you get upset with me. You are my friend," she said boldly. "This man doesn't have any right to treat you any other way but right. We all have watched you struggle for months to keep everything together—paying the mortgage, taking care of all the bills, working two jobs, never complaining when you had the right to. You kept everything together and made sure that we were all taken care of. Now it is your time to be taken care of. You shouldn't have to work two jobs. He should be doing that, and whatever it takes to make you happy and comfortable. That's a man's job, and until he does right by you, I won't have any respect for him, and I'm pretty sure no one else will, either. If your stepsister finds out what happened, you know she will be furious. Have you told her yet?"

"Audra, please don't keep going on and on about this. I know what I need to be doing, and I don't get into other people's business, so why are you pressuring me like this? For months, if I couldn't talk to anyone else about what was going on in my life, I knew beyond a shadow of a doubt I could talk to you, as you weren't going to be judgmental. Now maybe that was a mistake. Please, can we talk about something else?" I asked with much attitude.

"No," she replied. "For once you need to listen to someone else, and that someone else is me. Why? Because for number one, I love you and care about what happens to you, and no, I don't want to see you hurt by anyone. Cee, you're going to have to listen to someone. If not, I'm afraid of the worst."

"And what is that, Audra?" I asked sarcastically.

"I fear for your life," she said.

"Fear for my life?" I laughed at her thought.

"Girl, you better wake up and smell the coffee before it's too late," she said. "This situation you're in is serious—it's like a time bomb waiting to explode. Do you hear me? You're acting like this is a joke. Look how he has stolen things from you time and time again and without remorse. Not to mention how he ran off with the car for about two days until your brother made him bring it back, and smoked up your mortgage payment, all for the sake of getting high. Now he has not only conned you into taking him back, but also made your brother feel so guilty about what he did to his hand that he, too, is under Mark's spell. What is it going to take for you to snap back into reality? Is it going to take someone to lose their life? You know how this man is when he is smoking that crack. He is only using you for everything that it is worth to him right now. He has you and your brother right where he wants you, like putty in his hands. It's almost like the two of you are under a spell, and if I didn't know any better,

I would think you both were smoking crack. How your brother could feel so sorry for this man, enough to trust him once again and live under the same roof, I don't know. But one thing is for certain. If I had the spell he cast on y'all, I could patent it and get rich overnight." She laughed out loud. "I love you, girlfriend, and only want the best for you. That's all," she concluded.

"Audra, even though I know what you're saying may be true, you haven't been around Mark since he has been home to see the change in him like I have. He is much more caring, taking time with Terry, and making plans and preparations for this baby. Every day he comes home in such a good mood. Just yesterday he told his mom in front of me that we were getting married, and she was so happy for us."

Mark's mom, Mrs. Davis, was a very quiet and conservative woman in her early sixties with long, straight jet black hair and high cheekbones. It was apparent by her golden-reddish skin tone that she was mixed with Cherokee Indian. Mark's mother was a very sweet woman who never interfered in our lives. She always made my favorite dish—Eggplant Parmesan—and to me, she was the master chef. This special dish always put a smile on my face and she knew it. Often she would comment about her unborn grandchild by saying that she didn't want me craving for Eggplant Parmesan because my baby's head may be shaped like one. That tickled her to no end. Mark's mother was a very sweet woman whom I really loved. I don't know what made me love her the most, the fact that she was very quiet and sweet, or the fact that she minded her own business. She never questioned me about what was going on or happening in my life, which if she did, I would not have told her anyway. Her house was only about a five-minute walk from where we lived, and I relished the thought of her being so nearby. This way she could spend time with her grandchild and get to see him or her grow up and do all the things grandmas do for their grandchildren. Mark had several brothers and sisters, all scattered out across the country. His whole family was looking forward to the birth of our first child, as Mark was the second-oldest son. By looking at his family, my friends would often comment to me how beautiful they thought my baby was going to be because his family was part Cherokee Indian. It didn't take my friends to tell me something that I already knew. This baby was already destined to be beautiful, first of all because it would be our child, regardless of what it looked like on the outside, and if the baby looks like a monkey, to the mother it is still beautiful. Haven't you ever seen some babies that were just plain ugly, and all you could say to the parent was "Oh, that sure is a healthy child," or, "Look at the baby," but nothing else of great significance. Well, rest assured the parent already knows but if they are like me will never admit it.

None of my friends had ever really seen any of my family, except my father before he passed away and my brother Chad. When I relocated back to Paterson, New Jersey after returning home from the military, it was just the two of us, me and my baby brother. Together we felt we could conquer the world. Most of my family were in the South and scattered all over the country, just like most of his. But at least Mark had his immediate family right here in the same town. Sometimes this made me feel so lonely, and I longed for the day when my immediate family would be close by. Every expectant mother wants her family close by to share her joy. For me that idea was just a mere thought, as my closest family was hundreds of miles away.

Being that my family is so far away, lately Mark has been going out of his way to do extra-nice things for me. Just yesterday he fixed me breakfast in bed and gave me a red rose. I thought this was so sweet of him. Regardless of what anybody thinks, me and my man are going to make it through these hard times and prosper. Before you know it, we will both be standing on top of the world. Nothing makes disbelievers madder than proving them wrong. And that's exactly what we are going to do. This man means the world to me.

Right now I know Terry doesn't fully trust him, and it's going to take some time, but in due time he will. What my child has to realize is that everyone makes mistakes. I refused to tell him all the bad things about Mark. I just told him what I felt he needed to know, and that was that every couple goes through problems and assured him that whatever Mark and I were going through, it had nothing to do with him. He seems to understand, even though he is such a young child; he has the mindset of an old man. From day one he has always been this way. One thing for sure, though, is that no matter what I know, this child, as young as he is, knows what it means to be trusted, for it has been months since he started keeping my money and not one dime has ever been misplaced or lost. Terry made me feel proud to know that I, his mother, could have so much confidence in him. Each time I did, he never once let me down. There was only one time I can recall that he did lose the money, but it was made out in a check that I gave him to hold for me, and somehow by mistake it got washed up in the little blue jeans he had on earlier that day. My baby forgot to take the check for $500.00 out of his pocket and proceeded to wash his pants with it in the pocket. By the time I came home, he came running to meet me at the door to tell me what had happened to the check. I could tell by the look in his sad, puppy-dog eyes that he was scared and thought that he was going to get a beating. You could hear the sound of fear in his raspy voice as he held his head down to tell me. "Momma, something bad happened today. Please don't get mad at me. I made a mistake and the check got washed up. See?" he said as he handed me the check, all balled up like a dingy white piece of cotton. As I looked at my child I could tell it worried him no end for something like this to have happened. But, I assured him that everything would be okay and that Mommy could get that check replaced. The next day I called the place where the check had been issued and informed them of what had happened. They told me if I came down and showed proper ID they would re-issue me another check for the same amount. This little boy was too thrilled to know it was just that simple. After hugging and kissing him about ten times, I told him how important it was to be careful and that he still was my favorite banker. What else could I do? After all, this kid had kept my secret for months and this was the first mistake ever. "I could not have expected too much more, for no one is perfect," I reassured him.

Right now I'm getting sleepy so I guess I'll write more later. Talk to you later, Mrs. Diary. If Mark had any idea I was letting a seven-year-old kid run around with sometimes anywhere from $500 to $800 in his pocket, he would flip for sure. In my mind, I know the first time he jacks my child for some money to buy that stupid crack, I'm going to try to knock his head off of his body. Good night, Mrs. Diary.

April 23, 1986

Dear Diary,

Today Mark and I came to the conclusion that it would be best if he didn't cash his checks on payday and that he would just bring his whole check home to me and then we could go and cash it together. This way he wouldn't be tempted to get high. Right now he is taking his recovery one step at a time, going to a support meeting every night, and making sure that I know where he is at all times. Lately when he comes home he's not hungry and can't eat—says his whole body aches. And let's not even begin to talk about sex. I can't remember the last time we touched each other's bodies. To me Mark doesn't have a desire for it—I'm trying to hold on and be strong, so I barely mention it to him. Even though deep inside I'm craving for his touch, I refuse to force myself on him. It was just a few months ago when he had the same symptoms, and I think it was withdrawal from his addiction kicking in again. So of course you know I'm kind of on edge, because I know what happened before. Except this time I feel he is much stronger and can handle himself before he would go out and get high again. He knows how much it almost cost him the last time.

The more he shows me that he is strong, the more I want to be there to support him. I'm determined to prove that we can make it, and know that he feels the same way, too. It is through the love I see in his eyes and the sincerity that he shows when he takes me into his arms and looks into my eyes that I know he really means it this time. My friends all think I'm crazy for giving him another chance, but who are they to judge me and what I want to do in my life? They need to be concentrating on their own. I know that they love me and want the best for me, but what they must also understand is that this is my life, and if I make my bed hard, then I'll just have to lie in it. No, I'm not trying to be cocky because Mark and I are back together; I'm just being real about how I feel and what I need right now. And what I need right now is love and comfort not only from my friends, but my man also.

May 1, 1986

Dear Diary,

It's been days since I have written and I almost feel guilty. Lately I have been so busy between work and trying to get things ready for the birth of my baby. I only have about two more months to go. Each day I'm getting more and more excited, looking forward to seeing this little girl. I think it's a girl, and no one can change my mind. Most people who look at my stomach say it's a girl, especially the older women. I have heard it so much until I'm convinced. Now, if it's a boy, I will be totally surprised and disappointed, for my mind is made up, and I don't want any more children. I always wanted one of each sex, the perfect little family.

Right now, I don't know who's more anxious, me or Mark. Yesterday when he came home he took me out to dinner and said maybe we can go to New York to see my Aunt Stella. Now, that would really put a smile on my face.

Here I am, sitting here writing, and almost forgot today is the first of the month again, and I dread it in a way. My tenant Mary, who lives on the first floor, is always complaining about not having any money, and when it comes time to pay the rent, she is totally broke. Always talking about how she had to spend all her money on her light bill. Mary is in her early fifties and looks great for her age. She has a pecan-tan complexion and is about five feet, six and one-half inches tall. If it wasn't for the three missing teeth in the front of her mouth, she would be a knockout. If you wanted to know what was going on in the neighborhood or three blocks around the corner, just ask her. Everybody else's business was hers, whether they knew it or not. There was no shame in her game. She had three children who lived with her, one daughter and two sons. Being that all of her children are older, over eighteen, they held steady jobs, and there was no reason for their momma to be crying broke on rent day. She wasn't crying the other day when I saw her stepping off the bus with about four or five new outfits hanging over her shoulder, the ones she had just bought from the department store, Jacob's. This store where she shopped was one of the most exclusive ones here in Paterson. And by the smile on her face, she couldn't wait to get home to show them off to me, of all people, the landlady, the one she would be telling in just a few short days that she didn't have the rent money. By the way she dressed, you would have thought she had a pocket full of money. The only reason she cried broke on rent day was so we would feel sorry for her and give her a break on her payment. The fact that all three of us had purchased a house at such an early age made us feel guilty to really lay the law down to this older woman as to what we expected from her as a tenant. No matter what, she knew how to get on our weak side to get what she wanted (by offering us home-cooked meals), and that was always more time to pay her rent. Mary knew how to put down the crocodile tears and make you feel guilty about something that was rightfully yours, the rent money. Something she knew she had to pay no matter where she lived, whether it was my house or someone else's; that fact remains no matter where you go. It's a part of life, plain and simple.

This woman could cook her butt off and use it to her advantage every time. Whenever she was cooking something good, you could smell the aroma creeping up the back staircase, working its way into my nostrils. Being that I am pregnant and greedy, mind you, it didn't help me to be the best at controlling my thoughts. At the time, my stomach overruled any decision I made. If it smelled good, it must taste good. And it worked like a charm every time. Sooner or later the time was going to come when we would have to make a decision on taking her to court to get our money. Each month she started paying us later and later. First it was by the fifth and then after that first month, the next was like the twelfth, and each month after that it was strictly downhill, paying us whenever she felt like it. Sometimes it would be almost the twentieth of the month. By the time she would get around to paying us the rent, the mortgage would already be paid and it would be almost due again. But this didn't matter to her. She could care less as long as she could look good to go to work every day at our expense. One day her luck is going to run out. I don't care how nice she is; I have to look out for my family and can't afford to be blinded by her shrewd kindness. If it's not one thing, it's another. The gentleman that sold us the house tried to forewarn us about her, but no, we wouldn't listen. Boy, do I wish I had! It would save me some of the heartache I'm going through now.

Sometimes our money is so tight from paying all our bills we could barely afford to pay our mortgage. Remember, this was not a one-family house or two-family house, but a three-family house, the one that I was determined to buy regardless of how expensive the utility bill was. If I knew then what I know now, I would have waited or bought another house. Nevertheless, all three of us made the decision to get it, so no need for crying over spilled milk now. No need in thinking about it now; it's getting late and Mark will be home soon. So, I might as well start dinner. Gotta go, will try to write more if I have time. Talk more tomorrow, Mrs. Diary.

May 3, 1986

Dear Diary,

I just got off from work, and my feet are so swollen from standing all day. My boss told me to sit down and prop my feet up, but I couldn't stay still long enough to do that. She told me that if I was hardheaded one more time when she asked me to sit down and prop my feet up, she was going to tell the boss to sign my disability papers early. Can you believe that? I think she's just afraid that I might have this baby at the office; that's all it is.

My boss, Barbara, was from Ireland originally. Her hair was as red as a carrot top. By looking at her, she didn't appear to be a day over forty-five and was about five feet, four inches tall. You could tell by her old-fashioned ways that she didn't think pregnant women should really work, and the best place for them was at home. To let her tell it, her dad did everything for her mom, and her mother never had to work outside the home (that's only because her daddy wasn't on crack). I'm not trying to be funny; I'm just being real. Do you think that if her dad were on crack back in the day, her mom would have been able to sit at home? I don't think so, girlfriend. Of course, I would be able to stay home, too, if my man was responsible and not on crack. I love my boss dearly, but right now she is getting on my nerves with every little thing and is clueless about anything that is going on in my life. Every move I make, she is right on top of it, always asking me if I'm in pain. I know I'm as big as a tick and starting to look like the

Pillsbury doughgirl and that I'm getting ready to pop open any minute, but there's no need to treat me like I'm handicapped. Pregnancy does not make you helpless. I know. I should be grateful to have a boss like her, and Mark says that I should stop complaining and be thankful. But how can I, when every five minutes someone is asking, are you okay? Do you want to sit down? Can I get you anything? Do you need me to put that away for you? As sweet as all of this sounds, it was annoying after a while. My job was making me useless to them. I no longer felt they needed me and my emotions were running away; I guess I didn't want them to spoil me for fear that, once I had the baby, I wasn't going to be the center of attention anymore.

It's almost 5:00 p.m. If I can put this diary down, I can get some work done, like cook dinner. Usually by the time Mark comes home, everything is together. The house would be cleaned and dinner ready. Today is just a lazy, hazy day meant only for me to loaf around and do whatever I want, and that is nothing right about now. Mark will just have to understand that there will be days like this. After all, I'm not superwoman nor am I trying to be. I need a break, and today is the day. For so long I have worked two jobs just to maintain; now it's his turn to pick up the slack and be happy that I'm giving him another chance to be the man he should have been from the beginning. I'm going to take me a nap, and by the time I wake up, maybe he'll be home and prepare a meal for me. If nothing else, I deserve it. Good night, Mrs. Diary.

May 7, 1986

Dear Diary,

Yesterday, Mark came home late and seemed a little upset. I tried to get him to open up and talk to me and make him realize that communication is the key to a good relationship. No matter what I said, he clammed up even more. To me this was not a good sign and it alerted me that something was going on with him that I needed to know about. The more I pressed him about telling me what it was, the more he denied that anything was wrong and told me to stop bugging him. He sure has some nerve, especially after he didn't come home until 11:00 p.m. the other night and told me that he worked late, and his ride left him, and he had to catch the bus home. I asked him why he couldn't call me. He told me that it was too late, and he didn't want to disturb me. After listening to him, I told him how ridiculous that was and made him promise me that it would never happen again. For the first time in weeks, he looked at me as if to ask, who did I think I was? The anger that built up in him after I made that statement was shocking and threw me for a loop. His response was, "Cee, who do you think you are? Telling me what to do, telling me when I can come home? You are not my mother and can't tell me what to do. Don't ever feel like you own me. Just because you're pregnant and carrying my baby does not give you or anybody else the right to tell me what to do," he yelled. "And don't forget!" he screamed from the top of his voice, demanding that I respond. "As a matter of fact, I'm going for a ride—where are the keys?" he asked angrily. "If you want to go, you can, and if not, I'm going without you."

He really knew how to spoil a nice evening, something I had been planning all day. I thought that maybe by the time he came home, we could have a nice, quiet dinner, then maybe take a ride to New York so we could look at the skyline and just have a relaxing evening while rolling along, listening to some Jazz.

Evidently before he got home, he already had things that he wanted to do planned in his head. The first thing he did, from the moment he walked in the door, was start a silly argument so he would have a reason to leave. By the time his voice tone changed, I already knew it was the crack addiction kicking in. This time I knew for sure that I could no longer afford to be in denial because it would cost me dearly. After everything he put me through, he was acting like I owed him something when it was just the opposite—he owed me. Just who did he think he was, acting this way? And what made him think I was going to accept his behavior again? At this stage in the game, this man felt like no matter what he did I was going to accept it, and after all, haven't I? Inside, I didn't want to give up, but in reality I had already done just that by not giving my own self the opportunity to prove that I could make it without him.

No one deserves to be treated the way he's treating me. He had gotten so used to mistreating me that it was just plain natural for him. Most men at least tried harder to please their women when they were pregnant and prove that they were real men. Not this brother— he didn't care, especially after he had taken a few hits of crack. He could have cared less. When I looked out the window and saw him pulling off, I already knew that I wasn't going to see him anytime soon. For me at that moment, a sigh of relief swept over me. I was almost at the point where I didn't care if he ever came back. It was only a few days earlier that I felt and thought so strongly that he had changed and together we could conquer the world. Boy, what a fool I was.

Here I was, wanting to prove everyone wrong—my brother and anyone else who knew what was going on in my life. Right now, at this moment, I know for sure that he will never change and that I'm the only one that can make the difference by changing me and the way I feel. It's up to me, and I pray that God will give me the extra strength this time to get out of the mess that I have gotten myself into. This is insane; how can anyone be so blind as to let this man who is a drug addict take over her life and have so much control when he didn't have control over what he is doing with his own? It is time for the spell he has me under to come to an abrupt end. Knowing that he is probably gone for the night should make it easy for me to go to sleep, for I know it'll be at least a day before I lay eyes on him again. This time I really hope my brother does not find out because if he does it will create nothing but more problems, something I really don't need. I'm getting too close to having my baby and don't need any confusion and fighting around me or my child.

May 9, 1986

Dear Diary,

Terry seems so sad today. I know he suspects that something is wrong with me, for I have been quiet all day. From the time he woke up this morning and knocked on my bedroom door and came rushing in and jumped up on my bed, I knew my child already knew that

Mark had taken the car and left. By looking into his eyes, I could see the hurt and pain he felt for his momma. Even though he didn't say a word, he didn't have to. It was already evident in the way he held his head and kissed me on the cheek. I tried to pretend like I was still asleep, but it was hard to do with him rubbing my back.

"Momma," he said in a raspy voice, "I love you and I will die for my momma."

Little did I know at the time that this child really meant what he was saying. As I rolled over and pretended that I had just woke up, he grabbed and hugged me. I sat up in bed and rocked him back and forth and told him that I loved him, too. That day we both cried. I don't know if I cried because I knew all the pain I brought into his life or because of how sweet and understanding this child was. How could any decent mother or parent let their child go through this like I have? I must have been out of my mind. No one should love anyone so much that they let their child suffer, I thought to myself.

"Terry, Momma is going to be all right, and I need you to continue to be strong," I told him while holding him close to me. "I'm not going to let anything happen to you or your little brother or sister," I assured him.

No matter what I said, he continued to repeat what he had said earlier, "Momma, I love you and I'll die for you." All I could ask myself was, what made my child think this way? And why was he so persistent about it, making sure I understood every word he said as if I didn't hear him the first time. Finally I could not resist the urge to ask him why he said it again.

"Son, I know you love me, but why are you telling me this over and over again?"

"I'm so afraid that one day you and Mark are going to get into an argument and he may hurt you and the baby," he said.

By now he really had my attention. "What makes you think that Mark will ever harm me, sweetie?" I asked.

"Momma, I don't trust Mark. He is always arguing and fussing with you and making you cry. I'm tired of seeing you cry, Momma, and I hope Mark never comes back," he said with a tremor in his voice. "Why does he fuss with you all the time?" he asked. "Please, please, if you never get me anything else for my birthday, Momma, please get me a solid wooden baseball bat. That's all I want," he said with a serious and stern look on his face.

For a moment I thought it was cute, until I actually thought about the reason he really wanted it. When it really started sinking in as to why this child of only seven years old wanted this so badly, it made me want to cry. I could feel the pit of my stomach churning from the notion. This little boy, whom I thought had no idea or was clueless as to the situation I was in, was ready to hit a home run and Mark's head was going to be the ball. What do you say or tell your child when he is fearing for his momma's life? For Momma is all he has and knows. [My child loved me, and I couldn't fault him for feeling the way he did. His little heart was aching for his momma, and the pain was killing him to see her this way. Here I was, too blinded by love to feel the pain that my child was feeling for me, not knowing that it was driving him insane and planting unpleasant thoughts in his head. The seeds of violence were taking form and I was in such denial, I refused to see it. Thinking that my little Terry was too young and innocent to conceive certain ideas, and that he would not think or commit a violent act. (Mothers out there, please wake up before it's too late.) When a child, especially a son, feels that his mother is in danger and being threatened, his first instinct is to protect her from all harm. Even though he was young, he had the courage of a lion and the heart of a lamb. My baby had no fear from day one. As long as he had Momma, he felt he had everything. Just like any child who had a bond to their mother would. His feelings were only normal. It was me, the abnormal one, thinking that it was impossible for a child of his age to feel the way that he did.]

It's been almost two days since Mark left and wrecked the car. Sooner or later, I knew this was going to happen. He had only been gone away from the house for about 45 minutes when the phone rang and it was him on the other end, all upset and nervous, telling me that he had an accident with the car and that it wasn't his fault. Telling me that he went to press on the brakes and the car wouldn't stop and he hit the curb. To tell the truth, the only thing I miss is the car. Once I got over the initial shock of him being in an accident with my car, the only other question lingering in my mind at the time was if he was getting high at the time of the accident. Here it was, only one month later, and the car of my dreams was totaled. Little did I know that the damage was going to be estimated at over $5,000 to fix it. My whole world was rapidly crumbling, right before my very eyes, and I was too thick-headed to see, so blind I couldn't see the forest for the trees. If he doesn't come back, I'll be all right.

After he wrecked the car, can you believe he had the audacity to call me on the phone, crying, trying to convince me that it wasn't his fault and that if I had taken the ride with him, none of this would have happened in the first place? The nerve of this man. He had the gall to beg me not to tell my brother or Jeremy about what had happened. It's starting to feel good not having him around. I have gotten so used to him running off that this time was no different than any other time; I don't even worry about him like I used to. My feelings have changed, and enough is enough.

To tell the truth, if I hadn't gotten myself into so much debt, I probably would have never, ever taken him back in the first place. Fear of having bad credit and losing everything consumed my thoughts day and night. Paying a mortgage, car note, new furniture, car insurance, light bill, water bill, cable, grocery, and you name it terrified me; just the thought of two people, my brother and myself, doing all this terrified me. Especially on my salary of only $5.25 an hour—my brother was only making about $6.40 an hour. Mark had a pretty decent job and brought home the real bacon, when he wasn't out blowing it on getting high. The man made really good money and with overtime he would bring home over $300 some weeks, and that was after taxes.

In a few minutes, I guess I'll get ready to go downtown so I can pay on the layaway for the baby. Nothing is going to stop me from doing what I have to do right now. When Mark comes back with the car keys, I'll be more prepared than ever to give him a piece of my mind and let him go forever. No man is worth the headaches he has given me, I thought, as I stood at the mirror combing my hair, convincing myself over and over again that it was going to be different this time.

My dream car was no longer a dream, but now, thanks to him, a wrecked car. I had to prove I was driving the night of the accident, for this man didn't have a driver's license, so he couldn't even call the police to file an accident report. What in the world am I going to do? How ams I going to convince anyone that I am seven months pregnant and totaled this car, which didn't have a scratch on it. That's right. The car didn't have a scratch on it and yet the whole "Alquote frame" was cracked in half. The impact of the car hitting the corner of the curb at such a high speed caused so much damage to the A-frame that anybody in their right mind would have known that with that type of impact, if I had been driving more than likely it would have caused some bodily harm not only to me, but my unborn child. Tomorrow I have to call the insurance company and tell them what happened. It's going to be hard filing a claim without the police report. How am I going to get anyone to believe me, I thought to myself. Without a real report to back me up, I knew I would be fighting a losing battle. Somehow or other, I'm going to have to convince them that this is for real, no matter what they say. I have to get this car fixed. Who wants to commute by bus all day long when you could have a luxury car to ride in? Not me, and that is for sure. Too many years have come and gone with me standing in the rain, sleet, and snow to catch a bus; the thought of this makes me ill. I'm getting too old to be starting over again.

Thoughts of the first time I spotted my dream car clouded my mind as I got dressed to go to the insurance company so I could file my claim. They made it clear that they wanted to see me in person. Maybe they wanted to see if I was who I said I was. Whatever the case, I knew I had to be prepared for all of their questions and skepticism. While getting ready, I stood in front of the mirror and rehearsed in my mind what I was going to say. This was hard for me to do, and to tell the truth I was scared to death. What if they caught me in a lie? I would have been the one paying the price for something I didn't do. How could this ruthless man named Mark Davis let me take the fall for something I didn't do? One thing I had to face for sure was that if I did tell the truth, my insurance company would not pay for the repairs to my car and I would have been stuck paying for a bill of over maybe $5,000. There was no way I would be able to pay this large sum of money to get my dream car fixed. Mark seemed as if he didn't care, and that made me even angrier. His only response was that it wasn't his fault and I should be happy that he was okay; at that moment, I could have cared less. This man had no guilt, shame, or remorse about what he had done and how he made me feel. He seemed at ease with the fact that we no longer had transportation. If this was true, he was one sick individual.

May 13, 1986

Dear Diary,

Yesterday was a long day. My car insurance company wants me to go meet with the head adjuster in their claims department at the corporate office located in Newark. If this happens, I'm headed for nothing but pure disaster. This means that they are going to investigate me inside out. Right now I don't need any added stress to an already complex situation that could have been eliminated from the beginning. Everything that has happened so far I could have eliminated, for there was no reason for things to get so out of control. Poor little Terry hasn't been the same since he found out about the car. His whole demeanor has changed, and I sense his pain just like any mother would about her child. It's been a long time since I've seen him like this. Lately he has been so quiet I barely notice that he is in the house. Every time I look at him, I can feel the hurt and pain that he carries on the inside. There is not one day that goes by that I don't show him my appreciation. At times, just like any mother, I have to be hard on him and make him be responsible for his actions. Some of my friends tell me I'm too hard on him and should give him a break. I'm afraid that if I do what they suggest, my child will become a statistic just like so many others.

When you are a single parent, it is hard to raise children in this day's society and expect it to be like it was when our parents grew up. Thinking back when I was a child, the neighbor was given permission to spank you if you did something wrong, and dare you to tell or talk back. Now in today's society, you better think twice before you hit anybody's child, including your own. Parents are almost losing the right to discipline their own children. And children are so rude and disrespectful; they are telling their parents that they will call CPS (Child Protective Services), better known to all in the big city as Social Services. Once CPS gets in your business, it's just like having a bad toothache that you can't ever get rid of. Some parents have lost their children to Child Protective Services under false claims and others lost them to drug addiction or physical, mental, and emotional abuse. To hear people talk about the horror some of their friends experienced with CPS can be unreal. There were cases where the mother was a single parent and had to work and her child was a latchkey kid, meaning that the child would get home from school maybe two or three hours before the parent. Someone reported this to Social Service, and the parent lost custody of the child, and now they are in foster care. That's only one story. There are so many I can't even begin to tell you. In many cases, the children were protected through CPS, and in other cases, the parents became the victims because they simply could not afford after-school care for their children. Just thinking about losing my child gives me goose bumps, and I pray that something like this will never happen to me. I can't imagine going through the thought of losing someone so dear and precious to me.

Let me put this diary down so I can get some work done around here. Sometimes I start writing and can't stop. It's almost like this diary is my best friend at times, for I know it can keep all my secrets that I dare not tell anyone else. Well, Mrs. Diary, it is getting late and I have so much to do before I lay my head down.

May 18, 1986

Dear Diary,

Today I received a call from the head claims adjuster at the corporate office, demanding that he schedule an appointment for me to come in so he can go over my accident claim with me. His main question was, how could this car be totaled and not have one scratch on it, and the damages come up to over $5,000, and the driver, who was seven months pregnant at the time, walk away without a bruise, scratch, police report or anything? He told me the only way he was going to sign that check for me to have the repairs done was if I met him in person. By this time my hands were tied. This man was curious and wanted to know every detail from the moment I stepped into the car until I called them to report it. "Lady, are you telling me that you were actually driving this car, hit the curve going 45 to 55 mph, the car jumped the curb, the impact broke the A-frame in two, and you didn't receive not one bruise. Are you swearing to me that this is what happened?" he asked so clearly and boldly. As hard as it was, I had to look into this man's face and tell him a straight-faced lie, something that I really feared doing, but knew I had to so the insurance company would pay. Telling lies is not one of my specialties, and it was very hard to look Mr. Garrison in the eye and be dishonest.

Mr. Garrison is in his early thirties and a very handsome, distinguished-looking man—and, let's not forget, also a very flirtatious man who smiled from the time I walked through the door until the time I left. His well-groomed hair and neatly trimmed sideburns told of a man who was into pampering himself. Looking at his hands and how they were manicured said a lot about a man's character. My first impression would be a lasting one, like the seductive cologne he wore. Mr. Garrison was a true gentleman and was always so nice to me, treating me like a lady from the moment he welcomed me to step inside his office. At first I didn't know if he was being nice to flatter me so he could get the information he needed or if this was just his personality all the time. He made me feel welcome and told me to tell the truth. When he asked me what really happened to the car and told me that he knew I was lying, I had no choice but to 'fess up and tell the truth and that I did. In between sobs, I told him what really happened. At the moment I was confessing the truth I felt like a weight had lifted up off of me. Even though I knew I was ruining any chance of getting the insurance company to cover my expenses for repairs, at least I felt good knowing that I had done the right thing and didn't have to worry about a lie coming back to haunt me later.

After confessing the truth to him, my stomach was growling; it growled so loud, in fact, I knew he had to hear it. That's when he asked me out to lunch. I jumped at the offer. If he hadn't asked, I was soon to ask him out myself. This little life inside of me knew how to get what it wanted when it was feeding time. If this baby is this hungry now, imagine after it's born! It was hard for Mr. Garrison not to laugh as he looked at me and helped me up out of my comfortable seat. It was so comfortable, in fact, I probably would have liked it better if he had ordered something to eat in instead of going out. Today, I must say I know God was with me because before I left, this man told me to expect my check for the amount of $5,465.85 in the mail within the next five to seven business days. What more could I ask for? Now the worst was over, and I could take the ride home with a smile on my face knowing that everything was going to be all right. It's amazing how faith can move mountains. Just keeping the faith helped to see me through.

May 21, 1986

Dear Diary,

It's been about a week since I have actually had anything to say to Mark. Even though we sleep in the same bed, I have nothing to say. He acts as though he doesn't owe me anything, and it doesn't seem to matter to him. When he gets off from work he barely says a word and comes home with an attitude. My brother doesn't know what happened to the car and thinks that it is in the shop for repairs. There is no way I can bring myself to tell him the truth. If he finds out, I would have to move out of town. It's no problem for me to keep this secret because my brother works at night, so when Mark gets off from work, Chad is just leaving to go. And when he gets off, most of the time I'm already in the bed asleep. The only time we have to see each other is on Thursday and sometimes late in the evening on Saturday if I stay up late.

I'm so glad Chad's eye has healed pretty nicely and you can barely see the scar. For a moment I thought he would have to have plastic surgery. That would have broken my heart. Since the accident he has become very protective of me and Terry. I can tell by the way he acts, and if he is off from work and knows that Mark is around, he won't go too far out of my sight. For many reasons, he doesn't trust Mark and has every right to feel the way he does. Every chance he gets he lets me know by telling me how he feels about the situation I'm in. Yes, my brother loves me, but I'm grown and need to make my own choices in life.

Yesterday when Mark came home he picked an argument for nothing; the only reason he did it was because he knew today was payday, and if he started a good enough argument, he felt it gave him the right to keep all his money and not give me any to pay bills. Right now, I'm at the point where I'm tired of protecting his secret and could care less if he keeps every penny he makes. I wish he would just leave. If I didn't fear for my life, I would have left him a long time ago, but fear keeps me here.

Believe it or not, staying in an abusive situation doesn't make it better; it only gets worse with time. Fear of the unknown will make you hurt your own self. Once fear sets in, it is hard to think about anything else. The only thing you think about, day in and day out, is what if I leave, how can I leave? Where will I go? How will I survive? *[I know all those questions all too well, as I was a victim—remember? Remember one thing: the longer you stay in the situation, the longer the abuse will continue. It will only end with change. That change is something you have to find within you.]*

May 22, 1986

Dear Diary,

My hands are shaking as I write these words on this paper; I have to tell somebody what happened last night. Mark came home from work and started an argument. At first I tried so hard to ignore him, fearing that Terry would hear us and get scared. The last thing I want is my child upset, crying, and scared to death thinking about what is going to happen to his momma. Mark was so angry—I could tell by the look in his eyes that he wanted to do something awful to me. He had me locked up in the bedroom, screaming and cursing at me and demanding that I give him his money back, and threatening me as to what he was going to do if I didn't. There was no way I could give him his money back. I had already given it to Terry for safekeeping. Mark told me that I had five minutes to show him his money or he was going to choke it out of me. By the time he told me this, I was shaking like a leaf and thought that I was going to pass out for fear of what he was going to do to me. No matter how loud I would scream, no one but my child would hear me, and the last thing I wanted was for this man to abuse my child, too. Thinking quickly, I pretended like I couldn't breathe and needed some fresh air; my forehead was covered with sweat. When he reached to open the door, I dashed toward the slight opening, only to see my child standing there crying. He had already heard Mark threaten me. Looking into my child's eyes, I could sense his fear and we both decided to run for it. Terry ran in front of me, reaching his tiny hand out for mine so he could quickly guide me down the steep, dark stairway.

The hallway light that lit the staircase had blown out the night before, and trying to find your way in the dark down those steep stairs was very frightening. By the time we made our way to the front door, I could hear Mark calling my name and cursing at me, swearing to fulfill his promise to choke me to death. Upon hearing those chilling, horrible words, my son looked at me as he quickly closed the door behind us and motioned for me to move out of the way. There was a 2 x 4 piece of plywood about four feet long lying by the door as if someone had left it there purposely for me. Without having time to think, I grabbed it and when Mark ran down the stairs I hid silently behind the door, waiting for him to open the storm door so I could let him have it. When he opened the storm door and I saw his head, I swung; lucky for him, I missed; he ducked just in time.

That day I was the one pretending that his head was a baseball. I was at the point where I was sick and tired of being sick and tired of putting up with someone else's mess. It was hard for me to believe that I swung at this man and missed, hitting the wall and breaking the board in half. That's just how hard I swung it. The surprised and angry look on Mark's face told the story. "I hope you took your best shot," he said. "Cee, is that all you have?" he said as he continued to chase me and my son. Terry was already on the other side of the fence, standing in front of the balcony, stretching his arms out for me once again to come with him. At that very moment, without thinking and with nowhere else to turn for safety, I had no choice but to climb up on the front porch balcony and jump off, not knowing whether I was going to land on top of the four-foot fence that surrounded our house or on the sidewalk. When my feet hit the ground and I realized I was okay, there Terry was, anxiously waiting for me with tears in his eyes as he grabbed my hand and made sure I was all right.

"Momma, are you okay?" he whispered as we both ran to safety in the dark. Mark was so high from crack and whatever else, there was no telling what he had done if he would have caught us. The only reason he gave up on chasing us was the fact that maybe he was too high and feared someone would see him since we were out in the open, and that they would find out that he was a ruthless and cold man. His secret reign of terror would be in the open. I'm convinced that was the only thing that saved me and my son's life tonight. Terry was brave in my time of need and displayed no sign of fear. Inside, I knew he was trying to be strong for his mother. This little boy loves his momma and was going to make sure she was okay.

As nosy as my neighbors are, where were they in my time of need? Here it was, almost 11:30 p.m., and my son and I were running for our lives. Not even one wino on the corner. I couldn't help but wonder where everyone was. The leap from the porch to the ground was about six feet; my heart was beating so fast and as scared as I was, I'm surprised that I didn't hurt myself and that I didn't start hemorrhaging. All my life I had been a tomboy, and I guess my being in the military helped, too. For it was some of those G.I. Joe tactics I used to lower my fat, wobbly body to the ground as I leaped off the front porch balcony. Sometimes when fear grips you, you forget certain things—such as I'm seven months pregnant and shouldn't be doing this. At the moment, your only concern is survival. This Beast Master, Mr. Mark, could have cared less how scared I was or if me or the baby were safe. His only concern was in getting his hands on that money he had given me to pay the bills. How cold and heartless was this man I had come to love so much? Here it was, only thirteen months into the relationship, and this man I had grown to care about and love so much had become known to me as the Beast Master, someone I began to despise.

If it had not been for my son, I don't know what I would have done. Together we both walked around in a daze, not knowing what to do next. Too afraid to tell anybody and too proud to give anyone the right to interfere in our business. We both were so dependent on each other and the bond we had was special. To me, Terry became my hero and protector. The situation he was placed in was unfair and unfit for any child his age. Instead of going outside to play with his friends, here he was, lingering around the house waiting to see what was going to happen to his mother. My child's life became consumed with fear. Fear of the unknown that he felt sooner or later would take his mom's life. No child should ever have to experience what he did. How can a parent or parents expect a child to go to school, function, and get good grades under this kind of pressure? No matter what, Terry was managing.

When I came home from work, together we would count the money he had for me to put in the bank. And on rent days I would leave a note for my tenants to give him the rent money. It was almost as if he had a regular job being my banker. Our secret was so well kept that no one had the slightest idea that this little boy that was barely four feet tall was a powerhouse filled with information and secrets. Secrets that I knew he would take to his grave if it came down to that.

As we turned the corner, I could see the taillights of a car pulling up in front of our house. I knew it had to be my brother and his friend just getting off from work. Most nights when he got off, he would sit out in his friend's car and drink a beer before coming upstairs. Tonight, I knew that Terry and I would have to put a quick one over on Chad so he wouldn't suspect anything unusual. While walking down the street, quietly and calmly, slowly approaching our house, we both looked at each other's reactions and managed to smile and started small talk to appear as if nothing had happened. Of course, my brother knew whenever he arrived home most times I would be in bed asleep, but tonight was different. Before he had a chance to recognize who I was, I went over to the car and started a conversation with him and his friend, asking all kinds of stupid questions, not giving him any chance to suspect anything. If I'm thinking right, I would say that they were a little bit tipsy, and if so tonight, that is all right with me. You can't imagine the relief I felt knowing that he was not the least bit suspicious about me being out so late.

May 23, 1986

Dear Diary,

Today I didn't go to work. My side was aching and I know it's from me leaping off the porch last night. My whole body is sore. Terry was purposely late going to school this morning. He was determined that he was going to stay home with me. I had to make him go. Despite how hard he begged and cried, I had to make him go. He is so afraid that something bad is going to happen to me. Mark wasn't home when we returned last night; I guess he stayed at the "crack house." My brother has been knocking on my door all morning and I haven't responded, so I know he probably thinks that I'm out riding around. He still does not know what happened to the car yet. And if I have to tell him I guess he won't know.

It's been a long time since I felt as scared as I did last night. It was almost like being on a roller coaster that was zooming out of control. Right now my life is full of heartache and pain, something I never imagined. I'm so tired of living a lie, and every day I think it will get better, but it's only getting worse. Why am I fooling myself like this? If my family knew what I was going through, they would make me pack up my things and leave him for good. But I know this is my problem, not theirs. Even though Mark has threatened me repeatedly, I only thought that he was just talking and trying to scare me so he could have his way with me and make me give him back the money he had already given me to pay bills.

Now, as each day goes by, he is getting colder and colder. Becoming someone I don't even care to know. I'm starting to have some really ugly thoughts about him. Yesterday I found myself wishing he would get hit by a "Big Mack" truck. This man knows I'll soon be eight months pregnant, and he watched me as I jumped off that porch that was six feet up off the ground. How could he be so cold? What was going through his mind? I could have gotten seriously injured or, even worse, died. Let's make no mistake about it. This man was cold and ruthless and could have cared less. The only thing he had on his mind at the moment was where was he going to get the money to buy his next hit.

After that last incident with him and my brother, I thought he really wanted to change for the better. For the life of me, I wish that something would change him. I don't know what it's going to take for him to snap back into reality. We tried counseling, NA, you name it. At this very moment I wish he would vanish, and that's just how I feel. I wish he didn't make me feel this way. How could something that started out to be so right turn out so wrong? Tomorrow I have a doctor's appointment. We both were supposed to be going together. Deep down inside, I hope he doesn't show up. The way he chased me and Terry last night, I don't want to see his face anytime soon. To me, he has become the monster in the horror story.

My son, no matter how brave he is in front of this man, fears for my life. Terry has become so good at hiding his emotions and putting up a brave front, pretending that he is okay. But, late at night I hear his soft cries. Mentally, emotionally, and physically, the strain of the lack of sleep is taking a toll on my child. Just the other day, the teacher sent me a note stating that Terry is sleeping in class, and his grades have fallen to a D-average. It's very hard for me to fuss at him, knowing how much he is actually going through to keep his mother's secret and protect me. My eighth month is approaching fast, and I know that soon the hardest part will be almost over and I can start a normal life. Today, I'm going to try and do something really special for Terry so he'll forget about last night and not be tense.

My nerves are getting the best of me and my fears are getting stronger. Who knows what tomorrow may bring? The mechanic from the repair shop at the car dealership where I bought the car called and informed me that they ordered the parts for my car, and because it is a foreign car that they rarely repair, it was going to be at least a three-to-six-month wait before they would be able to start. When I heard this news it really put a damper on my day. Sooner or later I will have to tell my brother the truth, but for now I'm going to hold out for as long as I can. Turmoil on top of turmoil is the last thing I need, for there is no telling what might happen next. Good night, Mrs. Diary.

May 24, 1986

Dear Diary,

Terry came home, running up the stairs all the way, nonstop. By the time he reached the top step he was out of breath, running hard as if someone had been chasing him.

"Momma, Momma," he called out anxiously, "are you here?" From the way he sounded, I thought something terrible had happened.

"Yes, baby I'm here," I replied, meeting him at the door, asking him what was wrong.

"Nothing's wrong, Momma. I just wanted to make sure you were here. I worried about you all day in school," he said.

Looking at his face, I could see the white traces of where the teardrops lay on his face. My child had been crying, and I know every tear he shed was for the love of his momma and the pain he felt she must have been going through. "Hey, little boy, I'm here and your momma sure is glad to see you," I said, hugging his neck so tight and planting sweet kisses all over his little tear-stained face. As he looked into my eyes, I could see his love for me beaming through like it was the sun glowing on the moon. "Terry, you are my angel," I said as we both walked into the kitchen so I could fix his special treat. This little boy loves biscuits—hot, cold, he didn't care. As long as they were biscuits.

"Momma, did you go to the doctor?" he asked while talking with a mouth full of biscuit and rubbing his tiny hands on my belly, trying to feel the baby kicking.

"Yes, baby, Momma went to the doctor," I said.

"Is the baby okay?" he asked, still chewing.

"Yes, the baby is fine."

"Did the doctor tell you if it was a boy or girl?"

"No, Terry, I won't know until I have the baby," I said.

"Where is Mark, Momma? Did he go to the doctor with you?"

"No baby, he didn't."

"Good," he said, "I hope he never comes back. He is so mean to us. Momma, please don't take Mark back," he begged. "We always have fun when Mark is not here."

In my mind I couldn't help but think about the tragedy of going through giving birth to this baby alone. Right now, if anything, I need a friend, someone I can talk to. The last time I talked to Audra she really laid it on the line, not feeling sorry for me, and told me like it really was. Good night, Mrs. Diary.

May 27, 1986

Dear Diary,

In a few days it will be the first of the month again. The months seem to zoom by so fast. And the time is getting closer for me to drop this load. I know this has to be all baby. My doctor told me that I had gained a total of forty-five pounds and that this baby should weigh between seven and eight pounds. Hopefully I'll lose this baby fat and still be able to get into my old clothes. I'll cry if I can't. Before I became pregnant, I had just gone on a mad shopping spree, trying to buy everything in sight that I could afford. All I want to do is get back in shape—mentally, physically, and financially. It's been a while since I have worked my second job, and I miss the money, to be honest. When I was working two jobs, I didn't miss the money Mark blew so much because I had backup. Now I don't know how I'm going to make it. I hope and pray that he will come through with flying colors. Maybe when I have the baby he will change. I can't imagine him continuing to live foolishly. No one can go on like this forever. Not even him.

June 6, 1986

Dear Diary,

As I lay across the bed thinking about what I'm going to name my baby, I can't help but think about everything that has happened. And how relieved I am at the progress my child is starting to make in school. In a few more short weeks he will be getting out for summer vacation. Maybe my Aunt Janice will want him to come down South to visit. This way he will have some fun and get to see his other little cousins that are about his age. He really needs some spark in his life.

He is too young to be carrying his momma's problems and taking on the responsibility of a grown man. I thank God for my precious little angel everyday; I adore him. For he has given me more than I feel I'm worthy of. And that is his undying love for his momma. Sometimes I wonder how my child can love me so much when I have subjected him to such an abusive life. Only the man upstairs knows.

June 7, 1986

Dear Diary,

Audra came home from work in a really good mood and told me to get dressed, that we were going to take the kids out for pizza and ice cream. This is going to make Terry so happy. We have fun when we all go out together. I have yet to tell her about what happened the other night and realize that if I do, things might explode around my house. The last time we spoke about Mark and my situation, she really let me have it and told me how she really felt. Since that time we hadn't talked about too much of anything. Our conflicting work schedules kept us from spending any real quality time together, so anytime we get a chance to have fun, that's what we do—have fun.

The kids really enjoy themselves when they get together and are in a world of their own. Nothing else seems to matter to them right now, and it makes me feel so good when I can see a smile on their little sweet faces. It brightens my day, especially to see my child for once not having to worry about his mother.

Even though I was a little disappointed in Audra for scolding me a few weeks ago, I couldn't help but forgive her and realize that she is a true friend who was only concerned about my well-being. Friends like her are very rare and I wouldn't trade her for anything else in the world. She was always there when I needed her the most and never betrayed me. I'll forever be grateful to her for this. No one else understood me like she did. To me, like I have said before, she was priceless. Her smooth California personality and style was so laid back, you knew exactly where she was coming from when she laid the facts on the line, never beating around the bush about anything. It was a delight to have her around. There was no way I could stay mad at her if I tried. When she was in a room, you felt it come alive. I wish everyone had a friend like her so they, too, would know this feeling. The joy of friendship can be so enlightening, and I feel so special for having her in my life. One day, I hope I'll be as good to her as she has been to me.

It's been a few days since I have seen Mark, and right now I could care less as to where he has been, as long as he doesn't bother me or my child. I'm so glad my brother has been putting in a lot of hours at work—I barely get to see him. He has yet to ask me about my car or anything else. Sooner or later I know the cat will be out of the bag and he is going to find out about everything—I dread that day happening. As long as I can be discreet about what is going on, then and only then will I be okay. If my brother or Jeremy had any idea that I jumped off the porch the other night and was chased by Mark, my life would become a nightmare. The longer he stays away, the better things will be.

Today the baby kicked so hard I thought for a moment he was going to kick his way out. Whatever it is, a boy or girl, I know one thing for sure—this baby is going to be strong. And right now my only worry is if this baby will be healthy. The only thing I can do is pray and have faith that it will be.

June 10, 1986

Dear Diary,

Can you believe it? Today, out of all days, when I came home from work, guess who the cat drug in? You guessed it, Mr. Mark. He had the nerve to be lying across my bed, snoring as if he hadn't slept in days. The nerve of this man. He has been gone for about ten days or more, has not called home once, and is bold enough to show up here after everything he has done. Especially after the last fight we had where he chased me and Terry. This man has got to be out of his mind. What kind of monster is he? How in the world can he be so cold and ruthless? And return home as if nothing has happened? I can hardly bear the sight of him, and I can only imagine what Terry is going to think and feel when he comes home and finds out that he is here. Right at the moment when my child was getting comfortable with the fact that Mark was no longer around, here he is, showing up again. What can I say to make him understand that I had nothing to do with Mark returning and that he and I must continue to keep our secret about what happened no matter how mad or disappointed he gets? Asking my child to hold all of this inside was a mother asking a lot. Still, the fact remained that for our safety, we both had to be silent. For silence was golden, and that's what I had drilled in his head for months, not realizing what type of affect or impact it would have on him. In a way this was selfish of me. But, what other choice did I have? Who else could I have trusted as much as I trusted him? Whirling thoughts of how Mark is going to react when he awakes are driving me insane. What can this man possibly say to me now? Where is he going to tell me he has been for the last almost two weeks? Or is he going to act like it doesn't matter? There are so many questions dancing around in my head unanswered. Nothing would make me happier than if he left me alone to live my own life. I have come to the realization that he isn't going to change, and all the wishing and hoping is not going to make a difference.

June 13, 1986

Dear Diary,

It's been almost three days since Mark returned. He has been trying to apologize and trying to make me feel guilty by saying things like, if I didn't make him mad, everything would not have gotten so out of control that night we argued and he left. He told me the only reason he left was to give me some time to think about how I was mistreating him and making him feel like he was a little boy by asking him so many questions and that he should be allowed to ask for some of his money back to do as he pleases. Now, you know this man is taking it a little too far by saying this, and if the truth be known and I weren't pregnant right now, I would have smacked him right upside his head for thinking and talking nothing but pure ignorance. How does he sound, telling me something so stupid and ridiculous that he should be arrested just for the thought? Where does he get off thinking the way he does? Has his crack addiction fried his brain? What is he going to come up with next? By looking at him, you can tell he hasn't been eating regularly; his face is already thin, and now it's all sunken in and his teeth are beginning to decay badly. His eyes are bulging out of his head, making him look almost twice his age. It is hard for me to believe that this handsome man I had come to love so much at one time is starting to look like one of the hobos on the street corner, someone I would have never given a second glance.

My brother told me that my stepmom wants to see me, and I can only wonder if she knows what's going on. Knowing her, someone may have told her by now. It's hard for me to keep anything from her, for she can tell by the look in my eyes if something is wrong. Never failing to be wrong once. She is something else, always making sure that I'm all right and fixing me something special to eat whenever I go to visit her. Her new apartment in the senior citizens' building was so nice and cozy, nestled up on the third floor. When you stepped off the elevator, the floors were so clean you could almost eat off of them. The reflections that danced around from silhouette to silhouette told of how shiny the white marble tile floors were. Clara was so proud of her new apartment and welcomed anyone who wanted to come in—even the neighbors she didn't know down the hall. As the saying used to go, she never met a stranger. It's been some time since I have seen her last. I think it was just the other day I spoke with her on the phone. Of course, she scolded me for not visiting. When I do, she will be filled with about fifty questions, so you know I'll have to be ready and prepared to answer everything as if it is really her business anyway. How can I hide so much from her? My intuition tells me that she suspects something, but isn't telling me. Usually she just sits back and lets you think that she doesn't know anything and waits until you have spun your last web of lies before she will let you know that she actually knows the truth, making you feel like a complete fool. If I know anything, I know this for a fact. She has done it so many times, over and over again. I watched her catch my stepsister Joyce in a bunch of lies, but that never stopped poor Joyce. Each time she would try to fool my stepmom, I already knew what the outcome was going to be.

Sometimes I catch myself thinking about the time when I was

nineteen years old and had lost my apartment and I was homeless. I guess Terry must have been about eighteen months old, and here I was, wandering from girlfriend's house to girlfriend's house for a place to lay my head, too afraid and filled with too much pride to let anyone know what was really going on in my life. Afraid that people would think I was a failure if they knew the truth about me. One day, here I was on top of the world, and everyone so proud of me, and at the time I was only nineteen years old.

I remember going to visit Clara one cold and windy Sunday in March right before spring had set in. This was years ago when she used to live on Governor Street. After spending a restless day of wondering where my baby and I were going to sleep later on that night, I remembered the first thing she asked me that evening.

"Cee, I heard you moved into a new apartment—tell me all about it," she said. I purposely pretended like I didn't hear her talking to me and continued to stare at the TV, hoping she wouldn't repeat the question. The more I pretended not to hear her, the more fascinated (or curious, should I say) she became. Peering at her from the corner of my eye, I could tell she was looking straight through me and saw the scared little girl who didn't know what to do and was too proud to say that she and her baby were homeless. As I sat on the bed that day pretending not to hear her, she got up from her favorite E-Z chair and headed toward the kitchen, not saying a word. Finally, I could hear her light, cheery voice calling me, telling me she had something to show me. As I approached the narrow hallway leading toward the opening in the kitchen, I saw the shadow of her slender body leaning against the doorway that was opened to the left of the kitchen—the one I never paid any attention to and barely knew existed. When she opened the bedroom door she was leaning against, the odor of mildew hit me dead in my face. The black net that was hanging from the walls and ceiling filled with dusty cobwebs told a story, and the psychedelic, bright pink paint on the wall told of an era where someone was into the Parliament Funkadelics, and that couldn't be anybody other than my crazy stepsister Joyce.

Before I could say a word, she said, "I know this room is a mess and no one has slept here in years, but if you want to, you can have it. I'll only charge you $25 a week, and that includes me watching the baby while you work. It's going to take some cleaning and a good imagination to fix it up. What do you think?" she asked, watching the look of shock on my face.

Thinking back now, I don't know if I was shocked because the room was such a mess and looked horrible or because I was delighted to have a warm place for me and my baby to lay our heads.

"I'm going to let you decide," she said, with a warm and gentle smile that showed much love and support.

At that moment my heart was skipping a beat and relief swept over me as once more the Lord answered my prayers. How did she know I was homeless? Until this day, I have no earthly idea. Can you imagine this woman knowing exactly what I needed without asking me or saying a word? God knew what He was doing when He planted her into my life. Not taking too much time to think, I happily accepted her offer, knowing in advance that this room needed some real, real fixing up. Just looking at it made me tired, and I knew in order for me to get it to where it was suitable for me and my child to be comfortable, I would need at least $10 to $15 in cleaning supplies if I wanted it to look and smell decent. I took the last few dollars I had and went up to the corner store and bought cleaning supplies so I could start what would be a three-to-four-hour job, but I got it done by midnight. Before I went to bed I had already mopped the floor three times, wiped down walls, knocked down cobwebs, changed linen on the make-believe bed. I say make-believe because it looked like a pull-out sofa, but it was so old it was hard to make out what it really was! Can you imagine that? Looking back now, I remember how grateful I was to her for taking me and my child in. Eventually, I knew my father would find out and I would have to explain to him what happened and how I got myself into a situation like this in the first place. Maybe I'll wait until tomorrow to go see her when I am rested and feel up to all the questions she's going to ask me. Well, for now I must say good night.

June 15, 1986

Dear Diary,

My head is still spinning from what happened last night. I can't believe that I'm still alive and breathing, much less sitting here writing about it. Yesterday started out to be so lovely. I went to visit my step-mom like I had planned and we had such a nice visit. She had made some hors d'oeuvres—deviled eggs, my favorite—and I stuffed my face like there was no tomorrow. I was so full, I felt like an over-stuffed tick, ready to pop any moment. She really knew how to spoil a pregnant woman and make her lazy.

After returning home from my visit with her, I felt so rejuvenated and refreshed. My mind was clear and free from all thoughts of the horrible things Mark had put me through. There was nothing that was going to spoil my mood and change the way I was thinking and feeling at the moment. At least this is what I wanted to think. Re-turning home with a smile on my face and laughter in my heart be-cause of the conversation my stepmom and I had made me giggle as I opened the gate to the fence surrounding my house. Giggling all the way up the front porch steps I felt like a high school teenager act-ing silly. Terry couldn't help but laugh at me not being able to stop the laughter. He laughed because I was laughing, and to be honest, it felt so good to see a bright smile on his face. As we both got closer to the door, we looked at each other hoping and wishing the same thing—that Mark wouldn't be home so we could relax in peace, not having to worry about what he was going to argue or pick a fight about. Relief swept over us as we stuck the shiny, silver key into the door and realized that we were home alone—it made us feel so good that the Beast Master was gone. Oh boy, what a sigh of relief that was. I felt as if a weight had been lifted off of me, and I began humming and singing, thinking nothing but positive thoughts about my future and how bright it was going to be after I had my baby. Traveling from room to room to make sure Mark was nowhere around, Terry came happily running into my room. It was so funny to see how glad he was to know that Mark was not at home. We both started singing, looking into each other's mind as if we could read what the other was thinking.

"Momma, can I sleep in your bed?" he asked, much excitement in his tone.

"No Terry," I replied. "Now go and take a bath and get ready for school tomorrow," I told him.

Before I could finish getting the words out of my mouth, I could hear Mark's voice as he climbed the stairs. My heart dropped and I became speechless, pausing in midsentence, hoping he didn't hear the happiness in our voices and wondering if he had overheard any of our conversation about how happy we were that he was not around. For a moment, fear consumed my thoughts, not knowing what frame of mind this crazy man was going to be in. Mentally and emotionally, I had to prepare myself for whatever may come, not letting on to my son about how scared I really was. No matter how brave I tried to be on the outside, on the inside my soul was crying, overflowing like a well filled with many tears, enough to start a flood.

As he got to the top of the stairs, my heart started to beat rapidly and I could once again feel my body began to tremble. I'm eight and a half months pregnant and starting to look like I'm going to have this baby any day now. My clothes are feeling smaller and I refuse to buy anything else to wear. It's been a while since Mark has even touched my stomach to feel this little bundle of joy I'm so proudly carrying. It's almost as if he doesn't really care. How can this man be so cold and non-caring at a time like this? Thinking back, I can't even remember him asking me about my last checkup. He used to care so much; even if he did smoke crack, he was concerned about his unborn baby. When he first found out I was pregnant he rubbed my stomach all the time and used to stick his ear to my stomach to see if he could hear the baby moving. Then there were the times he would talk to the baby. To me he was so cute and sweet when he used to do that. I remember the mornings when he would get up and fix me breakfast in bed and let me sleep late, telling me I needed the rest and that he would fix dinner, too. Especially when he first started going to his NA meeting, he made me feel so special, it was a delight to hear his key in the door. And now, this very moment, all I feel is resentment for being so gullible and naïve—how could I have been so stupid?

Mark's first reaction when he came home last night was calm and peaceful—he seemed to be a different person, trying to convince Terry that he was just upset the other night and that he would never get that angry again. Then asking Terry to forgive him and saying that he was going to try to be a good role model from now on and to please give him another chance. His words seemed so sincere, but not yet convincing enough for me or my son. By the way Terry looked at him, I could tell that he didn't believe one word this man was saying—the hurt in his little eyes told how he really felt. This man had played far too many tricks; for me, he had more tricks than a magician at the circus. Yet he had enough guts to try to cast his last spell on me and my son, only for us to laugh in his face. We both giggled as Mark made a plea for us to trust him and give him another chance for the hundredth time. I just flat-out told him no, and that once I had my baby I was leaving him.

Once the words about me leaving him came blaring out of my mouth, I could feel the fury about to come on, but it was too late to take back what I had already said. Within seconds of me telling my plans, he went into a rage. All of a sudden, out of the blue, he asked me for the rent money I had collected from the tenants on the third floor. I tried to pretend like I hadn't collected the money and convince him that I was telling the truth. He yelled and screamed out loud, shouting to the world how much he hated me and wished I was dead. Upon hearing those words, I decided that enough was enough and that I didn't have to stand there and listen to him curse me out in front of my child. As I turned toward the staircase, I could feel his presence following me, demanding that I stop and listen to him. Looking around, trying to see where my child was, I ignored Mark. Pretending that he wasn't there and trying to block him from my thoughts, I called out, "Terry where are you? Let's get ready to go to Aunt Joyce's." As I turned the hallway light on to see if he was on the balcony, not hearing him respond made my heart flutter, wondering where my child was. All of a sudden I heard him knocking at the back door.

"Momma, let me in," he cried.

"Baby, where did you go to?" I asked.

"I went to visit Mrs. Audra and I told her you wanted to see her," he said.

I knew what my child was trying to do. He was trying to make Mark believe that any minute Audra would be coming downstairs; this way nothing bad would happen. When Mark heard Terry inform me that my friend Audra may be on her way, he really started cutting up, cursing my child as if he had lost his mind. With his eyes filled with tears and refusing to cry, my baby held my hand and walked toward the doorway leading to the staircase.

"Momma, let's go for a walk—come," he said, walking in front of me. The faster we walked, the more Mark screamed and yelled, continuing to call out my name and curse my son.

"Cee, come back here," he demanded. As I continued to ignore his plea, he became more bitter, following behind, telling me that I would regret it if I didn't stop and come back. Fear consumed me and I gave in to his demand and returned back up the stairs, standing directly in front of him as he stood at the top of the stairs facing me while Terry was already at the bottom step waiting for his momma so we could make our escape. I began to beg him to stop fussing in front of Terry and making threats on my life.

"If you want me to stop, give me the money you collected from the rent," he yelled, "and I'll leave you and your nappy-headed son alone," he said, heartless and cold.

"You make me so sick—I hate you, I hate you," I yelled while tears streamed down my face. The horrible words he had said about my son taunted me and yanked at my heart.

"Why don't you leave, Mark, so we can all be happy?" I cried.

"Why don't you make me leave, Cee?" he said with a voice full of raging anger.

Staring at each other eye to eye as I stood on the second step from the top, Mark yelled, "Better yet, you leave—and I mean leave now!"

Without any warning, he did the unthinkable, shoving me down a flight of twenty steps. At that very moment I saw my whole life flash before my eyes, and as I was falling, I could feel my unborn child kicking inside of me almost as if he, too, sensed death and was begging to live. The only thing I remembered about the fall is that before I was pushed, I turned around and looked at Terry standing at the bottom step with tears in his eyes and reassured him that everything was going to be all right. If it had not been for my son saving my life, I probably would have died.

As I sit here writing in this diary, I can't help but wonder how he saved my life. He is only about four feet tall and maybe forty-five pounds. Tiny as he is, I'm surprised that I didn't trample over him and kill him instantly from the impact. I know beyond a shadow of a doubt the mere fact of me being alive today is a miracle and God must have sent an angel to shield me from death—and that angel was my son. Terry is still in shock and hasn't spoken all day.

By the time the ambulance had arrived to take me to the hospital, Mark had already concocted a story, telling the EMS attendant that I slipped and fell down the stairs, not giving me or Terry a chance to say anything, making sure he was right there by my side, crying and pretending while squeezing my hand so tight, trying to appear to be such a concerned father. Pleading for the life of our baby and begging God to let everything be okay, he made sure that Terry and I didn't open our mouths. My child cried, as he knew the truth and held it inside for fear of what Mark may do later. The look of disgust was all over his face as he searched his thoughts, seeking answers as to why Mark did such a horrible thing to his mother. Even though he was scared, too, his quick thinking saved my life and that is something I'll never forget. After being checked over and over again and x-rayed around three times, the doctor finally gave me the okay to go and released me into Mark's custody, telling me to go home and stay in bed and to take it easy and if I start to spot, come back to the hospital.

So many "what if" thoughts clouded my mind. What if my son hadn't been there to rescue me? How could a child his size save my life when my whole body was falling down a flight of stairs, out of control? What would have happened if I had died? How could this man that professed to love me so much be so mean and cruel as to hurt me the way that he did? Did he mean to push me? And why? Nothing or no one could answer those questions for me as I lay resting in bed, feeling lost and full of pain, hurting from the inside out. I thought I knew this man and never thought he would be capable of doing something like this. Oh boy, was I wrong—just how wrong I was, no one knew but me. My son came into the room and laid his head on my stomach with much quietness, as if he had lost his very best friend. His little eyes reeled with sadness. And all I could do was gently stroke his head and hold him close to me, letting him know that Momma was okay and how much I loved him. Looking into his eyes, I knew he was also filled with many questions as to why, but he dared not say a word.

That night we both were thankful that I was alive. This was a secret that I never wanted anyone to know and if I had my way, no one would. As horrible as this secret was to keep, I feared what would happen if it was known. The pain searing through my heart was like a match someone lit to a bonfire. You could not imagine what a fool I felt like—and a loser on top of that. Out of all the apples in the barrel I picked the rotten one. What was my family going to think once they found out the truth of how this man really was? In my mind, what was I going to tell my mother? Knowing that she, too, had already experienced such violent abuse, so much that it took her eyesight. Nothing could prepare me for what I would face once the truth was known. Here I was, almost ready to deliver, and my baby's daddy was acting like a complete fool. A stranger I no longer wanted or chose to know. Only time can heal the wounds that are festering inside my heart.

June 16, 1986

Dear Diary,

My girlfriend Audra came downstairs to visit me and I really was glad to see her. She said Terry told her I needed some company and I wanted her to come and visit with me. Of course, we were both happy to see each other. Whenever she steps into a room, the sun is sure to shine. We talked as if it had been ages, and I begged her for butter pecan ice cream, which she went and bought for me. I enjoyed it thoroughly. She made my day. Not once did she even mention Mark's name; that made me feel extra special.

A few hours after she left, Mark came home and kneeled down by my bedside, holding my hand and begging for me to forgive him. I felt nothing but cold chills and numbness to the pain he caused inside my aching womb. He made my heart ache and my life so full of grief. He was hateful, harmful, and filled with a nasty, filthy habit—his addiction to crack cocaine. Those little white rocks of powder caused you to lie to yourself, your momma, wife, children, and whoever else that got in its way—crack cocaine doesn't discriminate. It doesn't care about color, nationality, or origin—not even religion. I'm so glad Audra does not suspect anything is wrong with me. She thinks that this is just normal for me to be in bed this time of day.

June 20, 1986

Dear Diary,

My brother has not been around too much lately. I think he may have another girlfriend or he is working a lot of overtime. It's been a while since we talked about anything. If he knew that Mark pushed me down a flight of stairs, I know there wouldn't be anything that could stop him from the unthinkable. And there wouldn't be anything I could do to stop him this time. He would go and get my god-brother Jeremy and it would be like World War III for sure. All I want right now is for things to blow over with no commotion.

When I listen to other women bragging about what they would do if they were in an abusive relationship, I can't help but wonder if they would really do everything they say or would they, too, be shaking in their boots just like me? My girlfriends would often say, "Girl you know if my boyfriend ever hits me, that's it" or "I'm never going to let a man hit me and get away with it—he'll be in jail." They made it seem so easy just to simply call the cops and get rid of the problem, but what I always wanted to know is what happens when that man gets out of jail and comes back home? Did they think he was going to be locked up forever? I'm pretty sure if that was the case, my girl-friend Audra would have had her husband Pee Wee locked up a long time ago. Especially after some of the fights I have overheard. Plenty of times I wanted to call the cops and have him arrested.

No woman or man deserves their spouse putting their hands on them. So many women have lost their lives over domestic violence and thinking about that now, it is the last thing I want to happen to me. Somehow or other, I have to get out before it's too late. Each day this man is becoming more and more possessive, especially since my fall. He tries to make sure that he is with me all the time and monitors who visits me, informing them that I need my rest and he will give me their messages. One more month seems so long to me. Having this baby sooner than the original due date would be a blessing in disguise. More and more, I'm beginning to believe that this is a bad nightmare that is never going to end.

June 29, 1986

Dear Diary,

It's getting harder and harder to try to write anything without Mark finding my diary and ripping it apart. He is very insecure and doesn't trust anyone. We have yet to talk about the incident, and can you believe that he is trying to convince me and my son that it was just a careless mistake and that I was so clumsy I accidentally tripped over my own two feet? How ruthless can this man be? Evidently he must think I'm crazy enough to believe him. Terry refuses to go outside and play, always making up excuses and cuddling up next to me as if he is going to read me a bedtime story. He is so sweet; I couldn't bear the thought of making him do something he really didn't want to. Every day it became routine for him to play Mommy's doctor, laying his little, round head against my stomach to listen to the baby's heartbeat and feel the baby kick. Also, mind you, asking me a thousand questions.

July 3, 1986

Dear Diary,

My doctor called to check on me. I assured her that everything was okay and that I wasn't experiencing any real pain or spotting. I also informed her that I was getting plenty of rest and staying off my feet. In another week it will be almost time for me to go on maternity leave and believe it or not, I will be more than ready. At first I thought I would work until my due date, but lately, with the way things have been going, I don't think I can last. My feet are starting to swell really badly and I'm beginning to feel pressure pain in the lower part of my stomach. Just the other day I overheard one of my co-workers talking about the surprise baby shower they were planning to have for me at work. From what I overheard, it sounds like they are planning to throw out the red carpet for me. If my supervisor knew that I had any idea that they were planning to surprise me, she would be so disappointed. It's getting hard to pretend like I don't know what they're planning, but I have to. It's so sweet of them to think so much of me. When I walked into the bathroom, my two co-workers, Bonnie and Michele, did not see me and continued on with their conversation detailing what type of icing and the color of the trim for the cake. Everyone knows I had my heart set on a little girl. So of course you know the color of the trim will be neutral (yellow or green) no matter what I want. Hopefully I will last until my shower.

I try to walk a little more each day so I can soothe the pain I'm experiencing. The doctor told me that exercising will help. Only fifteen more days and counting. Sometimes I think Terry is more excited than me; he has his own little calendar and is counting also.

By now I thought maybe my aunt would have asked for him to come down South and spend the summer. It's very unlike her not to call and let me know if she wants him to visit. Maybe she is too busy working and doesn't have time. After raising all of us and everybody else's kids, I guess she needs a break. I can't blame her; if I were in her shoes, I would need a break, too. For as long as I can remember, my Aunt Janice has been raising children, being that she never had any of her own. She was that aunt who never raised her voice, but you knew what she meant just by looking at the expressions on her face. When we were kids she would send for all of us to come to Philly so we could spend the summer with her. This woman loved children. It would not only be me and my two bratty brothers, but my other three first "bad" cousins by my mother's baby sister, Dot, who lived in Brooklyn. My Aunt Dot's kids were better known as Babe's Kids; the reason I say this is because no matter what, my cousin Tracey was a tattletale, Little William was a snotty-nosed crybaby, and the baby boy Sid just stayed into something all the time, always threatening to tell if he couldn't have his way. Which, of course, made me very mad, especially due to the fact that I was just beginning my puberty years and was starting to smell myself.

My Aunt Janice told me and Tracey, who was about three years younger than me, that we were responsible for my younger cousins and that they had to go wherever we went. Now you know that really put a damper on things and spoiled our fun. I remember the time when my baby cousin Sid made me and Tracey mad, and we held him down and cut a big patch of his hair by accident and we got scared silly and tried faithfully to glue the boy's hair back on with some Elmer's glue. Of course you know this little boy was awfully, awfully upset at us and, like always, threatened to tell—that is, until we convinced him that the glue was going to help his hair grow back, and if he told he would wake up to a bald head for real.

Thinking back now, those were the fun days, when we would sit out on the stoop playing hopscotch, double dutch, jacks, giant steps, and hot peas and butter while waiting for the ice cream truck. Aunt Janice was a hard-working, attractive woman in her late thirties and stood about five feet, two in her bare feet. She and my Aunt Theo, who was her mother, were only sixteen years apart and appeared to be sisters. Most of the time it was my Aunt Theo who would travel the distance with us to our destination, making sure that we arrived safely and were out of her hair for a few months.

Just sitting back, thinking about all the fun we used to have, me and my cousins, is so delightful now, but back then I didn't think so. Sometimes it's good to remember the small and simple things in our past that gave us so much pleasure, and right now that's what I'm feeling. For a moment while writing this, I almost felt like a little girl filled with laughter, happiness, and the joy of peace and serenity that comes with the pleasures of being a kid and enjoying the fact that someone else is responsible for taking care of you and making sure that you are safe from all harm. The love we were showered with as children made us feel so special. We felt that no other child had more love. All of my aunts took turns sending for us every summer; if we weren't in Philly, we were in Brooklyn with my Aunt Dot. Now, my Aunt Dot was the baby girl, and every Thanksgiving you can rest assured that she is going to tell one of her famous stories. The most favorite one of all is the one about the little girl who chased me home when I was five or six years old and beat me up. Every year I had to get prepared as she told this story to all my family and friends. Now that I'm of age, I thought that it would stop, but you know how that is. No matter how old you get, you are still a child to them. It sure feels so good just lying here reminiscing about the good old days. Wish that could last forever.

July 8, 1986

Dear Diary,

After today I'll only have ten more days until my due date. My stomach is so tight and round. My stepmom says that it's a girl; everybody else is convinced that it is a little boy. I'm so glad that someone else besides me believes that it is a little girl. Right now my heart is set on a little girl. If it is a boy, I don't know what my reaction is going to be. Hopefully I won't be upset; after all, it will be a part of me, regardless. I'm praying that this baby will have my ways, if nothing else.

More and more each day, I'm beginning to feel like I don't have any privacy. Just the other day Mark came home and asked me what was I doing and what I was writing about. Some things are private, and every woman should keep a journal, diary, or whatever. This is special to me. I would hate to know what would happen if he ever found out what I was really writing in this book and that I called him the Beast Master. Thinking about it now, I don't think I would live to tell about it. My diary is my outlet; I can talk to it and tell all my deepest, darkest secrets and never have to worry about anyone finding out.

July 15, 1986

Dear Diary,

Today it was so hot, and each day it is getting more and more humid. It's getting harder for me to stand on the corner and wait for the bus, especially after getting used to having a luxury car to ride in and zoom everywhere I wanted to go. Being without a car has really put a strain on me, trying to get back and forth to work. Terry has yet to complain and tries to make me feel that it is okay with him if we have to walk to the moon and back. I don't think my poor child knows how long it will be before Mommy will get her car back. His only concern right now is waiting for Mommy to give birth to his little sister or brother. Every day his little face is starting to shine brighter and brighter, and by the looks of it, he is starting to get his glow back.

Lately, Mark has been quiet and trying to stay close by the house in case I go into labor. It's been a few weeks since we have had anything to say to one another. If he doesn't have anything to say, neither do I. Yesterday he went and got some of the baby things off of layaway. He even bought me my favorite treat, peaches and cottage cheese, trying to butter me up. Yet, still and all, we both barely spoke a word. If he only knew what I was planning in the back of my mind and how much I disliked him. There was nothing that could prepare him for the way he made me feel. Once I have this baby, my life is going to change for the better, and I'm going to leave.

While standing on the porch talking to my next-door neighbor, I felt a sharp pain in my lower abdomen. For a moment I thought it was a possibility that I may be going into labor, but as time went on, it slowly disappeared. As I stood on the porch holding my side, appearing to be hurting, she asked if I was all right, only to hear me reply that I was okay.

"Cee, please tell someone if you're in pain," she insisted as I chuckled with laughter, assuring her that I was okay. I didn't want her to sound off a false alarm, which would only end up with me being whisked off to the hospital in an ambulance and sent back home to wait my turn due to false labor. To me that spelled nothing but sheer embarrassment. It's getting late, and Terry has fallen fast asleep in my bed. This little boy is hard to wake up once he is out like a light. Well, tomorrow morning when he wakes up, he will be in his own bed.

July 16, 1986

Dear Diary,

I almost forgot that it's about time for me to renew my driver's license—I have two more days before it will be expired. How in the world did I forget something as important as this? Maybe Mr. Thomas down the block will take me to DMV if I ask. In the morning I'm going to ask him if I don't forget. Lately I have been forgetting quite a few things, and that is only because my mind has been preoccupied with everything else that has been going on in my life. Before I go to bed I'll tell Terry to remind me, and I'll also write it on a little sticky note so I can remember. One thing for sure is that I can't afford to be without that. My license is a critical and vital part of my life. I don't know how anyone functions without one.

July 18, 1986

Dear Diary,

Yesterday, I was so busy I forgot all about going to renew my license, the very thing I tried my best to remember. Now I'm in a frantic rush, trying to take a shower so I can get dressed and go to DMV. Terry ran down the street and asked Mr. Thomas, my next-door neighbor, if he would take me. He said yes—if I could be ready within an hour, he would take me and only charge me five dollars. To me that is a blessing because DMV is about fifteen miles from where we live. Every day Mr. Thomas made pretty good money just sitting around his house playing taxicab driver for anyone that needed a ride. Even the boosters who needed a getaway car. I'm surprised he hasn't gotten busted yet for riding around with hot goods in his car. Well, that is his problem—he will have to deal with it if he gets caught. Mr. Thomas knows how much time it is, and if that happens, he will be almost one hundred when he gets out. He is almost that now, no offense. And right now he has a lot more nerve than me. He doesn't care who asks for a ride, as long as they have his money right; distance is never an issue. As I scurried to get ready, I never once noticed the date on the calendar; the only thing I can remember is that today was my deadline to renew my license, and I had to take the written test—something I dreaded with a passion.

After arriving at the DMV office and waiting in the long line for what seemed to be forever, finally I could hear my name being called. There was a sigh of relief as I approached the examiner for him to ask me about fifty questions, so I thought. Things would have been different if I wasn't changing my license over to another state. Even though this exam wasn't too long, neither was it too short; my patience was growing thin as I twisted and turned in my seat, hoping not to be noticed. My pencil became a drumstick as I continued to annoy others while they tried to focus and complete their exam. To me this was just a waste of time.

I grew restless as my stomach started to ache and I could feel my tension rising. Concentration was the last thing on my mind as the pain continued to grow stronger, demanding that I quit and go home. Without trying to disrupt anyone, I politely stood up and walked over to the examiner and turned my blank test paper in. Stunned, the examiner asked me what the problem was, and I told him that I would come back and complete it when I felt better. This little nagging pain in my stomach would not go away. It didn't matter what I tried, the pain grew more and more intense until I started to ache all over. Of course, I didn't want Mr. Thomas to know how bad I was starting to ache, for fear of his age and not knowing whether he could handle being told that I may be going into labor. This man was almost seventy-five and had already had three heart attacks, and I was not going to be the one to give him a fourth. Even though he had nine children and about twenty grands, you would think by looking at him that he could handle anything, and here it was almost 3:00 p.m. and it was getting to where I wanted to moan out in pain, but had no choice but to hold it in. If this pain continues I'll have no choice but to tell someone that I think I'm going into labor. I could hardly wait to get out the door and to the car to go home.

When the car pulled up to my block, the pain had subsided, and to tell the truth right now at this moment is not the time for me to have this baby, for all day my taste buds were calling for steak. After freshening up when I returned home, I put my mouth-watering, tender, juicy steak with sautéed onions and green peppers into the skillet, filled with some brown, rich and creamy homemade gravy, made with the special ingredients in the recipe which my late father had passed on to me when I was much younger.

My dad was the best cook in the world and would more times than not outcook my mother and my aunts. Pop had learned how to cook from the best—my great grandmother, Mrs. Annie Scipio. When it came to cooking, my family's name was at the top of the list—I guess that's where I get it from. More times than not, that's where I spend the majority of my time. Creating recipes has always been one of my favorite pastimes, staying up until the wee hours of the night just to figure out the ingredients and think about how I could improve upon the taste. It became a hobby and an obsession to see how far my imagination could go and where it would lead me. Since my Aunt Theo would never let me cook when I was younger, I made a vow to myself that once I got out on my own I was going to cook everything under the sun. Little did my aunt know that all the years she thought I couldn't cook, I had been peeking through the window watching everything she was doing. It wasn't until I turned twenty-three years old that she found out that I knew her secret recipe for her famous spaghetti sauce. Aunt Theo made the best spaghetti sauce of anyone I knew. She could use the same sauce and put it into about twenty different recipes, making something unique and special each time. It got to the point where I would notice people asking her what ingredients she used, and for one reason or another, she would always pretend she didn't hear them and talk around the subject. I hate to say or think this about her, but to tell the truth, she was just downright stingy when it came to sharing a recipe. She may give you a piece of it, but you could rest assured it wasn't going to be the original, making you wonder what you did wrong or what you forgot to add. I was one of those people who always knew that in order for me to get what info I needed for a recipe from her, all it required was to pretend that you weren't paying attention to what she was doing and in the meantime watch her like a hawk and have a memory like an elephant.

For some reason, right now my mind is on food and I'm beginning to feel like I haven't eaten in days. The sweet peas are almost ready, and the rice is just right, steamed to perfection. Stirring the gravy surrounding the steak, I could tell it was very tender and tasty as it fell apart with each motion of the spoon. Just the aroma that filled the air made the baby inside of me kick even harder, it seemed. At least that's what I want to believe. Now, to be honest the last thing I want right now is the fact or possibility that I might be going into labor, and if the latter is true, this means I won't get to eat any of this delicious food that I have sweated so hard to prepare. Rocking back and forth as I stood over the stove, trying to make sure that nothing burned, the pains in the lower part of my stomach were growing stronger and stronger until I was ready to go anywhere so that someone could relieve me of what I was feeling, and right now that was pain that was getting more unbearable by the moment. I'm only one second short of yelling out for someone to call a taxi, but I'm too embarrassed to go in an ambulance and want to be incognito. I was hoping and praying that if this is the case, I will have a chance to eat something I've cooked. I have sweated too hard, especially today. All day I have been craving for steak, and it's at my fingertips and I can't even take one bite for fear that I just may be in labor. Mark will be home shortly and if I'm still hurting by then, I'll get him to go with me to the hospital. This way I won't have to go by myself.

Terry is outside playing, and it's been so long since he has really enjoyed himself without having to worry about me. The last thing I want to do is get him all worked up about me going to the hospital and have it be a false alarm. He has been through enough; even though I know going into labor now would be exciting for him, he will also be worrying if I will be okay. That's a little momma's boy for you.

Today is the day that the truth will come out about how Mark really feels. If I'm in labor and he is genuinely concerned about me and the well-being of our unborn child, I'll know. Tasting the steamy, hot, dripping, brown gravy with a spoon only made me want more; temptation to fix a hearty plate dangled in my head, while pain surged through my body until I had no choice but to scream out in pain, dropping my empty bowl on the table and alarming my tenants that something was wrong. I could hear footsteps running up the steps. It was Mark. Finally he was home and at least if I had to go to the hospital, my mind would be at ease.

"Did I just hear you screaming?" he asked, a concerned look on his face. "Cee, please answer me." he said. "Now is not the time to clam up—I need you to communicate with me. For days you have not said anything to me."

What did this man think? After pushing me down a flight of stairs, what was I supposed to say to him? As I rubbed my stomach, hoping the pain would go away, I couldn't help but notice the sincerity in his tone, but wondered in my mind what trick he was going to pull next. This was not the time to think about Mark and his crack addiction. It was time for me to be thinking about calling an ambulance so I could get to the hospital, because the pains were already starting to get sharper, and I could feel the pressure at the lower part of my stomach. Mark went into the bedroom to call an ambulance and to get my overnight bag so when they arrived, I wouldn't forget anything. It's about 7:45 p.m. and I'm beginning to have second thoughts, thinking that maybe I just have a bad case of gas. I told Mark that maybe this is a false alarm and he needed to call the EMS back and cancel; standing there, looking me straight into my eyes, he flat-out told me no and that I was going to the hospital anyway. Before I knew it, the sounds of the sirens and bells and whistles were blowing, and guess what? They were coming for me. My face was flushed with embarrassment as I took Mark's hand and he lead me down the stairs, walking in front of me, making sure I was careful not to trip and fall this time. *Like I had done a few weeks earlier*. By the time we reached our front door and he opened it, you could see all the nosy people who lived on my block and the next few blocks over, waiting to see what had happened and who was getting into the ambulance. You could not imagine how embarrassed I was as I hid my face behind his shoulders, wanting to take off running and wishing that no one had seen me. The EMS attendant reached out to take my hand as I climbed into the back of the ambulance, too shy to look him in the face.

"Ma'am, what is your name?" he asked as I sat up with my head resting against the wall, trying to pretend that the pain had subsided, that I was okay, and trying to reassure him that I only had a bad case of gas.

"My name is Cee, and I don't know why my man called the ambulance—I told him not to," I said boldly. "Now he is going to make me look stupid."

"Why do you say that?" the attendant asked.

"Well, for one, the pains have stopped and I'm having second thoughts about going to the hospital," I said.

"When is your due date?" the attendant asked.

"To be honest, my doctor said the July 20 and I said July 18."

"Ma'am, if that is the case, then don't you think you made the right choice by calling us, because you just may be in labor. After all, today is July 18."

Here it was. The day had finally arrived for me to bring this little booger into the world, and I was not ready. I don't know what scared me the most, everything you go through to have a baby or not knowing if my child was going to be healthy or not. The suspense was mounting.

By the time we arrived at the hospital, it was 8:00 p.m. and I was rushed into the emergency room to be checked by my doctor, only to be told that I was in labor and to find out that this baby would be delivered in the next thirty minutes. I was speechless and unprepared. My soul wanted to cry.

"How could I be in labor when my water hasn't even broken?" I asked the nurse as she prepped me, making sure that she had checked all my vital signs and whatever else.

"Sometimes this happens," she informed me. "The water may break only a few seconds before you deliver," she said, but your contractions are so close you could give birth at any moment."

Any moment, I thought to myself, frightened me even more. Here I was, hoping for the best and preparing myself for the worst.

"I'll be right back—if you need anything, just press this little buzzer," she said as she left the room.

Before she could get outside the door, I could feel something warm trickling down my legs. I knew from the warm sensation that my water had broken, and regardless of whether I was ready or not, this baby was coming and there was nothing I could do to stop it. Without thinking, I pressed the buzzer. The nurse returned so quickly, it was almost as if she had never left.

"Ma'am, what is wrong?" she asked as she rushed over to my bedside.

"I think my water broke," I informed her.

Pulling the covers back to check, she assured me that yes, I was correct, and that it was time for her to get the doctor. She didn't have to leave the room, just push the button and key in a code, and before you knew it there she stood, all ready to wheel me down to the delivery room. Everything was happening so fast, I didn't have time to think about where Mark was—or if I even cared.

"Cee, are you all right?" I heard a voice calling out very softly, looking up as the nurses rolled me down the hall on the stretcher. I could see that it was Mark walking briskly alongside me with tears in his eyes, telling me that everything was going to be all right and that he was going to be in the delivery room with me. No matter how hard I tried to stay angry, I still had a soft spot in my heart for him. After all, he was still my unborn child's father. Holding my hand and giving me comfort while he stroked my face made me think about the time we first met and how in love we used to be.

Dr. Lambert came over to ask me how I was feeling and when was the last time I had a strong contraction. I told her it had been about six minutes. She told me to tell her when I had the next one so she could time it. No sooner did the words come out of her mouth than I screamed out in pain. My contractions were getting closer, until they were about three minutes apart. As the nurses strapped my legs in the stirrups and Mark held my hand, the doctor was instructing me to get ready to push hard with my next contraction. The first time I pushed, it seemed to take all the life out of me. Even though this was my third time giving birth, it seemed like my first. One thing I was certain to find out that day was no matter how many times you gave birth, each was different. And for some reason, this one was very different. The pain seemed to be so much greater than any I had ever experienced with my prior pregnancies. After pushing and pushing for what seemed to be forever, I was beginning to think I was going to experience some unforeseen complications. "Why is this baby so stubborn?" I asked, screaming out loud in terrible pain with the next hard contraction. "Please—I don't care what you do, Doctor, just get this baby out of me," I cried.

Mark looked shocked at the fact that I actually begged the doctor to cut this baby out. I was so tired from pushing and the nurses and doctor telling me that any minute I was going to have this baby, and nothing was happening. My mind started thinking terrible thoughts and I was already thinking the worst (that something was wrong with my baby). Adjusting the mirror that was attached to the wall, angling it just enough so I could see the birth of my child, the nurse asked if I could see and if I needed her to adjust it any more. I sadly told her no, all I wanted right now was to do what seemed almost impossible and that was to give birth. My poor body was drained from all the strain, and I was at the point of giving up and demanding that they give me a cesarean. How much more pain were they expecting me to take? With the next hard contraction, the doctor told me for what seemed like the hundredth time that this would be it. Mark was standing by my side, holding my hand, cheering me on, and telling me to hold on, that it would soon be over, and that he could see the baby's head, and by the way the hair looked, he thought it was going to be a girl. More and more, my heart was beating rapidly, thinking that just maybe I would be happy after all.

"Cee, I know you can do it," I heard Mark say out loud.

"One last push is all you need," the doctor insisted.

As I looked at the clock on the wall, it was going on 8:30 p.m. Pushing hard and with all my strength, I could feel my body being relieved of all the pressure. Finally my baby had made his grand entrance amidst all the hoopla and was getting his first pop on his butt, as he cried for dear life. This baby had a set of lungs. Whether it was a boy or girl, it didn't matter now, because I had a sudden migraine headache.

"Congratulations, you have a baby boy!" the doctor exclaimed.

Tears flowed down Mark's face while he looked at me and told me how beautiful I was and that our child was precious. Knowing that I should have been thrilled watching my baby being placed on my stomach for the very first time, all I felt was the throbbing in my head robbing me of what should have been a joyous moment.

"Can you please remove him?" I asked the nurse. "Right now, all I want is something to get rid of this migraine headache," I said.

Everyone was shocked at my request and looked at me like I had lost my mind.

"Please, will someone get this hollering baby?" I said, getting angrier and angrier at the thought of being ignored.

"Okay, Momma, we will take him and finish cleaning him up. We won't be able to give you anything for your headache right now, but maybe within the next hour or so."

"Why is my baby screaming so loud?" I asked.

"He is okay," the doctor replied. "He has ten fingers, ten toes, and is a healthy, beautiful baby."

"Yes, he is," I replied as I watched the nurses cleaning him up, preparing him for his first ride down the hall to the nursery to rest with about twenty other little fellows just like him. No one could imagine the happiness that flooded my heart to hear the doctor say that my baby was healthy.

"Thank you, God, for answering my prayers," I murmured to myself.

Today turned out to be a beautiful day after all; nothing could have made me happier. This meant no more worrying about "what if." All had gone well, and now I could finally begin to move on. Lying in the recovery room, I could see Mark standing over me, confessing how sorry he was for putting me through so much agony and pain. My mind was numb and my head was still slightly aching. Looking at him and thinking about how mean he had been to me and my child, I felt no remorse for him and for a brief moment started feeling depressed. If he only knew what my plans were.

"Cee, I know you don't believe me, but I'm going to be a good father for my son," he said. "You'll see," he promised, while holding my hand and staring straight into my eyes.

Of course, I was speechless; there weren't any words left for me to express myself other than "Beat it." Exhausted and mentally drained, I asked Mark if he would ask the doctor how much longer before I would be able to get into a room. Mark came back and told me what the doctor said and that it would be another ten minutes before my room would be ready. It had been a long time since I'd felt this exhausted, but at the same time, it was a relief.

July 19, 1986

Dear Diary,

Waking up this morning, my body was so sore, and I'm experiencing so much pain. The nurse that checked me said that it is normal for me to be in pain. She told me that many mothers experience what they call "after-birth pains" (stomach muscles contracting back to their normal size) when they have their second baby. Believe me, it is no fun; the pain I was experiencing felt like labor pains. The more pain I felt, the more depressed I became, until I just lay in bed, crying. I was crying so hard I didn't hear the nurse coming in with my son for me to feed him. When the nurse came into my room and brought the baby over to me, my stomach was hurting so bad, and even though I was still depressed somewhat for whatever reason, excitement filled me to be able to hold my newborn in my arms for the second time. Mark had spent the night at the hospital and was right there assisting the nurse while she prepared me to hold my baby. This handsome little fellow had a head full of curly hair and a round face, with the same caramel complexion as his father. He had all of his father's features, and resembling me very little. Pulling his soft, neat blanket back, I could feel his warm and tender skin while I traced the outline of his tiny body and held him up and rubbed his cheeks next to mine, loving him gently. My baby boy kept his eyes closed, but you could tell he enjoyed the attention by the way he responded, stretching his arms and legs, trying to wake up as I counted every finger and toe. Feelings of thankfulness filled my heart. I felt very blessed to know that my baby was healthy, especially after everything I had gone through and the terrible thoughts of "what if" for months. All those thoughts of not knowing whether my baby was going to be healthy or not left my mind for good. Even though I was thrilled at the birth of my son, deep down inside I must admit I started feeling an emptiness that just wouldn't go away, no matter how hard I tried to fight it. After the nurse came to take my precious baby boy back to the nursery, I felt an overwhelming feeling of depression coming on; to be honest, I have never once remembered feeling this way. Why was I getting so depressed on the spur of the moment? I had no idea. Maybe tomorrow, when the doctor comes in to examine me, I can tell her what I'm experiencing and find out if it is normal for me to be feeling this way. Thoughts of being disappointed I had a boy and not a girl entered my mind briefly, and the more I lay in bed trying not to think of anything, the more the thought of disappointment entered my mind, and how I had planned and hoped for a little girl—my heart's desire.

Mark could not understand why I was depressed and thought I was being selfish because I didn't express how I was feeling to him. How could I tell him how I felt and expect him to understand? Truth be known, more than likely he was the root of the problem. Tomorrow Mark and I will have to choose a name for our son; right now, I don't have any names in mind. All the names I picked out were for little girls. I was not prepared for a boy; no matter how happy or excited I try to pretend that I am, it's not working. Before I know it, another day will have come and gone and the thought of naming a baby boy was just not in my agenda. Lying here, thinking about it and watching my roommate in the next bed cuddling her newborn baby girl, makes me more depressed by the moment. Why couldn't they have placed me in the room with another mother who had a little boy? Why a happy, jovial mother who's so thrilled and tickled pink that she had a little girl? Is this my punishment, I thought to myself. At this moment all I'm feeling is resentment and anger. How could some people be so lucky, I thought to myself. There is no way in the world that I'm going to try again for a little girl, especially with the Beast Master. I would have to be insane to even contemplate that thought.

July 20, 1986

Dear Diary,

I could hardly wait for my doctor to examine me this morning. When I informed her of how depressed I became right after giving birth and that I had never, ever felt that way before, she probed for a better understanding and asked me if there was anything going on in my life that I wanted to talk about. She also informed me that I may be experiencing postpartum depression, and she told me that a lot of mothers experienced this after giving birth—some more traumatic than others. She said that I wasn't the first or the last that had experienced this, and that it was nothing to be worried about, and that in due time it would subside and within a few days I would be okay; if not, she would give me a prescription to help me keep it under control. Medication was not something I was ready to agree to. Could it be that serious, I thought to myself.

"What exactly is postpartum depression?" I asked Dr. Lambert while she continued to check me.

"Postpartum is a depression that quite a few women experience after giving birth the second time. It just depends, and sometimes, you may cry more often than others," she stated. "One moment you're happy, the next moment you're sad. Is that how you feel?" she asked.

"Yes, that's exactly how I feel," I said. "One moment I'm happy and ready to take on the world, and the next moment I'm crying nonstop for about an hour. At first I thought maybe it was because of my disappointment with having a baby boy. I'm so glad you explained that to me," I told her. Relieved that it was something else, I was not acknowledging that the postpartum depression was actually worse than what I thought.

"You'll be okay tomorrow," Dr. Lambert said with a smile in her voice.

"Are you sure?" I asked. "The nurses aren't going to come and take me away in a straightjacket?" I asked sarcastically.

"No, they're not," she replied.

"Okay, then I believe you. Now I can rest."

Preparing her paperwork so she could retire early, Dr. Lambert informed me that I should be able to go home tomorrow. Now that's the fun part, I thought, while trying to conjure up a name for my handsome baby boy weighing in at seven pounds and twenty-two-and-a-half inches. To me he was such a handsome little fellow, even though you would not have thought I felt this way about this little boy a few days earlier when I had a migraine after giving birth to him.

So far the only visitors I had had were my brother and Mark. Everybody else was too busy working, but I understood. At least I'm trying to fool myself that this was the case. Tomorrow, I'll be going home anyway, so that's okay. Right now, if I do anything, I need to get some rest before I go home. If I'm blessed, this will be a good baby, one that won't have his days confused with his nights. Remembering the sleepless nights when Terry was a baby made me mentally tired;

he was a hollering baby. Bringing the house down when he cried. Waking up everyone. Holding my newborn baby in my arms, he appears to be such a peaceful child, one who could care less about what went on around him. Please, please, let this be the case when I get him home, I said to myself.

July 21, 1986

Dear Diary,

Morning could not come fast enough, and the excitement of Terry laying his eyes on his newborn baby brother for the first time is going to be so special I can hardly wait. Now I know why no one came to see me; they were all waiting to visit me right before I went to sleep last night. I had three visitors: first, my old friend Frank came by to suggest a name for the baby. He told me I should name him Antwan, which is a cute name and maybe just might be it after I talk it over with Mark. I was almost about to drift into a deep sleep after Frank left when I heard someone lightly knocking on my door.

"Cee, is it okay if I come in?" From the sound of the voice I could tell it was my godbrother Jeremy. "Hey, girlie, how are you feeling?" he asked. "I'm sorry I haven't had a chance to come see you before now. Guess what?" he asked anxiously. "I have a beautiful name for my godchild," he said.

"I'm listening Jeremy—what is it?" I asked.

"Take a guess," he said.

"Jeremy, right now I'm not in the guessing mood," I said with a smile on my tired face. "Okay, Cee—I was thinking that maybe you could name the baby Antwan." When I heard the name Antwan, I started laughing nonstop—for a moment, I could feel my stitches pulling.

"Why are you laughing?" he asked.

"Well, for one thing, you are the second person that has recommended that name."

"Oh, really?" he asked. "Who else chose that name?"

"For starters, do you remember my old friend Frank?" I asked.

"Frank? Where in the world did he come from?" Jeremy asked as he laughed out loud.

"What's so funny, Jeremy?"

"Well, Cee, seems like this guy always shows up when you have a baby. What's up with that?" Jeremy asked, still continuing to laugh out loud until tears were flowing down his face. "Girl, you could be in South Africa, and Frank would be right there. Now I have much love for that brother because no matter what, he has always been right there for you and Terry. Do you think that you two may hook up someday?"

"Jeremy, don't be ridiculous," I said, trying to hold back my laughter.

"Other than your ex-friend recommending the name, do you like it and do you see anything wrong with the name Antwan?" Jeremy asked.

"Nothing," I said. "It's just that you are the second person today to suggest that name. Is Antwan supposed to be the hot name this year?" I questioned.

"I have no idea," he said, looking mystified. "Being that I'm the child's godfather, don't I get the first choice?" he asked, looking at me with a slight grin.

"Jeremy, let me think about it," I said.

"Okay, Cee, think about it."

"And you have to remember that Mark has the final say," I told Jeremy.

Just the mention of Mark's name changed the whole expression on Jeremy's face.

"Speaking of Mark, he should be here shortly so he can help me pack. The doctor said I can go home tomorrow, and you know that Terry is going to be so excited to know that Mommy is coming home with his new little baby brother."

"Has Terry been up to visit you yet? Jeremy asked.

"No, he hasn't—I want to surprise him."

"Surprised he will be," Jeremy said. "Well, Cee, I'll stop by the house to see you tomorrow. If you need anything, please call me. You do have my phone number?" he asked.

"Yes, I do," I replied.

"Did Mark ever get the bassinet that you told me you wanted?"

"No, not yet—he told me that when he comes to pick me up tomorrow we will stop and pick it up."

"Do you have the car seat? You do know that it's mandatory in the state of New Jersey to have one," he said.

"Yes, Jeremy, I know the law, but thanks for being concerned," I told him.

"Cee, I'm getting ready to leave, and like I said, if you need anything, please give me a call."

"You know I will," I assured him.

No sooner had he closed the door behind him than in steps Mark, all bright-eyed and bushy-tailed, looking like a little kid filled with excitement and joy. The glow on his face made me feel good. Looking at him, he appeared to be well rested.

"So Cee, guess what I have been thinking about? The name for our son, and I finally have it."

"Okay—what is it Mark?"

"Antwan," he replied.

"You have to be kidding, and this is a joke?" I asked.

"No, I'm not joking—I think Antwan is a rather nice name."

"Mark, do you know you are the third person to suggest that name?"

Shocked, Mark looked disappointed. "Who else suggested that name, Cee?"

"For starters, one of my old friends, and then Jeremy, my godbrother," I said.

"Well, well, I don't know whether that's good or bad, considering I'm the last one to recommend the same name for my son."

"Right now, Mark, to be honest, I think Antwan is a beautiful name, and at least our child will be able to spell it without having to use an encyclopedia."

Smiling and glowing with happiness, appearing to be happier than he had been in a long time, Mark agreed. "Okay, baby—well, Antwan it will be," he said. "Do you have any suggestions for the middle name?" he asked.

"Of course not—it was hard enough to come up with the first name. Whatever you decide will be fine with me."

"Are you sure?" he asked, trying to be sincere and sarcastic at the same time. "Doesn't it feel strange for the both of us to be talking about our son?" Mark asked. "Cee, I want you to know how sorry I am for putting you through so much hurt and misery. I promise— from here on out I'm going to be good to you and our children. I know what type of man you need, and I'm going to be that man you never had in me before. Baby, just hold on and give me another chance," Mark begged. "Girl, I love you and I want to give you the world. You have seen the hard times with me and put up with all my nonsense: now it's time for me to put up or shut up. Cee, believe it or not, when I laid eyes on our son for the first time, feelings I never knew existed were aroused within me. Antwan has not just my blood, but has your blood also flowing through his veins, and he needs both of his parents, not just one. Give me a chance to prove to you that I can be a good man. Life would not be the same without you, and I don't even want to contemplate the thought of living alone. Please, please, baby, forgive me, and find that special place in your heart for me again. I promise you nothing but true joy and hap- piness. Give me a chance to spoil you rotten. If nothing else, Cee, you deserve to be spoiled," Mark said.

Nothing he said moved me, and even though I looked at him with a smile on my face, in my heart I felt no warmth. Thoughts of all the hurt and disappointment clouded my mind. How could anyone in their right mind forget the mean and cruel things this man did? Did he think that he could wave a magic wand and everything was going to be all right, I thought to myself as I lay there resting, waiting for my doctor to come in and sign my release forms.

Dr. Lambert usually made her rounds to my room between 8:30 and 9:00 a.m. She has to know that I'm anxious to go home. Just thinking about how excited Terry is going to be is a thrill in itself.

Mark started packing all my things while I continued to get ready for my trip home. "Double-check everything, Mark, to be sure we aren't forgetting anything. By the way, I forgot to ask—how are we getting home?"

"I figured we would catch the bus," Mark replied.

"Catch the bus? Have you lost your mind? Did you forget I have stitches and my butt is sore?" I asked, looking at him as if he was the dumbest man alive. Thinking to myself, if it hadn't been for him and his foolishness, I wouldn't have to think twice about how I was going to get home because I would have my car. But no, he had to do something stupid like get mad, run off like a spoiled brat, and wreck my car. Now, here it is the day I'm leaving the hospital with my newborn for the first time, and we are subjected to riding on the city bus. How embarrassing and unacceptable! But, I have to accept blame, being that I let it happen. Girlfriend, girlfriend, no matter how much he begged and pleaded, I felt nothing but numbness in my heart and relief that I had given birth.

Finally, the moment had arrived for my doctor to visit and sign my release forms. Entering my room with a cheery smile as always, Dr. Lambert asked how I felt and if I was still having bouts of depression and if I thought I needed a prescription. I reassured her that I would be okay and medication was the last thing I needed.

"Well, you are all set to go," Dr. Lambert said, handing me the final papers to sign, telling me congratulations and informing me of my first follow-up appointment. "Take it easy and I will see you in a few weeks," she said.

As the doctor turned to leave the room and I peered down the hallway, I could see the nurses preparing my baby for his first trip home. Mark appeared a little more excited than me. The moment had come for little Antwan to be placed in my arms. As I sat in the wheelchair, waiting for the elevator to arrive, looking at my baby and how beautiful he was sent chills through my body.

It was a relief to step onto the bus and find that it wasn't as crowded as I thought it was going to be. Most people just stood and stared at me, wanting to ask whether it was a boy or girl and asking if they could see the baby. By the time the bus arrived on my block, I was exhausted and my butt was sore, even though Mark had brought a pillow for me to sit on. It wasn't really helping too much, no matter how hard I wanted to believe that it was.

Looking out of the window, I could see Terry outside playing with his friends; my heart fluttered to see my child so happy. It had been months since I had seen him this happy. When he lays eyes on Antwan, he is going to be so excited; all he has ever wanted was a little brother or sister and now he had his wish come true. Anticipating Terry's reaction, I could barely contain myself when it was time for me to pull the buzzer. Mark stood up and held my hand when the bus approached our stop. Making sure that our baby boy was covered up and that I was okay, he led me off the bus, proudly holding me by my arm and watching the glow on Terry's face when he realized that his momma was coming down the street with his new baby brother. To see the look on Terry's face put a smile in my heart. Skipping all the way nonstop until he was standing right in front of me, smiling and hugging me around my waist, this kid was so excited and it showed.

"Momma, I missed you, and you know what? I thought about you every day, and today I just knew you were coming home! Can I hold my little brother when we get upstairs?" he asked. "What is his name? Does he look like me?"

Terry was filled with a hundred questions before I could even answer one. Being honest, I don't know who was more excited, me for getting through having the baby and preparing to move on with my life, or the fact that now my oldest son had a little brother to play with.

"Terry, of course you can hold your little brother once we get upstairs, sweetie, but right now, please don't ask any more questions until your dear mother can sit down and rest her feet. I'm so tired."

"Momma, I'll help you get some rest," he said, looking all innocent. "While you sleep, I'll watch the baby."

Now, this little boy knew he was too much. Here it was, I hadn't been home for a hot second and already he was volunteering to once again take care of me and his little brother. It felt good being home. Looking around the room, I could tell that Mark had really cleaned up everything and had already put the baby bassinet up. Mark made sure I was relaxed and insisted that I change clothes and put on something more comfortable. Pulling out an oversized Japanese silk kimono, I slid it over my head and immediately when the fabric brushed against my skin, it felt so good. Without any hesitation, Terry barged into my room, anxiously waiting for me to get settled in so he could hold his little brother for the first time.

"Terry, Mommy wants you to be relaxed and sit over here so I can show you how to hold Antwan."

Sliding his pudgy little body over, he stretched out his hands to embrace his brother for what would be his first but not last time. "Momma, I got him," he boasted, trying to be a little man so full of pride and joy. The expression on his perky face told of his happiness. Rocking back and forth while holding his brother, he made promises.

"Antwan, I'm your big brother—I'm going to take care of you and my momma, and no one is going to hurt you," he said.

Listening to him made me blush with happiness. For this little boy, my son, to be so young, he had the mind of an old man and meant every word he said.

"Momma, guess what?" he asked. "I'm not going back outside to play anymore. I want to stay home with you and Antwan."

"Terry, I know you want to be there for Momma, but you need to go outside and play, too. I can handle things inside."

Sooner or later, I knew the newborn syndrome was going to wear off and Terry would be back to his old self after about a day or two. It felt so good to look at the two of my children together and to know that both were healthy and strong. My insides were bubbling over with joy for the happiness I felt.

July 29, 1986

Dear Diary,

If I'm dreaming, please don't wake me up. This is too good to be true, Antwan is sleeping all day and all night; sometimes I have to wake him up to change him and wake him up to feed him. Before Antwan even has a chance to get cranked up good in the middle of the night or early morning, I can hear Mark's feet hitting the floor, and when I try to get up so I can attend to the baby, he is telling me to lie back down so I can get some rest and that he has the baby. To be honest, I think that is so considerate. Antwan is such a good baby.

I can't believe it, considering that Terry was a hollering child. God has truly blessed me this time, if I must say so without sounding biased.

Mark is so good with Antwan, even bathing him when he gets off from work. Believe it or not, I don't think Mark has gotten high since I had the baby. I have never seen anyone so happy to be a father. You would think by looking at him that he was the only one to have a newborn. Every day he comes straight home from work and wakes Antwan up and just holds him and stares at him as if he is totally amazed. In my mind, I can't help but wonder, is he amazed that the baby is healthy and normal or because he is so precious? Remembering back just over a month ago, this was the same man who didn't care whether I lived or died. And now here it was—he was so in love with this little bundle of joy. Was he trying to impress me and make me think that he was for real and that all the bad was in the past? Whatever he was doing, no matter how bad I wanted to believe it wasn't getting next to me, it was, and I could feel it. Not wanting to display any real emotions and make him feel that I was giving in to his kindness, I tried so hard to be non-caring. But the harder I tried to be cold, the more it didn't work. It was so hard trying to be non-caring when this man was displaying so much love and affection, feelings that I hadn't seen him express for quite some time. Maybe he is starting to come around, after all. Whatever is happening to him, I hope it continues because it feels so good right now. From the look on his face, anyone that knows Mark knows that he has changed.

July 30, 1986

Dear Diary,

Today, Antwan is twelve days old and growing like a weed. Since his birth he has been such a good baby; when my girlfriends start telling me how they feel sorry for me and that I need a break from Antwan keeping me up all night, I have to put them in check real quick and let them know that my son is like the golden child, never really waking me up at night, and that his father gets up with him more than I do. No matter what time—day or night, one thing I have to give Mark credit for is the fact that he is really a good father to the baby. Last week we discussed the baby-sitter arrangements when I go back to work. Mark agreed that we would take turns taking the baby to the baby-sitter, telling me that he would take Antwan in the morning and that I could pick him up in the evening. I can't begin to tell you how relieved I was to hear that. Sitting here thinking about his proposal, it did sound rather great, even though we hadn't yet decided on a baby-sitter. I bet over the past four months my stepmother must have recommended at least two or three, and for the life of me, I don't know why I didn't follow through on getting their phone numbers. And now I almost feel "stuck like Chuck," without a baby-sitter. Mark told me that he is going to call my stepmom and get the number of the baby-sitter she recommended so we can set up an appointment to interview her for keeping Antwan and possibly watching Terry when he gets out of school. From everything Clara has told me about Mrs. Toby, she sounds like just the type of baby-sitter I'm looking for. Clara says that she used to keep Joyce's oldest son, "Baby Darrel," when he was only six weeks old and that Joyce always talked about how good she was with babies and how she took time out of her busy schedule to teach the older children who ranged in age from three to six years old; these were her after-school kids.

Rocking my sweet baby in my arms brings back so many memories. Antwan is such a good baby. Sometimes I want to pinch my child to see if he is real. Looking down at his tiny body, I can't help but notice how much he looks like his dad. The resemblance is so noticeable, until it's like me looking at myself holding a baby Mark in my arms. Laughing to myself, I can't help but think out loud, what a fool Mark would be if he tried to disown our son. Every judge in America would throw the book at him for being so ignorant. Well, good night, Mrs. Diary.

August 2, 1986

Dear Diary,

Today turned out to be nice. Mark and I went to meet the baby-sitter, Mrs. Toby, and everything we have said about with her seems to be on a positive note. Mrs. Toby appears to be in her late sixties and weighs about 380 and only stands about five feet, three. Watching her handle all three of the children she was keeping and noticing how well-mannered they were, Mrs. Toby seems to be the very informative baby-sitter, the type any mother would relish to keep for dear life. Not trying to be nosy, but overhearing part of a conversation she had with one of the other children's mothers when she arrived, alerted me to how attentive she was to the children she kept. Most of the mothers that came by to pick up their children while I was there couldn't stop talking about how she spoiled them and how much they loved her for taking such good care of their precious ones. When we first walked up to the porch, she could hardly introduce herself, for she was too busy reaching for Antwan and asking about ten questions all at once, not coming up for air, not one time.

"How old is the baby? What is his name? Is he spoiled?" she asked. Boy, this lady didn't waste any time beating around the bush. Mrs. Toby was straight to the point.

"Which question do you want me to answer first?" I asked her, smiling the whole time.

"You can start by telling me how old the little prince is," she replied.

Responding to her question, I answered, "Almost three weeks old."

"Where do you work and what are your hours?"

"I'm a receptionist, and I work for an inventory control company out of Hackensack, New Jersey."

"In case of an emergency, who should I call?" Mrs. Toby asked.

"My stepmother, Clara," I replied.

Placing a smile on her face, little did she know that it was her first impression that won my attention and gained my trust. Believe it or not, this woman, better known as Mrs. Toby, was great; this woman was so confident that I was going to choose her as my baby-sitter, and that's exactly what I did. Here she was, this lady who barely knew me, and yet was bold enough to reach her arms out for a stranger's baby. This show of affection won my heart over ten times, and Mark's, too. After taking a few moments to think over the idea of her keeping our child, we both felt secure in knowing that our baby was going to be left in good hands once I go back to work within the next few weeks. Tonight, I can rest good, knowing that I have accomplished my task of finding a great person to care for my children. Mrs. Toby was a miracle waiting to happen, and I thanked God for blessing me with the pleasure of having the opportunity to have met her.

August 10, 1986

Dear Diary,

I have three more weeks to wait before I go back to the doctor for my six-week checkup, and she already knows that I want to have my tubes tied, as we talked about this before I had Antwan. Dr. Lambert told me that it would be best if I waited for about six weeks after I had the baby before having a tubal ligation done. Right before I had Antwan, I went through so much with Mark until it made the thought of having more children a nightmare for me. No matter how nice Mark may be right now, I'll never forget all the horrible things he did to me, and my feelings toward him have changed. Mark is going to flip out when he finds out that I'm having this surgery done, but there is nothing he can do to stop me. For some reason or another, Mark feels like every woman who has a tubal ligation is out to play around with other men, being that she will no longer fear getting pregnant.

Sometimes, Mark can be so ridiculous with his thoughts. In about three more weeks it will be time for me to go back to work. Time goes by so fast when you're having fun, but when you are at work the time just seems to stand still. Why couldn't it be the other way around?

Dr. Lambert assured me that the procedure for the tubular ligation was a simple, same-day procedure and that I would be able to go home about four or five hours after the surgery was completed. My fear of the operation is mounting every day, as the days seem to go by so fast.

Before you know it, I'll be back at work and getting up about two hours earlier, just so I can get the baby ready to go off to the baby-sitter and Terry ready for school. Thinking of what my new schedule is going to consist of makes me tired. It has been years since I had to fix baby formula, pack a diaper bag, and make sure I packed enough milk and extra bibs, outfits, socks, and, of course, an extra pacifier in case he loses the first one. My first day back to work will more than likely be a trip—worrying about my precious baby all day long, getting on everybody's nerves, and worrying about little things.

Mark volunteered to pack Antwan's diaper bag and make his bottles. If I must say so myself, he has become a dynamite father for his son and is trying with Terry. From the looks of things, he has a long way to go to win Terry's trust, and I can't fault my son for feeling the way he does. Looking at my son and the way he responds to Mark, I can tell that he feels very uncomfortable and barely has anything to say to Mark. Sometimes I wonder if Terry will ever feel any different.

As a mother, I want my child to be happy and enjoy his life without fearing for his mother. He is such a wonderful child and a blessing and would be a joy for any mother to have around, I thought to myself as I played with Antwan and tickled his little tiny belly. Antwan has big, sparkly brown eyes that are so beautiful and mesmerizing. The glow on his caramel complexion told that he was a happy baby, always cooing and grinning. My baby looks just like his daddy and is a handsome little fellow if I must say so myself. Audra calls him her "Boo Bear," and whenever she gets off from work in the evening and comes home, her first stop is to my house to see Antwan, picking him up and talking to him as if he understands what she's saying. I couldn't help but notice the outfit Audra had on the other day and how much weight she has lost lately; her face is starting to look drawn-in and the area around her eyes is beginning to look a little darker. When Audra and I spoke the other day, we made a date to take the kids to New York on next Friday, after she gets home from work. A week ago on Friday, we had made plans to go to New York, but Audra became sick and couldn't go, so we decided that we would reschedule it to the next weekend, rain or shine. It has been so long since we have done anything together. To be honest, the last place Audra and I went together is to the park with the children. How could I ever forget that day? That was the day when she let me have it about Mark. Even though that day she told me how she felt about Mark treating me the way he did, she didn't seem like herself, for she was very edgy and nervous. If I didn't know any better, I would have thought that she and Pee Wee had an argument. Whatever is going on with her, she will tell me sooner or later.

August 15, 1986

Dear Diary,

Last night, after putting Terry and Antwan to bed, for the first time in months Mark and I lay in bed next to each other, talking until the wee hours in the morning. I must admit that it felt so good to be held in my man's arms. We both had forgotten about how wonderful it felt to lie next to each other. His body felt so warm and pleasant as we began to enjoy caressing and cuddling. Before you knew it, our bodies were intertwined with my legs wrapped around his. Stroking my hands along his high cheekbones softly, I could feel the smile on his face and the love in his heart, tearing down that wall of insecurity within me. And just as I could feel my body temperature starting to rise, wouldn't you know it, someone had to spoil our groove by ringing the bell. At first when I heard the doorbell, I told Mark to ignore it and whoever it was would go away. Here it was about 3:30 in the morning, and someone was bold enough to ring our bell and spoil our mood. Not only did they ring it once, but continuously until there was no way we could pretend like we didn't hear it and had no choice but to get up so we could see who it was, whether we wanted to or not. No matter how much I tried to convince Mark to ignore it, he was determined to go see who it was. Maybe I was just being plain old selfish by not wanting to spoil the mood, because I was too afraid that the special moment we had would be lost forever, and trying to recapture a stolen moment is something that is hard to do. Once it's gone, it's gone.

Sitting up on the edge of the bed, I stroked Mark's back as he continued to reach for his robe and slip on his bedroom slippers so he could go take the long walk downstairs to answer the door. Standing at the top of the stairs waiting for Mark to ask who it was as he peeped out of the peephole, I could barely hear the faint voice of a woman.

"Who is it?" Mark asked loudly. "Okay, if you don't answer this time, I'm not going to open the door," he stated.

"Please, please open the door," the voice on the other side of the door cried. "I'm dying—please, somebody help me."

As Mark turned the knob to open the door, I ran back up the stairs and went to peek over the balcony to see who it was standing on my front porch. I could not believe my eyes—it was Audra! Yelling down the stairs for Mark to open the door, I couldn't help but run back to the stairs as he opened the door for Audra to fall in. Shocked with disbelief at what we were witnessing, Mark yelled for me to get a cold towel and a glass of water while I listened to him begging for Audra to respond as he lightly tapped her on her face, trying to awaken her.

"Cee, come help me carry her upstairs," Mark yelled. "I think she's dying."

"Dying?" I said. While rushing down the stairs to aid my best friend, tears started to flow down my face while I tried not to panic.

"Audra, wake up, baby—please wake up!" I said.

"Please help me, somebody," she cried. "Mark, I can't breathe—please help me. I don't want to die," Audra pleaded.

Mark took Audra's pulse. By the time we carried her upstairs and laid her on the couch, we could tell her breathing was getting worse. I wanted to call an ambulance, but Mark told me not to; he said he knew what was wrong with Audra and for me to go into the kitchen and get an orange out of the refrigerator. Shocked at his request, I began to question him.

"Cee, *please* don't ask any questions right now! I'll tell you what's wrong with her later."

"Later?" I asked, "You must be out of your mind. Here she is, my best girlfriend, who may be dying, and you won't let me call an ambulance. The only thing you can say is, go into the kitchen and get me an orange and that you know what is wrong with my friend, and I'm supposed to believe you? What are you now, Mark, a doctor?"

"Please, Cee, don't give me a hard time about this. Your girlfriend Audra is suffering from dehydration."

"Dehydration? From what?" I asked.

"Cee, please don't ask that question," Mark begged, trying to appear all serious. "Cee, some things aren't meant for you to know. I'm pretty sure when Audra comes to, she will tell you what was wrong with her."

"What do you mean? Is there something you know that I don't? Mark, please tell me what is wrong with my friend," I begged. "You are supposed to be my man, and that means that we don't keep secrets from one another."

"Cee, I know that, and that's why it is so hard for me to tell you."

"Tell me what Mark?"

"Okay, okay; if you must know the truth—in order for Audra to be dehydrated the way she is, she had to be smoking."

"Smoking what?" I asked.

"She had to be smoking crack."

"Smoking crack? Now, Mark, that is a joke and you know that is a lie. I need for you to take that back. You know all too well that Audra is not smoking crack. How could you say something so horrible?" I yelled. "Just because *you* smoked crack does not mean that everyone else is, too," I said as I watched him storm out of the room angrily, while daring me to ask my friend to tell me the truth about something I believed beyond the shadow of a doubt to be a lie.

Barely moving as she lay on the couch in our living room, she seemed dazed and confused as I wiped her forehead with a cool towel and tried to give her something cool to drink. "Audra, wake up," I said. For a moment she seemed to be conscious, then the next moment she was out again. Mark rolled the orange I had given him until it was soft and juicy. He shook Audra and patted her face until she came to, then made her suck on the orange. What good that orange did I was soon to find out; it was almost like magic, watching her come to life and regaining consciousness. "Audra, are you okay?" I asked.

"Yes, Cee, I'm fine," Audra replied.

"What happened, and how did you end up on our front porch this time of the morning?" I asked her.

Looking at me with those deep brown, Betty Boop eyes, appearing to be more embarrassed than sad, for the first time since I had known her she was almost like a little girl, seemingly shy and quiet.

"Audra, please tell me the truth—don't lie to me. I've never seen you like this. Lately, I have noticed how much weight you have lost and those dark circles around your eyes and thought that maybe you were just working hard, but I know something else is going on. Girl, you are my buddy, and I need for you to be honest with me. Together we have gone through so much—please don't shut me out now. Let me be there for you—I want to be the friend you were to me when I was down and out. No matter what, Audra, I'm not going to let you down. I promise to be there for you, so please tell me what is wrong."

"Cee, you don't understand. I'm tired and can't take anymore."

"Tired of what?" I asked.

"I'm sick and tired of blowing all my money on getting high."

"Getting high on what, Audra?" I asked.

"Must I spell it out for you, Cee? Okay, if you want to know, Cee, I have been smoking crack."

Filled with shock and disbelief, tears formed in my eyes. Here was my girlfriend, confessing to smoking crack after everything she knew crack had taken us through. "How in the world did you, out of all people, get hooked on crack?" I asked angrily. "Audra," I screamed with much hurt and pain in my heart, feeling betrayed, "How could you do this to me? I believed in you and trusted you with my deepest, darkest secret, and here you're smoking crack, too! No, no," I sobbed as I tried to understand. Who else was smoking crack that I didn't know about as thoughts of misconception and betrayal boggled my mind.

"Please try to understand that I wasn't trying to hurt or deceive you, Cee," Audra begged. "You have to believe me, Cee. I would never do anything to hurt you. Cee, I thought if I gave in to my husband and his demands for me to try it that it would please him and he would stop beating on me. When he would start to smoke and demanded more money after he smoked up his paycheck and I wouldn't give him my money, he would get infuriated and start an awful argument which eventually turned into a fight and me getting a black eye. I got tired of the beatings, and one day he convinced me to try it and I started liking it. It became the one thing that we enjoyed doing together at first, and then after he would go to work on his third-shift job, my other girlfriend and her husband would come by and pick me up to go to New York and hang out with them. This way we could get more crack for our money. Instead of paying twenty dollars for a hit, we would pay only five dollars. Sometimes we would go back and forth to New York at least two or three times. And Cee, I hope by me telling you the truth you won't hate me," Audra cried.

"How could I ever hate you?" I asked her as we once again embraced each other with me reassuring her that I was her friend. "Audra, how could I ever turn my back on you?" I cried while we continued to embrace one another, rocking back and forth. For the first time in a while I almost felt like she was my baby sister. What I admired about her that night more than anything else is the fact that she confessed to the truth regardless of what she thought about the way I may have felt.

"Cee, I have never felt so afraid in all my life," Audra said. "After tonight I'm never going to get high again. I could have died on your front porch, and no one would have found me until daylight. The couple that I told you about earlier—I was hanging out with them, and the evening started off so nicely. We hung out in New York and rode around; at first, everything was okay. We had already made our first trip to get a few vials of crack, and then we came back to Paterson so we could just relax and smoke a little while we enjoyed riding around. Then all of a sudden, without warning, I started to breathe heavy and hyperventilate. When I told my friends that I started to feel sick, they told me I would be okay and that they were going to bring me home. The harder it became for me to breathe and I started hyperventilating more and more rapidly, I heard them say, let's take her home. I wanted them to take me to the hospital; they both panicked and dropped me off in front of the house and helped drag me to the front porch and just left me there for dead. They thought I was going to die."

"That was so lowlife and dirty—how could they have done this to you? Audra tell me—who did this to you?" I demanded to know.

"Cee, please don't ask that question."

"Girl, what is wrong with you? I'm trying to help you—don't you get it? If they did that once, they will do it again. Especially once they find out you are well. The first thing they will do is wait until you get paid and show up again."

"Cee, you don't understand what kind of problem it will cause if you find out."

"What kind of problem it will cause? Audra, it has already caused a problem, one in which you almost lost your life, and now here you are trying so desperately to protect these people who left you on my front porch to die. I demand that you tell me who they are! If you don't, that's only going to make me madder, and when I do find out, they will have to answer to me."

"Don't you have enough to worry about, Cee, without dipping into my business?" Audra had the nerve to say.

"*Your* business?" I asked. "You don't have any business," I yelled, "especially when you can show up on my porch at 3:30 in the morning half dead, and I'm not supposed to ask any questions? Now ask yourself, how stupid does that sound? Audra, you sound stupid right now, and as a matter of fact, until you tell me who left you on my porch to die, I don't have anything else to say to you. How dare you protect someone who had no regard for your life and left you to die! That's not a friend—that's a monster."

"Please, please, Cee, I don't need to be beat down right now. I'm already feeling bad about what happened and how I let you down."

"If that's true, Audra, then there wouldn't be any problem with you telling me who did this to you."

"Cee, no one could do any more to me than I have already done to myself. I'm the one who wanted to hang out and smoke crack cocaine. No one held a gun to my head and made me do it. Each time I took a hit, I kept thinking it was going to make me feel like I did the first time. But you know what? I could never get that feeling I had the first time."

"Audra, stop beating around the bush with me and tell me who did this to you. Look at you—have you looked in the mirror at yourself lately to see how bad you look?"

"No, I haven't," Audra replied.

"Your face is starting to sink in, and instead of wearing a size 9 or 10, you're starting to look like you could wear a size three. At first, girlfriend, I thought maybe you were going through stress from dealing with your problems with Pee Wee. But to find out otherwise— what I want to know now is, when are you going to wake up and smell the coffee? Audra, you are such a beautiful person, inside and out, and the last thing you need is to destroy your life with crack. What about your children? What's going to happen to them if you get strung out on crack? Please, Audra, be honest and let me help you. I can only help you if you let me. I know it's hard, but please don't shut me out."

"Okay, Cee. If you must know, it was Mark's brother Anthony and his wife," Audra yelled out, holding her head down in much shame.

My mouth dropped opened and my eyes must have looked like they were bulging out of my head from the shock. Even though I already knew that Mark's brother Anthony and his wife got high, it was shocking to find out that my girlfriend Audra was hanging out with them getting high, too. The reason that I was so shocked was the simple fact of how much she talked about Mark's brother Anthony's wife and how much she disliked her, and all along they were hanging out smoking crack together. What other dark secrets were lurking around the corner just waiting to jump out and shock me? Was my other girlfriend, Charlotte, getting high, too? Was there anyone who didn't smoke crack? Or was I in denial, and everyone around me was getting high and I was too dumb to figure it out? I trusted and believed in Audra so much; there was no one who would have ever been able to convince me that my best girlfriend was getting high on crack, much less hanging out with those lowlifes. I call it as I see it. To me, Anthony and his wife were lowlifes, leaving my girlfriend out on my front porch to die for fear she might die on them in their car. The nerve of them to just leave her like that! Shaking my head in disbelief at what Audra had just told me, I couldn't help how angry it made me feel and the disappointment that filled my heart. At this moment it seemed as though nothing but disappointment awaited me around every corner. By the time I thought I had one thing under control, something else popped up unexpectedly. Was the nightmare ever going to end, I asked myself while still trying to comfort my friend and make her feel that everything would be okay.

"Cee, please believe me. After the experience I have had this morning, I'm never going to smoke crack again. Please, please believe me," she begged. "Cee, you have to believe me."

"No, Audra, you have to believe in yourself," I told her. "Girlfriend, nothing will ever change until you change," I told her. "Audra, this is something you will have to do, and only you can do it."

"Do you think I can, Cee? That's all I need to know," Audra asked, appearing to be serious, more serious than I had ever seen her before.

"I need your support, Cee. Don't let me down."

"Audra, if anything, you know that I'm going to be right there for you. One thing I must admit and can't lie about is the fact that I'm shocked."

"I know you are, and you have every right to be, but I promise you that I'm going to change. You'll see," Audra promised as she hugged me and thanked me and Mark for being there for her. "Mark's quick thinking saved my life."

"What do you mean, *his quick thinking*?" I asked, looking straight at Mark.

"Remember when he made me suck on that orange? It awakened my taste buds and I stopped hyperventilating. If it hadn't been for him, I probably would have died. Whatever you do, Cee, please don't tell Pee Wee what happened to me—give me a chance to tell him myself."

"Now Audra, do I look like Boo-boo the Fool?" I asked. "Why would I tell Pee Wee about what happened—so he can start a fight? Ask yourself how you sound," I asked, laughing out loud.

"Okay, girlfriend, you have a point," she said while resting her head on the arm of the couch, appearing to be exhausted and in much need of a good night's sleep.

After hugging her for what seemed to be forever, I assured her that everything was okay and that I believed in her and would stand by her side.

"Cee, you're going to see the old me come back, the person who was eager to catch the bus to get to New York so we could show the kids a nice time. I miss those times, Cee, and I want us to be close," Audra stated while continuing to hold her head in shame.

"Hold your head up and realize you are only human, Audra. At least you are not in denial about your addiction and you're asking for help—that's a good sign."

"When I realized I could have died tonight, that made me snap back to reality quicker than I thought. I can't lie,"Audra said. "I was scared—it's been a long time since I've felt that way, Cee."

"Felt what way?"

"Like I was going to die. Cee, I was so scared."

"Audra, you had every reason to be afraid," I assured her. "Now, no more talking. I'm going to get you a blanket and cover you up so you can get some rest. We will talk more tomorrow. Good night, girl-friend, and remember I love you no matter what. Audra, you're still my buddy, and you can get through this, and you shall."

Nothing was going to stop me from believing that my friend Audra was going to change. If almost dying from smoking crack wasn't going to stop her, what would, I thought to myself. This woman was my friend and was there for me when no one else was. We shared tears, laughter, and the joy of just being the best of friends, and kept each other's darkest secrets. I would never in a million years have thought that Audra, of all people, was getting high on crack cocaine. Well, I guess that was a real wake-up call as to how deep this crack thing is. There was nothing that could have prepared me for what my girl-friend had just confided in me. How do you live with the thought of knowing your best friend's darkest secret is not only affecting her life, but now it's affecting your life also? Audra was bright, energetic, and such a joy to be around; all I could ask myself was, why? Why did she have to try that awful drug called crack cocaine?

The more I thought about the question why, the more anger con-sumed me until I wanted to lash out at someone, and that someone was her husband. But, there was no way that I could betray my friend, for I had promised her I wouldn't dare mention anything about what had happened to her husband Pee Wee. Inside my mind, the thought of knocking him upside his head for being crazy enough to get his wife hooked on an addictive drug like crack taunted my mind. What man or woman in their right mind would do something like this? Question after question drifted through my mind while I sat next to my girlfriend and watched her sleep. Looking at her resting so peacefully made me feel good that she trusted me enough to tell me the truth. No matter what, I made up my mind that I was going to be there for her, not just one day but every day. Thoughts of the times when I was depressed and she stuck by my side and pampered me, giving me hope, made me realize that we are all vulnerable to something at one time or another in our lives. To me, my friend Audra was a strong-spirited person who I believed could overcome anything, even crack cocaine. Sometimes, no matter how strong we think we are, we still need a higher power to intervene and that higher power is God. For without Him, we have already subjected ourselves to a greater struggle.

August 18, 1986

Dear Diary,

Antwan is a month old today. His little body is growing like a weed. For my baby to be only a month old, he is such a wonderful child. He barely cries, which is very unusual. Everyone tells me that I'm blessed that he is such a good baby. Mark has been such a great, supportive father, getting up in the wee hours of the morning, making sure the baby is fed and changed; he even bathes Antwan when he gets off from work every day. Taking care of Antwan is like a ritual for him. I think it's therapy for his addiction. Right now, I can't remember the last time Mark has gotten high. And to me that spells relief. With Terry and Mark helping me out with the baby, I can get more done each day.

Yesterday, before Audra went to work, she came and asked me if we were still going to New York on Friday. I was shocked; I thought maybe she would forget. I assured her that Mark had volunteered to keep Antwan and that our date with our kids on Friday was still on. The sparkle in her eyes and the glow on her face told me that it was an event she was anticipating. Watching Audra as she walked down the street to catch her bus for work, I could tell just by the way she walked and held her head up high that she was fighting to win her self-confidence back. The true Audra, the woman who made the sun shine in any room she stepped into, the woman who had so much confidence, and that win-win attitude that she could do anything. In my heart, no matter what, I know my girlfriend is putting up a good fight dealing with an abusive husband, his crack addiction, plus her own. And not to mention sometimes going to work with a black eye, and then coming home and trying to be a good mother to her kids. Thinking about her situation gave me a headache.

Here I am in the same shoes, trying to wear so many hats. I am a mass ball of confusion, not only for myself, but my children also. I just thank God at this point in my life that I didn't turn to smoking, too. What would happen to my children if I got strung out on crack cocaine? I asked myself as I stood over the sink washing dishes. My mind is numb from thinking about the situation.

August 20, 1986

Dear Diary,

Terry and Audra's two girls are so excited about going to New York. Every five minutes they are asking me what time their mother will get home from work. It's been a long time since I have seen our kids so happy. I assured the kids that when Audra came home she may be tired and need a few minutes to rest but once she got rested we would be leaving. Of course trying to explain this to three over-excited kids was hard to do. These kids were excited and filled with joy, anticipating the trip to New York. When Audra walked through the door you would have thought she was Santa Claus, the way their little eyes lit up and the smiles showed on their happy faces. Little did the kids know, but this sister was excited also, ready to take the 45-minute bus ride to the Big Apple.

Mark had volunteered earlier in the week to keep Antwan and told me to go out and have fun with the kids. I wonder if he would have said the same if I wanted to go out with some of my girlfriends to the club. Today would mark the first time I left Antwan, but I knew he would be in safe hands, so worry was the farthest thing from my mind.

"Momma, are you ready?" asked Terry, standing in front of me, grinning from ear to ear.

"Yes, baby, your momma's ready."

"Cee, I'll be ready as soon as I change shoes and touch up the girls' hair," Audra said while tiptoeing up the back stairs, trying not to awake Antwan. For the first time in months, I could feel my heart beginning to skip a beat just thinking about how much fun we were going to have in the Big City. When Audra came back down the stairs, the kids were ready, and it was off to catch the bus for our fun trip. Walking down the street, watching the kids skip and laugh, made the two of us feel so good. Trying not to think about what had happened to my girlfriend only a few nights earlier, I wanted her to feel comfortable as I reassured her how happy I was to have her in my life and what her friendship meant to me.

"Cee, you are the best, and when we are together we have so much fun. How I got caught up with the crack thing and let it almost destroy me, I don't know. But, one thing I do know is that I'm going to defeat this drug called crack cocaine. I refuse to let it ruin my life and rob me of our friendship. For now, let's concentrate on having a ball."

"Remember the last time we went to New York?" I reminded her. "Remember how much fun we had? Think about all the food we ate until we were miserable—and how cold it was."

"Wasn't that around Christmas, Cee?"

"I think it was."

"Remember how excited the kids were as we walked along the streets all decorated for Christmas and peeking in the windows at the displays?"

"And oh, let's not forget everyone's favorite—it was the display in the Macy's window of Santa and Mrs. Claus, surrounded by the elves and all the fluffy white snow that was scattered on the ground," I said.

"Oh, girl that was gorgeous. Everything was so bright and beautiful, you could feel the spirit of Christmas in the air."

"Remember it was so cold when we got to New York, we had to buy the kids some more gloves and ear mitts. Girl, we sure had fun," I said, watching the glow in her eyes as she remembered the good time we had.

"Whenever we get together, we have nothing but fun, and to think I was ready to throw all of that away for a hit of crack."

"Audra, please stop beating yourself up. We all make mistakes. At least you realized yours—some people go through their whole life and never change. Today is supposed to be filled with fun, nothing less. So please find it in your heart to let it go, Audra. If you don't, you're going to be miserable, and that doesn't help anything. It only makes matters worse. And right now, look at our children and how much fun they are having, and we haven't even stepped foot on the bus yet." Finally, after waiting for almost twenty minutes, the bus arrived. We let the kids get on ahead of us and instructed them to go to the back of the bus. This way we could have more room and enjoy our conversation. Normally on Fridays the traffic to New York would be backed up for miles. This particular Friday the bus arrived in New York so quick, we were ten minutes early. Stepping off the bus, I knew if nothing else, we had arrived in the Big Apple.

Nothing but tall buildings for as far as you could see outlined the sky, and the bright lights shimmered onto the water, giving off a double reflection. Audra and I both made a promise that one day we would work up enough nerve to go to the top of the World Trade Center. Thinking about it now, I would have to be awfully intoxicated or just drugged. There is no way I would go to the top of the Empire State Building; not the fourth, tenth, or twelfth floor, but, all the way up to the top. That's nuts, I thought to myself. Still, it was a challenge that lingered in the back of my mind, and from the looks of it, Audra must have had the same thought and was waiting for me to bring up the subject.

"What are we going to do first?" asked Terry and Audra's oldest daughter, Eva.

"Well, for starters, let's just walk around and get the feel of the city, and then we will take it from there," I said, watching the twinkling glow in their eyes.

Strolling along 42nd Street, passing the movie theater and about twenty restaurants, from the expression on the kids' faces, we knew it was time to decide on a place to eat. After three choices, we all agreed on Chinese. The restaurant we chose was nice and quiet. The atmosphere was so pleasant and delightful. Everyone decided to try a different dish so we could have the pleasure of sampling from each other's plates; this was fun. When the food arrived, we all looked at each other and were ready to dive in. I didn't know how hungry I was until I went to take the first bite and on the floor it went. This made the kids laugh nonstop. Boy, was I embarrassed, but it didn't stop me from gobbling up the rest of my food—or anybody else's. Not one morsel was left on my plate. By the looks of it, you would have thought that I was starving and hadn't eaten in days. To be honest, it has been such a long time since I tasted such great Chinese food that I can truly say was scrumptious. This food was beyond words. Everything was cooked to perfection; the meat sitting on the bed of fried rice drenched in sweet-and-sour sauce, surrounded by colorful red and green peppers for decorations, was tender and juicy and my egg roll was crispy and filled with succulent shrimp. The vegetables were fresh and tasty. My plate was so empty you could see your reflection in it. So does that tell you how good it was, or what? Audra tried her best not to laugh at me as I sat across the table from her and the girls, trying to unzip my pants so I could breathe. No matter how hard she tried not to laugh, she couldn't hold it in. It was embarrassing to have everyone poking fun at how silly I was by being so greedy. I was always taught that it was proper etiquette to leave at least a morsel or two on your plate so as not to appear to be greedy. But, in my mind I paid for this food, not my aunty, my granny or anyone else, and I was going to enjoy it to the fullest. And that I did.

After everyone finished eating and the waiter approached the table to give us our bill and pass out fortune cookies, we each took one. As we opened the wrappers to find out what good fortune awaited us, the kids were excited to read theirs first. So we started out with Audra's baby girl, Lydia, and let her read first. Lydia was six years old and had a mind of her own, always wanting to be first at whatever there was to do. Sitting attentively as little Lydia read her fortune, we burst out laughing, for her fortune made no sense for a six-year-old, but of course there was no way we could tell her that. Her fortune said that the man of her dreams would soon find her and that she would travel to many lands. Now how many lands was she going to travel to without her momma? And what man was she going to meet at six years old, barely able to read? We all laughed so hard we couldn't read one more, for we couldn't stop. Little Lydia was mad at us at first, but she soon got over it and joined us in our laughter.

When it was time to leave, we asked the waiter for a set of chopsticks so we could go home and practice how to use them and vowed that the next time when we came back to the Chinese restaurant we would eat with them.

All eyes were on me to give the order as to where we were going next. Stepping out onto the street, you couldn't help but notice all the vendors selling everything from jo-jo beads to books, tapes, tee shirts, kids' wear, and whatever else you wanted. And also, let's not forget the people who made an everyday living out of being professional beggars. Right now I bet most of those people had more money than Audra and me put together. Let's face it; some people were just beggars, and no matter how many times they heard a "no," there was a "yes" waiting around the corner.

Watching the glow on the children's faces and seeing how much fun they were having as they laughed and talked walking ahead of us made our hearts feel nothing but delight. These children of ours are the joy of our lives. Admiring them and how much fun they were having reminded Audra and me of how much fun we used to have as kids. Sometimes we have to let our hair down and become kids again with our children. There's nothing in the world that could give anyone more joy than experiencing the joys of parenthood. Even though it may not be for everyone, I knew it was for me, and by looking at my girlfriend I knew without a doubt it was for her also. We were all so full as we walked down the streets of New York, looking up at the World Trade Towers and pointing to the Empire State Building. The children were so intrigued and fascinated by all the bright lights and the people strolling along, just as we were. On every corner there was a vendor selling food, and to make matters worse, after walking around for a few hours, it was inevitable to want something else to nibble on. This time we agreed on shish kabobs—you know, the ones that have the onions and peppers on them. Um, um, they were so delicious. Even though we had eaten earlier, you know how Chinese food does you. It's only good for about thirty minutes and then you're hungry again. If I must say so, you're even hungrier the second time, trying to eat everything in sight.

After stuffing our faces for the second time, the children were ready for some type of activity, so Audra and I decided to let them choose what they wanted to do. From the looks of it they didn't have a problem deciding. The three of them wanted to go to the arcade and play video games. Audra and I both looked at each other, reading each other's mind, trying to prepare ourselves for a noisy, fun-filled adventure; at least that is what it would be for them. Going to an arcade in New York City was like a Tictac going to the zoo, filled with so many people you had to hold hands so you wouldn't get lost. Now, not only did we have to worry about holding onto the children, we also had to worry about holding onto our pocketbooks. Clutching our purses for dear life, we must have passed five or six arcades trying to find one that wasn't full. Thinking that the less people there meant more safety was not necessarily true.

I remembered a time when I got robbed in New York, and the people who robbed me were so friendly they didn't even have a gun. Just great conversation, and swindled me out of one hundred and sixty dollars. Of course, I was much younger and fell for the scam. We all fall for something, sooner or later. Well, that's another story in itself. Thinking about it now makes me laugh for being so silly.

Believe it or not, we finally chose an arcade and agreed to let the children play a few games for about an hour. Sometimes as parents you have to take the good with the bad. Audra and I stood back and guarded our children as they enjoyed their evening out on the town, laughing and teasing one another.

I knew it was time to go home when the corn on my pinky toe started hurting. It would be only a matter of time before it would start throbbing painfully. By the expression on my face, Audra could tell that my feet were beginning to ache and summoned the children to tell them that after their last game we would be leaving. To them she was the boogeyman, ending their fun by wanting to leave. When children start playing those games, they get so into it, they lose their sense of time.

Leaving the arcade after their last game, we could tell that they were getting sleepy, and if we didn't hurry up and get to the Port Authority to catch the bus, we would be trying to carry three sleeping children. Terry was yawning every few seconds and so were Audra's two little girls.

Finally arriving at the bus terminal, I went to purchase our tickets so we could save time and board the bus sooner. You cannot believe how relieved I was to see bus number 190 pulling into the terminal. My feet were overjoyed—so overjoyed I almost knocked one of the kids down to hop on and get a seat. Admitting it, I apologized, looking down at poor, sleepy little Lydia as she struggled to drag her tired butt onto the bus. Once this little girl got tired, it showed in all her actions. She was motionless and very grouchy. Marching to the back of the bus and taking a seat, we put all three of the children together so they could sleep, resting on each other for support. Looking at their faces made us smile and feel proud that we had taken the much-needed time out to spend with our children. Our babies needed our attention, and today we gave it to them.

The feeling I had inside made me bubble with delight, for I knew it would make Audra realize how much she had missed and hopefully this wonderful evening will make her want to do this more often. We can even make this a part of our weekly routine.

As the bus roared down Route 4, headed back to Paterson, we talked so much we almost missed our stop.

Waking the children up was a task; I realized once the bus stopped that we should have awoken our children about five minutes before we approached our stop. Now, trying to wake them up was hard, for it was almost 1:00 a.m. We had so much fun; we didn't want the evening to end and were trying to plan another date with the kids so we could have even more fun.

"Cee, I really enjoyed this evening. Girl, you made my day. It was only a few days ago when I thought I was going to die, and now I'm having the time of my life. Girlfriend, I love you and I promise you I'm never going to get high again," Audra said as we stepped off the bus with our sleepy children in tow. "Do you think Mark is going to be upset because it is so late and we are just getting home?"

"Of course not. Why would he? After all, he was the one to volunteer to baby-sit and Antwan is his baby, too, so him being upset is the last thing on my mind."

"Well, I know this may be a stupid question, Cee, but do you think Mark is still getting high?"

"Getting high on what?" I asked.

"You know what I'm talking about."

"Audra, in all fairness, I have to say I don't really think so, but I have to remember there were so many other times when I thought he wasn't getting high, and I was wrong. So now I'm taking it one day at a time and nothing more or nothing less."

"Where do you see your future with Mark?"

"Girlfriend, it would take a genie in a bottle to answer that question. One thing I do know for sure is that I'm not going to tolerate any more of his abusive behavior. Right now I think he is trying to do the right thing because he doesn't want to lose me or the kids. You know how the story goes, so don't act like you don't know," I said to her, flashing a smile.

"Well, are you two, you know, how can I say this? Are you two physically active?"

"What do you want, girlfriend?" I asked, laughing out loud. "Do you want a lie or the truth? To be honest, girlfriend, we probably would have been very physically active if you didn't disturb my groove at 3:00 in the morning."

"Is that right?" Audra asked, smirking under her breath, wanting to laugh. "Poor baby; I'm sorry I spoiled your groove, girlfriend," she said, all sarcastic, waiting for me to laugh at her silliness.

Opening the gate, I could see the shadow of someone pacing back and forth. By the looks of it, I knew without a doubt it was Mark and Antwan. Laughing all the way up the stairs, making much noise, Audra and I were curious about how long the baby had kept him up. Before we could reach the top step, Mark was standing there to greet us with a smile on his face, asking us did we have a nice time and where did we take the kids and if they had fun. It felt nice to know that he was concerned about whether we had fun or not.

"Mark, did Antwan keep you up? I saw you pacing the floor back and forth."

"Yes, he did, but only for a little while. Cee, you know how Antwan can be sometimes. Sleeping almost eight hours straight and at other times he just wants to be plain old nosy, trying to see everything in sight and bobbing his head all around like he knows what's going on. Overall, he was a pretty good baby. So good, in fact, I had to wake him up to feed him and also to change him. If I didn't wake him up, he would have slept through it all. Antwan had the whole house lit up from poop, and Cee, I was in the living room listening to some music and I kept smelling this funny odor—it just kept lingering right up under my nose. As I searched the house to find out what it was, guess what it was? Your son!"

"What do you mean, *my* son?" I laughed. "He is your son, too."

"Not when he stinks like that!" Mark laughed. Seeing Mark laughing like he was filled my heart with joy and hope. Hope that we could move on with our lives and leave the terrible past behind.

"Cee, I really missed you tonight while you were away, and I was looking forward to my baby coming home."

Upon hearing those words, Audra knew it was her cue to go upstairs with her sleepy children. Mark helped her carry Eva and Lydia upstairs, one on each arm. By the look on Audra's face, she was surprised that Mark was being so nice, displaying so much warmth. I know that once tomorrow comes, my girlfriend is going to have fifty questions for me. And I'm going to be ready.

Waiting for Mark to return downstairs, I decided to put on a pot of water for some coffee. Hearing his footsteps as he got closer to the back door, I couldn't help but think about how good it felt to be held in his arms and have his legs wrapped around mine the other night before we were so abruptly interrupted by Audra. But that was okay; I would do anything for my best friend and would do it over again if necessary.

While Mark and I sat at the kitchen table talking about old times and what we would do differently, we couldn't stop staring at each other. The look in his eyes I would know anywhere. It was the look of desire filled with passion. "Oh Boy" passion that I wanted so badly and yet was afraid to express for fear of giving in, only to be disappointed again. I could not stand another heartbreak, this I know. I had made a promise to myself that I was not going to take any more stuff from Mark and that I owed it not only to myself, but my children also. Pouring the water into the two mugs that lined the countertop, I could feel a strong presence hovering over me, and before I could place the cups on the table, warm hands were massaging my neck and shoulders. It felt so good to have his strong hands on my body. Trying to act like it didn't make a difference to me whether he touched me or not was not working. And being honest, this man knew what he was doing. In my mind, I knew I only had about two more weeks before it was time for me to have the tubal ligation, and I didn't want to blow my chances of having this surgery done by taking a stupid risk, without any type of birth control, and pop up pregnant again. I could feel my body temperature rising with every stroke of his hand and knew it would only be a few seconds before he would get next to me. Not wanting to give in, I demanded that he stop and told him I had to wait six weeks before I could have any physical contact.

"Cee, come on, baby. It has been a long time since we touched each other, and one time won't hurt anything," Mark begged. As he continued to caress me, the temptation was growing stronger and more intense by the minute. Inside I was screaming for someone to rescue me from this fire that was starting to burn inside of me. The last thing I wanted to do was give in to his needs when all I wanted was some sleep. I tried so hard to convince him that the time wasn't right. No matter what I said, it wasn't working; this brother was still going to try to have his way until I suddenly turned around and pushed him off of me. Shocked by my reaction, Mark was stunned and asked what was wrong with me. Not wanting to start an argument, I told him that I wasn't in the mood.

"You're not in the mood?" Mark questioned. "How is it you were in the mood the other night? And now you mean to tell me you feel nothing? Cee, please don't make me mad," he said, looking at me with disappointment in his eyes.

"It's getting late—let's go to bed, Mark, before Antwan wakes up. We have all day tomorrow to discuss this. By then you will have cooled off."

"Discuss what, Cee? That you don't want me to touch you, and sometimes you do and sometimes you don't? I'm not a water fountain, and you can't turn me on and off when you want," he said, trying to make me feel guilty.

"Right now is not the time to discuss this, Mark. If you continue to be loud you are going to wake up the children," I insisted.

"Wake up the kids? Is that all you're worried about? How about trying to think about why my woman doesn't want me to touch her—how about that, Cee? Is there someone else?"

"Don't be ridiculous, Mark—you are really being stupid now," I said.

"*I'm* being stupid? What about you? Here I sat all night and kept our son while you and your girlfriend and the kids went out, and you can't be considerate enough of my feelings to understand that I'm a man and I have needs and wants, too? What is so hard to understand about that, Cee? Is it that you don't understand or you don't care? And whichever one it is, I want you to tell me now. Don't try to play me for a fool! I'm going to ask you one more time—is there someone else?"

"No, Mark, there is no one else."

"If there is no one else, prove it to me."

"Prove what to you, Mark?"

"Don't be stupid, Cee, you know what I'm talking about."

"Well, if I knew what you were talking about, I wouldn't ask you, now would I? Mark, the last thing I want to do is to argue with you over something so stupid. Please, let's go to bed and talk about this tomorrow, can't we?" Walking toward the bedroom, I followed him in hopes of not going to bed mad.

"Cee, okay, come over here. I'm sorry, please forgive me. It was awfully selfish of me to try to force myself on you. You have a right to feel the way you do. After all, it was me who put you through those miserable changes and made your life a living hell. Baby, I'm so sorry, please forgive me. Baby, I love you so much, and you know you mean the world to me," Mark said as he kissed me gently on my forehead, trying to make up. It was cute seeing him blush like a child while pulling me close to him and wrapping his arms around me and holding me tight. "Cee, I'm going to show you what a real man is made of, and I promise you nothing but love. I know it's going to take some time for you to rekindle what you once felt for me, and in time, good things come to those who wait."

"Yes, that is true, Mark, but as I remember the saying, I think it goes like this: Good things come to those who wait, but not those who wait too late."

"So what are you trying to say?" Mark asked jokingly while we continued to hug and express our thoughts to one another. Realization of how we truly felt about each other started setting in, laying heavy on both of our hearts. Nestling into the bed and snuggling close up under the covers, we both went to sleep with a peace of mind and our legs wrapped around each other.

August 21, 1986

Dear Diary,

Waking up this morning to the beautiful sight of seeing father and son was so wonderful. Watching Mark hold Antwan as he fed him made me feel so good. It also made me feel like I had a real man. This man loved his son and it showed in the expression on his face as he held Antwan's little head cradled in the pit of his arm. Not wanting to disturb the two of them, I tried to ease out of the bed without disturbing them. If I had a camera I would have snapped their picture a thousand times. That's just how adorable they looked.

For the first time in months, I was starting to feel some hope for my relationship with Mark. Letting my feet hit the floor, I could feel Mark's hand reaching back to feel for my hand. Taking my hand in his while he held our son made me feel a warmness in my heart, something I hadn't felt in quite some time. He knew how to work on my emotions, especially when it came to our child. Seeing him like this, I couldn't help but wonder how long it was going to last and if his feelings were real. For a moment we both stared at our son as though he was an angel that we both knew in our heart was a blessing from God.

Rising to my feet to walk toward the bedroom door, I felt our room tremble; not paying it any attention, I continued to walk toward the kitchen, thinking that maybe one of my tenants was up early moving furniture around. Before I could get to the kitchen hallway, I heard a loud, thunderous sound. Frightened, I ran back to my bedroom, asking Mark what was going on and if he heard the loud noise. By the time I reached my door, the loud noise I had heard was even louder now, until it sounded like someone was not moving furniture, but throwing furniture. By the time Mark tried to lay Antwan down, it was too late; he had already woken up and was screaming at the top of his lungs. I could tell by the way my baby cried that something had frightened him out of his sleep. Antwan screamed so loudly, I had to pick him up while Mark went to the kitchen to see if he could make out what was going on. Listening carefully as he stood in the middle of the kitchen floor while I held Antwan, walking him back and forth, Mark signaled for me to go back into the bedroom as he could tell by all the commotion that someone was fighting. Moving quickly, I took Antwan back into the room and closed the door. Trying to rock my frightened baby back to sleep, I began to hear the voices of two people arguing, and from the sound of it, my girlfriend Audra was in rare form. You could hear her screaming for help and saying, "I'm not doing this anymore! It's over, I'm leaving. Pee Wee, please leave me alone," Audra cried.

Not being able to take any more, I finally went to the doorway of my bedroom and told Mark to go upstairs and break up the fight between my girlfriend and her husband. Of course, Pee Wee was Mark's friend and he didn't want to butt into his business, but right now, there was more to think about. Like for instance, they have two adorable little girls upstairs with them, watching them go through this turmoil. And more than likely, little Lydia and Eva were right there in the midst of this terrible war that their parents were in. Without further warning, Mark decided it was time for him to intervene by going upstairs and pulling Pee Wee off of Audra. From the sounds of it, you could tell that Pee Wee was hitting her pretty hard. Anger filled my heart, as Mark was moving a little too slow for me; I couldn't help myself and laid the baby down after he got quiet. Storming past Mark, I could feel chill bumps all over my body. How could this man stoop so low as to put his hands on a woman, especially in front of their children, and not feel any shame or remorse? Everything I went through with Mark flashed before my eyes. Knowing how much he took me through made me want to zoom upstairs to Audra's rescue. Reaching to open the back door, I could hear footsteps like a wild herd of horses running downstairs toward my door. Not wanting to be nosy, I moved away from the door, only to hear Audra yelling for Pee Wee to please leave her alone. Audra was begging for dear life, and for her husband to stop hitting her. The more she begged, the more he hit her. You could tell he was hitting her really hard from the sounds of the licks. Not being able to take any more of him abusing her, I could no longer hold my peace. Opening my back door, the look on Pee Wee's face told me that he was shocked and also high as a kite. Audra, on the other hand, was sober and fighting for her life, and there was no way I was going to let her husband lay another hand on her. Before I could say a word, both of them stumbled into my house, wrestling, with Audra hitting Pee Wee on the head. By the looks on their daughters' faces, you could tell little Eva and Lydia were scared to death and were screaming for their daddy to leave their mother alone. Not being able to take him abusing her anymore, I demanded that Pee Wee leave Audra alone and get out of my house before I call the cops. Not hearing one word I said, he continued to abuse her. Finally, when Mark did decide that enough was enough and tried to step in to break Pee Wee and Audra apart, it was at the wrong time. Audra grabbed hold of an old solid steel iron that was sitting on the edge of the sink counter and went to hit Pee Wee with it, only to miss him and bang Mark upside the head instead. Blood gushed everywhere, splattering on the wall, floor, and the couch. Shocked and dismayed at what happened, Audra was so upset and nervous she was shaking like a leaf on a tree. I was speechless and overwhelmed at witnessing the sight that had just occurred. Not being able to say a word, Mark fell onto the couch, holding one side of his head where the iron had struck. The blow was so hard I thought it had cracked his skull. The iron had hit the lower part of his head slightly above his left ear. The area that was struck started to swell immediately. Poor Audra didn't know what to do, and Pee Wee didn't make matters any better by continuing to fuss, telling Mark that it was his wife's fault, and that if she had never brought their problem downstairs none of this would have happened in the first place. Here he was, so ignorant of the facts of what had just happened, and so high on crack that I don't think he even realized what was going on. Did Pee Wee know that Mark was in much pain and may need to go to the hospital? Or did he even care at this point was all that I could ask myself. Audra went over to Mark as he lay on the couch holding his head, waiting for me to return with a towel.

"Mark, please tell me that you are okay. I'm so sorry. Please forgive me. I didn't mean for this to happen," Audra cried, tears flowing down her beautiful face. Pee Wee stood still in his tracks, just realizing that the blow was really meant for him. And if that had happened, he would be standing there with blood gushing from the side of his head instead of Mark's. Grabbing a white towel, Audra and I tried to calm Mark down as he screamed in pain.

I just knew from the way it sounded when that solid steel iron hit his head that it was going to be a lick that Pee Wee would remember forever, but instead it was Mark. Now here it was—my man was wounded from a lick that was intended for someone else, not himself. All because he was trying to break up a fight between a husband and wife who just happened to be our dearest friends. A fight that should never have started in the first place. No man has the right to put his hands on any woman.

"Mark, I'm sorry. Please forgive me," Audra begged as if she felt his pain.

I felt sorry for both. Sorry that my girlfriend had to endure such agonizing pain of the physical abuse her husband had subjected her to, which drove her to get so infuriated that now the throbbing pain Mark is feeling is the result. Pain that no amount of painkiller can take away. Looking at his head, trying to see where the blood was coming from, was hard because blood was everywhere. Rubbing his back and comforting him, I tried my best to appear calm and at the same time I was scared to death, not knowing if this man of mine was going to bleed to death or survive this trauma. Asking Mark if he wanted to go to the hospital was out of the question, and by the expression on his face I knew that he would be okay. Even though I felt he would be okay, a little piece of me felt for security reasons he needed to go get checked out. Mark was determined not to and was as stubborn as a mule, telling me he was going to be okay. Watching the blood drip down Mark's face, I felt so bad, and yet there wasn't anything I could do for him.

After about ten minutes, Pee Wee was still wandering around the house in disbelief, holding his head like he was the one that had gotten the lick instead of Mark. This brother had some nerve. Not once did he apologize to Mark for the terrible situation he placed upon us, not to mention the fear he caused in his children. How could any man be so cruel and uncaring? That's how Mark used to be, but looking at him today it made me feel proud that he was my man, even though he was the one to get clunked upside the head. Tears flowed down Audra's face as she repeatedly confessed her sorrow for what had happened. I felt so sorry for her and tried to comfort her.

"Cee, I'm going to leave Pee Wee," she confessed as we walked out onto the balcony, leaving Mark and Pee Wee alone inside the house so they could talk. "I can't take the abuse anymore, Cee, and my children are suffering, watching me go through this time and time again. Pee Wee gets high on crack, then wants to fight me because I no longer want to get high with him, making it easier for him to have control over me, being that we both would be getting high. I'm tired, and enough is enough. I'm moving back to California as soon as I save enough money. Yesterday I called my mother and told her that things weren't working out with Pee Wee, and my momma told me that if I wanted to I could come home and bring the kids."

"Girl, I hate that all of this is happening to you. Audra, you are such a beautiful person, not to mention a wonderful friend. I'm going to miss you dearly when you're gone, but if there is anyone that understands what you're going through, you know I do. I love you, Audra. Please promise to keep in touch."

"Cee, how could anyone forget you and your kindness? The fun times we shared, filled with laughter and joy I could never forget. Those memories are embedded in my heart forever. So Cee, please don't be upset if you come home one day and I'm not here. Just pray for me and my kids, for you know the reason more than anyone else."

Embracing my friend as we both shed tears, thinking about how much we were going to miss each other, I couldn't help but wonder if I would ever see her again. It is so sad, when you finally meet someone that you have so much in common with and love so much, to have to lose them so suddenly. Nothing could change what I was feeling at that moment. The emptiness of knowing that I was going to lose my friend placed a damper on my day, but I knew the only way for her to get out of that terrible, abusive relationship would be to leave.

Today was the saddest day I have experienced in a long time. Audra called a taxi and left with the kids; she told me that she would be back later to pick up some of her things and that she was going to be in Newark at a co-worker's house. She informed me that one of her friends at work knew of her situation and that she would be in contact. Watching her and the children leave was so sad. Little Lydia and Eva ran up to me to hug me and give me a kiss. There was so much hurt in their eyes; for a moment I felt their pain. Trying to hold back my tears as I embraced them one last time, I reassured them that they were going to be fine and that I would come to visit them soon.

Mark told Audra that everything would be all right and that his head was feeling much better. The swelling above his ear had formed a knot the size of a small walnut. Lying on the couch trying to relax, I made an ice pack for him to place on his head to reduce the swelling. I could tell he really appreciated all the attention I was giving to him by the way he looked at me and stroked my face so caringly. Seeing him this way, I couldn't help but feel sorry for him. This man, better known as the Beast Master, was now a gentle, tamed lion. Something I thought I would never see in him.

Pee Wee wandered around like he was trapped in a maze. When Audra left, it was so sudden, he didn't get a chance to stop her. We made sure that he didn't know. We had already called the taxi and it was outside honking before he even knew what was going on.

On the inside of my soul I was happy that my girlfriend had made her escape, happy to know that tonight she can lay her head down and not have to worry about anyone beating on her and subjecting her to the terrible, abusive drug called crack cocaine. Even though I will miss her dearly, it made me happy to know that she had gotten out alive with her children. No more was she a victim like so many others that were just like her and me.

[Today, there are so many women trapped in verbally, mentally, emotionally, and financially abusive relationships with no way out. It's not until you decide to take control of your own life and destiny through praying and asking God to grant you the strength and courage to fight for your own survival, do you find an end to this vicious cycle of repeated abuse at the hands of someone else. Remember, God is always there, and He does answer prayers. How well do I know about it? Right now, I feel that I'm a living testimony for all those who have experienced my pain and the crippling side effects of the emotional, physical, mental, financial and let's not forget the verbal, abuse that a tragic drug such as crack cocaine can have on someone's life.]

August 30, 1986

Dear Diary,

Today is Terry's birthday and he is eight years old. The smile on his face when he woke up this morning told of a happy little boy who was waiting for his birthday surprise. There isn't too much I can do with him because I just had a tubal ligation a few days ago and I'm still very sore. Dr. Lambert said that I would endure soreness for about a week or so, and then I should be ready to go back to work. Usually it takes about two weeks to get back into the swing of things after surgery. Mark has yet to find out that I had this operation. He thinks that I had a biopsy done—at least that is what I told him—so he is in the dark, and that is how I want to keep it. If he knew I had an operation done which wouldn't allow me to have any more children, he would flip. But, who cares? After all, it's my body and I'm entitled to do what I want with it. And right now, not having more children is the choice that I made, and I'm content with it. Terry is happy that he has a little brother, and this makes my whole world complete. Grinning from ear to ear with a tooth missing in the front of his mouth, Terry appeared to be as happy as a lamb, sitting on the edge of my bed feeding Antwan.

"Momma, are we going somewhere today? And when are you going to get your car back so we can go to New York to see Aunt Stella?" This little boy did not miss a beat with his questions.

"If everything goes right, baby, we should be able to go to see Aunt Stella in maybe another week or so. Once I get better, I'll go and pick up the replacement car that was promised to me by the dealer."

Excited and bubbling with joy, Terry's eyes lit up like a Christmas tree. "Are we getting another car?" he asked with a sparkling gleam in his beautiful eyes.

"Yes, we are, baby, and this time everything is going to be better."

"What do you mean by *better*, Momma?"

"*Better* meaning no more arguing with Mark, no more fights—nothing but good times," I promised.

Thinking back, it was just a few short months ago that this little boy named Terry wanted a solid wooden bat for his birthday, and now today, the same little boy could have cared less about any of that. He was happy and it showed. What made me feel the happiness was watching him make such a fuss over his little brother, and to know that he wasn't worried about his momma and what was going to happen to her anymore. The fear that had consumed his mind at one time was gone, and he was the little boy who was just that, a little boy.

Audra and I had planned on taking the kids to New York for Terry's birthday, but I know that's impossible now. Especially with me just having the surgery and not being able to get in touch with her. She promised that she was going to keep in touch, and now no one knows where she is. All along before she left, this is what I had feared would happen and it did. I don't want to spoil Terry's special day by telling him that I don't know how to find my girlfriend and his adorable little friends, Lydia and Eva. How do you tell your child that his friends, whom he loved and cherished so much and were a dear part of his life, have disappeared? For the life of me, I could not be the bearer of bad news. Right now all I want is for him to continue enjoying his day and looking forward to his surprise. My brother Chad bought him a remote control car, and I bought him some clothes and a basketball and gave him a card with some money in it so he can go and get what he really wants. And I know what he really wants, money won't be able to buy, and that's his two friends, Lydia and Eva. Tomorrow I will tell him the truth, but today is meant to be a happy one.

The birthday cake I made for Terry came out perfect, considering it's been a long time since I have baked anything from scratch. If I must say so myself, it looks delicious. My Aunt Theo used to say that once you learn something you never forget how to do it, and today I'm so glad baking a cake wasn't one of the things I forgot. Putting the candles on the cake, I told Terry to go outside and get some of his friends so they could join him in celebrating his birthday by eat-

ing cake and ice cream. Now you know he was to thrilled at that notion and flew down the stairs to fulfill my request. As he reached the
bottom step I heard him calling for me.

"Mom, what about Eva and Lydia? Are they coming, and when will
they get here?"

I was speechless once again with no words to fill the air. "Baby, I
don't know if they will be here. Maybe Audra had to work, and if she
did, Terry, I don't know what time she gets off. But, I'll make sure
enough cake is left for them when they do come over, even if I have
to put it into the freezer. Is that okay, baby?"

For the first time in awhile I saw a disappointing look come over
that sweet, innocent, little face. "Terry, don't be so sad. Today is your
birthday. I'm pretty sure wherever Eva and Lydia are, they are thinking about you," I told him. No matter what I said, it didn't change the
look on his disappointed face.

"Momma, it's not going to be a happy birthday anymore, and I
don't want cake and ice cream without them. It won't be any fun—
they were my best friends. The other kids—they are okay, but Eva
and Lydia were my best friends. We did everything together. We even
planned how we were going to double-team Mark the next time he
put his hands on you or Uncle Chad."

What my child said shocked me for a moment; then, just thinking
about it, I couldn't help but laugh at the notion of the three of them
on Mark's back.

"Terry, go on and get your other friends, and everything is going
to be okay."

Mark arrived home with hot dogs, rolls, chips, and drinks to make
it a real party. I wasn't planning on all of this, but if it makes my son
happy and relieves the tension of him missing his dear friends Eva
and Lydia, then I guess I'll have to play along. Singing "Happy Birthday"
to my oldest son and watching him blow out his candles as he closed
his eyes and made a wish, I reminisced about the day he was born
eight years ago. Boy, eight years have come and gone so fast; where
did the time go? Soon Terry will be a teenager. Sometimes I think he
skipped over the teenage years and acts so much older than his ac-
tual age.

July 14, 1988

Dear Diary,

While lying here on my back, staring up at the ceiling and the four dingy walls that surround me, I can't help but think about the tragic events that lead me to such a dreary place in my life. A place filled with the stench lingering in the air from the urine at the base of the toilet connected to the wall and so much noise; it's a blessing if you can get any sleep. Sleep these days is something one hopes and prays for and only comes at midnight when all the lights are out, if then. Never in a million years could anyone have told me that this would be my temporary home. Right now the only thing that gives me peace of mind and puts a smile on my face is the thought of my beautiful children and the good times Audra and I used to have when we went to New York. It's been two years since I've written anything in my diary. After Audra left, I lost interest in doing much of anything. Seems like just when I thought everything was coming together in my life for the better, something else was happening. I finally went to pick up my replacement car after Terry's eighth birthday two years ago, and that's when all hell broke loose. Mark was great up until I got that car, and that's when all my problems started. He became very insecure, and started accusing me of seeing someone else and following me around. Before I could even get into the house, he would start an argument and take the car keys and leave. By the time Mark started acting really ugly, Antwan was going on two months old and had to be rushed to the hospital for a very high fever. The day my baby got sick, I remember it like it was yesterday, because I thought I was going to pass out from the shock of what my baby-sitter was telling me when I returned after work to pick up my child. Just getting off from work and returning to the baby-sitter to pick up Antwan, I couldn't wait to see my precious bundle of joy, only for the baby-sitter, Mrs. Toby, to inform me that Antwan had been running a slight fever all day and that she thought I needed to take him to the doctor to get checked out. Hearing her words and running over to the crib where my baby lay, I picked him up and felt his forehead; he was burning up and I knew I couldn't wait and had to rush him to the hospital. Before I could walk out the door, Mark met me on Mrs.

Toby's front porch, and I told him what she had said. The look of fear was all over his face as we both jumped into the car and sped off hurriedly, taking our baby boy to the hospital. My hands were shaking and I couldn't stop crying as I looked at my innocent, adorable, sweet baby boy resting in my arms, not making a sound. Fear gripped my heart and flashbacks of what happened to my other son (Boo) almost sent me into a panicked frenzy. But this was no time to panic, and I had to get a hold of my emotions before I got carried away.

When I arrived at the hospital, Antwan's doctor was already there waiting for us. I had given Mrs. Toby the number and permission to call Antwan's doctor before I left her house, and told her to tell the doctor we were on our way with Antwan. Taking my precious angel out of my arms to place him on the table so he could be examined, Dr. Kim took his temperature, which was 104.

"With a temperature that high, babies can go into a seizure," Dr. Kim said while taking Antwan's pulse.

Mark wrapped his arms around me as we both waited patiently for the doctor to tell us what was wrong with our child. After examining our baby for about ten minutes, Dr. Kim called me and Mark into the room where they had my baby lying in a glass bassinet with a tiny little IV needle stuck in his arm.

"Mrs. Davis, I don't want to offend you or your husband with any of the questions I'm going to ask you, but for starters I must ask you this. Please don't be offended—like I said, this is something I have to ask you, and it is essential that you be honest with me."

"Okay, Dr. Kim, ask me whatever you have to. All I want to know is if my son is going to be all right, and why do you keep stressing the point of hoping you don't offend me with your questions?"

"Mrs. Davis, I think you need to take a seat, for what I'm about to ask you is very serious."

"Dr. Kim, please stop beating around the bush and ask me whatever it is you need to ask me."

"All right, Mrs. Davis, for starters please tell me if you were doing drugs when you were pregnant with your son."

"Drugs, what does this have to do with anything, Dr. Kim?"

"Well, Mrs. Davis, to be honest, I have no choice but to tell you the truth, but first I need you to answer my question."

"Dr. Kim, no, I didn't do drugs when I was pregnant with my son, and what does that have to do with anything?"

"Mrs. Davis, most times when a baby comes into the hospital with symptoms such as your son's, it is from the use of drugs while the mother was pregnant."

I could feel my blood boiling. Here this man was sitting in front of me, almost accusing me of being an addict. Shock and disbelief clouded my mind at the thought of his question. "Can you believe this doctor asking me something so stupid?"

"Mrs. Davis, as I said before, don't get offended. I'm still running more tests to try to find out what's wrong with Antwan, and we want to keep him overnight for observation. We have his fever pretty much under control, but your baby is dehydrated and his system needs to be replenished, so we are going to put him on Pedialite for now—until we get the test results back. So please don't be upset for me doing my job and asking you that question. It's part of my routine as a doctor." After Dr. Kim assured me that asking me that question was only routine, it made me feel a little better.

"Mrs. Davis, I'm going to assign your son a room, and you and your husband are more than welcome to stay overnight."

Mark has not said two words since he returned to the room. When Dr. Kim stepped out of the room, Mark left right behind him. He told me he was going to get something to drink, only to confide in me a few days later that he went and talked to Dr. Kim and confessed to him that he was the one strung out on drugs—not only on crack cocaine, but heroin also, making my poor baby what they considered back during that time a "crack cocaine, heroin-addicted" baby. When Mark informed me that he told the doctor he was a crack addict and that he also did heroin, I was shocked and could not believe what I was hearing. Nothing but pure fear ripped through my body like a blazing fire, out of control. Anger once again filled my heart; no wonder my baby slept all the time and barely woke up to be fed or changed. How could he wake up? He was still in a nod from all the drugs in his little body. Even though today, at this point and time in my life, not one doctor will admit that this is what had happened.

I'll never forget what Dr. Kim told me, revealing that my son would have to be in the hospital for about a week or so for treatment. To be exact, Dr. Kim kept him under observation for almost two weeks to make sure that everything was going to be okay. Sadness filled my heart when I learned that my baby came into the world with a problem, one I, his mother, was not aware of, nor could I fix. Shame filled my soul at my naiveté to the situation. Thank God for Mrs. Toby, bringing his fever to my attention and keeping me abreast of his activities that day. If she wasn't as attentive and checking on my baby every fifteen minutes or so, I may have lost him. The pain, plus the fear of losing another child, made me a basket case. I'm so grateful that Antwan was treated in time for his illness, which the doctor never wanted to tell me at Mark's request. How do you forgive your son's father for his addiction, and then turn around and find your baby is addicted and has to be treated not only for crack, but heroin, too? How do you answer for that?

Horrific thoughts danced around in my mind of how Mark had once banged my head repeatedly against a concrete wall until I felt like my skull was going to split open. And how about the times he came home so high on crack cocaine that he hawked from the pit of his stomach and spit on me until it ran down the side of my face and made me feel so filthy and low. Just sitting here, remembering some of the terrible things he has done to me, makes me sick to my stomach. The most frightening of all was when Mark chased me down the street with a gun, and I was so busy running for my life that I tripped and fell to the ground skidding all the way. As I skidded I could feel the burning sensation of the skin on my face as it was scraped against the sidewalk, removing a third of my skin, leaving a scar that would stain my memory forever. This man had some nerve, and let's not forget how he abused my oldest son Terry when Antwan was only three months old. Yes, that's right, let's not forget about that. Because today, I'm paying for it as I lie here reminiscing about all the terrible, terrible things he did, not only to me, but my children. That's right—he abused my beautiful, sweet, adorable son Terry, beating him so badly until my child went to school all bruised up and one of the teachers called Child Protective Services to investigate. I guess you ask, why didn't I know? How could I have known when my child hid it from me? I was working two jobs and by the time I got home from work, Terry was asleep; by the time I went back to work, he was still asleep and Mark would get him off to school.

The day I found out Terry had been physically abused, I was at work, sitting at my desk, when I got a disturbing and strange phone call from Child Protective Services, informing me that one of their caseworkers was downstairs in the lobby and on their way upstairs to pay me a visit. Dismayed, I convinced the caseworker, Mrs. Harrison, that I would take an early lunch to meet her downstairs in the lobby so we could talk. This particular day the elevator could not reach my floor fast enough, as I was curious to know what this woman had to tell me that was so important she had to come all the way to my job to see me and tell me in person. So many thoughts ran through my mind, the least of which was about my children, but perhaps my neighbors' kids or maybe she was trying to get information on my girlfriend Audra and her two children who disappeared without a trace.

As I convinced myself of more and more ridiculous thoughts of what it could be about, I began to feel better. Sometimes, it's always so much easier to assume the worst for someone else instead of yourself, and that day I chose to think the worst about everyone but myself. Stepping off the elevator, Mrs. Harrison was standing near the glass-enclosed entrance waiting to greet me. She was of medium height, a brown-skinned lady in her mid-thirties who wore a two-piece, double-breasted suit with matching shoes and purse; the glasses that framed her face made her look very sophisticated. This sister knew how to dress, if nothing else. Greeting me as I approached, she introduced herself and asked if I had a preference as to which restaurant I wanted to eat at. I told her I didn't care, and we both agreed on something fast so I wouldn't have to drive too far and wouldn't go over my 45-minute lunch break. By the time we arrived at the restaurant, the suspense about what she had to tell me was eating a hole through me. Not able to contain myself any longer, I just came straight out and asked her why she needed to speak with me and whose child she was inquiring about. Looking over her glasses as they slid down her nose, she said to me that we needed to be seated first and that she had some pictures she wanted to show me. Reaching the table to take a seat, I had forgotten all about food and that I was hungry. The only thought that consumed my mind was what is going on, and whose child is it? Believe it or not, the last thing I was prepared for was this lady to tell me she was here to talk about my child or my children.

"So what brings you here, Mrs. Harrison? Why do you need to see me?" I asked, while she continued to take off her coat and sip on hot chocolate.

"Mrs. Davis, it is about your son Terry."

"What about my son Terry? Is my child okay? Where is he?" Here I was, about to panic again.

"Mrs. Davis, did you know that your son Terry was abused? And that your spouse or boyfriend Mark Davis did it? Did you know that?"

"Where did you hear that lie?" I asked.

"Your son Terry came to school this morning and asked to speak with the teacher and told her what had happened to him. The teacher in turn requested that he go talk with a counselor, and the counselor contacted Child Protective Services."

Not wanting to hear what Mrs. Harrison was saying, I tried to block out what I didn't want to hear, and that was that my lover and partner in love, Mark Davis, had committed the ultimate crime by abusing my son physically. Tears welled in my eyes, as I so desperately wanted to believe that this was a horrible lie. As I wiped the tears with my hands, Mrs. Harrison reached into her purse and gave me a piece of tissue and then proceeded to show me the shocking pictures that Child Protective Services had taken of my son. Viewing the pictures made me sick to my stomach as I witnessed how badly bruised my son's little body was. Bruises were all over him—on his back, stomach, legs, behind, and arms. The only part of his body that didn't get bruised was his face. After viewing the pictures, Mrs. Harrison gave me the rest of the shocking news, telling me that I would be placed on observation, and they needed to talk with Mark to find out what made him do what he did to Terry. What could have made this man so angry he took it out on my son? So many thoughts and questions filled my mind as I searched and searched for answers.

"Mrs. Davis, I do hope you know that Child Protective Services have you and your child's best interest at heart. We want our children to be in a safe environment and protected from all harm. For the next thirty days, you and Mark will be under observation, and if we receive another report of any kind, we will have to investigate and may be forced to remove both children from your home. Do you understand what I'm telling you and how serious this is, Mrs. Davis? Do you have any questions?" Mrs. Harrison asked.

What was there for me to say as I sat there numb and dumbfounded, looking and feeling stupid? Here I was, feeling so distraught over what happened to my son; I could not even imagine how my son felt as he was the one to go through this horrible experience. From looking at the pictures, I knew his little body had to be sore and swollen. After viewing the pictures Mrs. Harrison showed me, it was hard for me to go back to work and function, knowing that my child had been abused.

That day I left work early so I could go home and hug my child and beg for his forgiveness. How could my son ever forgive me—or would he forgive me? This was my son, the one who swore to protect me, his mother, and here I was the adult and wasn't there to protect him when he needed me the most. My mind was numb from thinking about everything that had happened. Crying all the way home, I couldn't wait to reach the door and stick my key in, hoping that Terry was home. Running up the stairs, screaming out his name all the way, it felt like my heart was going to jump out of my chest. Every fiber of my being was hoping that he would greet me at the door, just as he had always done in the past, only this time I would be disappointed. When I walked through the door looking for my child, I found him lying down in his bed, facedown, trying to pretend like he was asleep. Rolling Terry over, I grabbed him and clutched his body close to me, holding him tight in my arms, rocking him and telling him how much I loved him, and that I was sorry and asking him to forgive me. Terry just looked at me as if he could see through the windows of my soul and knew how much I was hurting.

"Momma, I'm okay—why are you crying?" My son, even in his own pain and misery, was still trying to protect my feelings and acted as though nothing had happened.

"Baby, I know what happened, and you don't have to pretend for Mommy anymore. I know that Mark beat you badly, and I'm so sorry. Please forgive me for not being there to protect you. Terry, I promise you it will never happen again."

"Momma, I'm okay and it didn't hurt. Mark beat me because he said I was bad in school and I brought home some bad grades on my report card."

"Please, baby, do Momma a favor and pull up your shirt so you can show me where Mark hit you." Being obedient, Terry pulled up his shirt just like I requested. Looking at the bruises and whips that had turned into sores on his body made me sick to my stomach and filled with anger. Angry that I had been so blind; my child was abused as a result of me being so naive. Can you believe that my child, in his own agony, was still trying to be brave and protect not only me, but also his abuser, which happens most times with children who are abused? Abused children are so afraid to tell on the abuser. Sometimes they continue to suffer and take the abuse rather than tell, for fear of the consequences they may endure or what will happen to the abuser, or the parent if they, too, are being abused. God had blessed me with a beautiful son like Terry, and he was abused terribly, but still adored his mother.

After looking at the bruises that covered his body, I cried like a baby and begged him over and over again to forgive me. That day, you would have thought I was the child and he was the adult once again. Here was my eight-year-old son comforting me, handing me a tissue, telling me how much he loved me. If I must say so myself, God has truly blessed me.

Even though it's been almost two years since that incident, as I lie here writing this in my diary and remembering all these terrible things that happened, it still hurts and brings many tears to my eyes thinking about how my baby Terry suffered. Right now, I'm so happy he has gone to visit my Aunt Janice for the summer. This way he can have some fun, something he deserved for such a long time.

It would kill my son to know what has happened to his momma since he left. Maybe it was a blessing in disguise that he wasn't at the house when everything happened, but I know he would have understood what drove me to this point, as I'm sure he has grown sick and tired of watching his momma be sick and tired of dealing with a crack addict, and not ever having a moment's peace. Looking around me as I continue to write, all I see is the tormented souls of about twenty-five other women, all incarcerated for one reason or another.

Most of the women in here are younger than me and range in ages from eighteen to forty-eight. For the past ten hours, I haven't really talked to anyone, and I feel so alone, even though I know there are other bodies around me. At least, if nothing else, I can express what I feel on this paper without anyone knowing.

The sad thing is that my brother Chad does not even know that I'm gone or what happened to me. Hopefully by morning, someone will tell him what happened last night and where I'm at. Everything that happened last night was so fast and sudden; it was without warning. Life sometimes is so strange; it's amazing how one person can go from being totally happy to insane within a matter of seconds.

Returning home from work yesterday, Mark's brother Chris came by our house to invite us over so we could meet his new girlfriend and play cards. Mark and I both thought it was a good idea, being that it had been some time since we had done anything together. His brother suggested that we be at his house between 7:30 and 8:30 p.m. This way we could play cards and drink a few beers.

Arriving at Mark's brother's house, we were greeted by Mark's other sister-in-law, Joyce. She was in her early twenties. She was very outgoing and lots of fun to be around. This particular evening we took Antwan with us, so we wouldn't have to find a baby-sitter and rush home when we were just on the brink of having fun. No sooner did we start to play the first round of spades, than Mark's brother's girlfriend Lola mentions the fact that Antwan looks just like Mark. Blushing from ear to ear, Mark happily brags about his son looking like him and thanks her for the comment. Only then his ignorant brother, who had been imprisoned for two years, decides to say something stupid like, "That's not Mark's baby—that is my baby!" Floored at his response, Mark angrily jumps up from the table without saying a word and storms out the door with his brother laughing hysterically, only making Mark angrier. Shocked, I asked Mark's brother why he made such a stupid statement, which could cause me and Mark to fight. Chris just shook his head and said that his brother knew he was just joking and that Mark wasn't going to do anything to me. Dismayed at Chris for making such an annoying and unbelievable statement, I was speechless and picked Antwan up and packed his stroller so we could leave. Walking toward the front door, Chris's girl-friend Lola apologized and pleaded for me to stay and told me that Mark would come to his senses and be okay, and that he knew it was a joke. They thought that Mark was just overreacting, but what they didn't know was that this man had taken me through pure hell and was a jealous fool who was also strung out on crack, something that I dared not tell them for fear of the explosion it would create.

Mark's brother Chris had been imprisoned ever since he was a teenager and that's the only life he knew. He and Mark never really got along anyway, and from my understanding they didn't care for each other as kids. To me Chris always wanted to show off and prove that he was the better one, always striving to prove a point. Except this particular night was the wrong night to prove anything, espe-cially by insulting Mark's intelligence and telling him something so stupid such as Antwan is not his son. Chris knew before he opened his mouth and said something so stupid that it was going to start a fight. Not only did he insult his brother, but he also put my life in danger by adding salt to the wound. The last thing anyone should ever do is put someone else's life in danger by being ruthless, uncar-ing, and inconsiderate by saying something as terrible as he did. How could Chris be so senseless, and stoop so low as to tell a lie of this magnitude and know what type of impact it was going to have on his brother? To me, this brother could not have been thinking about my safety at all. The only thing he wanted to do was play a cruel trick on his brother by hurting his feelings and embarrassing him at my ex-pense.

Opening the door to leave, Chris walked over to Antwan and gave him a big hug. It took everything in me not to snatch my child away. But, I would have been wrong. After all, Chris was Antwan's uncle. Before I could walk out, I heard Joyce telling me to wait for her, that she would leave with me. No matter how many times Chris apolo-gized for his ignorance, I wasn't trying to hear it. This brother didn't know what he had done and what type of deathtrap he had set up for me to walk into. Chills came over me as Joyce and I walked along the street, pushing my son in his stroller, talking about what had hap-pened and how angry Mark was. I confided in Joyce that I was scared to go home, and that I feared that something bad was going to happen to me. Looking at me, I could see that Joyce was concerned as we circled the block where I lived three times.

"Cee, how many times are you going to push this stroller around this block?" Joyce asked.

"As many times as I need to."

Staring at Joyce, I told her that I felt as though something really terrible was going to happen. She reassured me that everything was going to be okay and that I was just paranoid.

"Cee, you're worrying about nothing—Mark knows he is Antwan's father."

Nothing Joyce said made me feel any better about the situation his brother Chris had placed upon us.

"If it will make you feel better, I'll come upstairs with you, and we can sit at the table and talk."

"Joyce, you don't understand—when I get home, Mark is not going to be in a talking mood. You don't know Mark. This man can be a monster when he wants to be."

Looking up at the sky, it was so clear—not one cloud, only the full moon glowing and the twinkling of the starlight. That night it was so quiet and peaceful, yet I felt so uneasy and nervous. Finally, after walking around the block one last time, Joyce convinced me to go home and put my sleepy baby boy to bed. Listening to her as she told me jokes to make me laugh, I almost forgot about the fear I felt inside. Sticking my key into the lock to open the door, I was relieved to be home and find that it was so quiet. Antwan's limp body felt heavier and heavier, the closer I got to the door. Carrying him up a flight of stairs wore me out. Joyce opened the door and went to Antwan's room to pull back the covers on his bed so I could lay him down. Passing by my bedroom to get to the kitchen, Joyce asked me if I felt okay and if I wanted her to stay for a few minutes. I told her no, and assured her that everything would be okay because my brother was home.

"Cee, being that you told me everything is okay, I'm going to leave. If you need me, just call me. Please don't hesitate," she said.

I was so busy trying to sneak into the house without waking anyone up that I didn't notice the fact that I hadn't undressed Antwan.

To be honest, I don't know if I had forgotten or was too afraid I would make too much noise and awaken Mark. Regardless, it was too late for me to do it now. Antwan was asleep and it didn't matter to him that he still had his clothes on. My baby looked like an angel, sleeping so peacefully. He will be two years old in a few more days, I thought to myself as I headed off to my room, hoping that Mark would be asleep. Trying to open my bedroom door without making any noise was almost impossible, as my door was swollen and it took more pressure to open it. Once I got the knob to turn, I pushed on the door slightly harder; then I gradually lifted it up so it wouldn't squeak. Tiptoeing into the room, too scared to turn the light on, I undressed in the dark. Fearful that Mark would wake up, I tiptoed over to the bed and got in, trying my best not to make a sound for fear of what might happen. After getting into the bed, my next task was to get comfortable by wiggling my tired body up next to the head where Mark lay resting. Boy, was I happy he was asleep, I thought to myself as I finally was in a comfortable position, rolling over onto my side to go to sleep. Lying on my side closest to the window at the foot of my bed, I could feel my body tremble as I felt the heat of Mark's body next to mine. I was so nervous as I felt him roll over, facing my back as I lay still, almost too afraid to move, much less breathe. Mark's warm breath was up against my back and sent fearful chills down my spine. My heart skipped a beat as I could feel the presence of his hand touching my shoulder, shaking me gently at first, trying to see if I was asleep. Pretending that I was asleep and couldn't be awakened irritated Mark, and made him try even harder to wake me by not only shaking me, but now tapping me on my face, telling me to wake up and that we needed to talk. After about three firm taps to my face, it was time to stop pretending and wake up, for I could see that his profound anger was progressively making him get more aggressive. Trying to gather my composure while I lay on my side facing the window, I felt Mark's anger beginning to grow out of control as he forcefully rolled my body over with me facing him eye to eye in the shadows of the dark. Looking directly into my eyes, Mark told me how disappointed he was because I didn't deny what his brother Chris had said about him not being Antwan's father. Screaming at the top of his lungs, Mark demanded to know why I didn't leave immediately after he did, and why didn't I deny what his brother had said in regard to Antwan being his child.

"First of all, I didn't feel like I should have to explain anything to you, Mark, because to me it was already self-explanatory. Your brother was locked up when I conceived Antwan. So how could you have even thought something that stupid? Mark, I thought you believed in me. How could you think I'd be that ruthless?"

"Cee, don't test me and try to make me look stupid. I know how women are, and you're no different." Upon hearing those words I was hurt and sat up in bed, holding my head and wondering when there was ever going to be a time in my life when I would be truly happy.

"Cee, I didn't make you do anything you didn't want to do. So let's get real. You know that you have another man," Mark yelled.

"Another man? Where is all this coming from?" I asked as I attempted to get out of bed and reach for something to cover my semi-nude body. I felt the pressure from Mark's hand grabbing my arm forcefully and demanding to know why I was getting up. Too scared to tell the truth with my heart doing monkey flips in my chest, I could barely talk.

"Cee, did you hear me ask you where you are going? I'm not going to ask you again." My mouth could not open fast enough for me to explain to him my need for a glass of water.

"So now all of a sudden you want a glass of water?" he asked hatefully.

Wiggling my tired and sleepy body down to the foot of the bed, I reached over to the chair where my clothes lay resting. As I managed to sit up on the edge of the bed in the dark with only the reflections from the moonlight falling upon the waxed tile floor, I could feel the presence of Mark's hands getting ready to violate my body. Sitting on the edge of the bed trying to put on my favorite sweatpants, I was terrified at the thought of what Mark may be planning to do to me. I could feel him getting up out of the bed right behind me. Before I knew it, he suddenly snatched the sweatpants I was holding out of my hands and dared me to get up. Scared to death with my heart racing in my chest, about to explode from anticipating his actions, I jumped up to turn the light on. Reaching out in the dark to feel for the switch, Mark snatched me by my right arm, causing me to lose my balance, and that's when he hauled off and slapped me so hard in my face that I dizzily fell onto the floor, holding my head in my hands, trying to soothe the pain and stop the stinging sensation that was burning my skin, as it felt on fire. Mark hit me so hard until it left a big whip mark that I could trace with my fingers along the side of my face. While stretching my eyes desperately, trying to adapt to the darkness so I could see where he was standing, I wondered what Mark was going to do to me next. The harder I tried to stretch my eyes so I could regain my sight, the only thing I could see was the tiny circle of stars that were spinning in front of me. I saw red ones, white ones, blue ones, yellow ones, and also green neon-colored stars. For a moment I almost felt like I was in a disco with the psychedelic strobe lights. Remember those? Those were the lights that made everyone look like they had lint balls on their clothes.

It took a few moments for me to get myself together. Being momentarily blinded for a few seconds from someone hitting me in my face really did something to me, as it made me angrier than I had ever been in my whole entire life. All I could think about as I sat on the floor, too dazed to move, was how my mother must feel having to live in the darkness every day, and now here I was, letting a man abuse me and put his hand in my face. Just those few seconds, when I was temporarily blinded, scared me pretty bad. Terrifying thoughts of how my mother had been beaten blind clouded my mind. While trying to gain my composure as I braced myself up against the wall, I could feel Mark getting ready to strike me again. Anger seared through my whole body and sent chills up my spine, as I could feel my adrenaline starting to flow, with me getting madder and madder at the thought of how my beautiful mother was abused, and the suffering she has to endure for the rest of her life, all because of an abusive man. The mere thought of how my mother has to suffer, not just one day, but every day for the rest of her life, adjusting to living in a world of darkness, filled my soul with rage. Now here I was, her oldest daughter, also being abused. Mark scared me so much until I began to feel like a rat backed into a corner, and I knew in order for me to get out I had to come out fighting. No more was I going to tolerate his abuse, not at any cost. No matter what it may cost me. This man was at the brink of driving me insane, but he didn't care. Crack co-caine had him so wrapped up that it had fried his brain and made him numb.

After knocking me down to the floor, he began to feel cocky and strong, boasting about how he would cause me bodily harm. Laughing out loud and hysterically, Mark began to boast about what he was going to do to me as he followed me into the kitchen as I pursued a glass of water. My mouth was so dry it felt like cotton. I could feel the cold evil of Mark's presence as he walked more closely up to me, watching me as I stood facing the sink, reaching up to open the cab-inet door. Taking out one of my favorite goblets to drink from, I ran the water until it was nice and cold. Standing next to me, Mark looked down on me, waiting to see my response. He sensed my fear and played on it. At that very moment, something came over me and I could feel warmth from one tear rolling down the right side of my face; without thinking, I turned around and looked at Mark eye to eye as I warned him that if he ever put his hands on me again, he would regret it for the rest of his life.

Laughing out loud with the look of hatred written all over his face, Mark yelled out loud, "Look out, world, Mrs. Big Bad Cee is going to kick my a—"

Oh, to him it was so funny, so funny in fact that he pushed me. But at the moment, I was madder than I had ever been before in my life. I reached onto the table and grabbed that same wine goblet I had been drinking from and slammed it up against the table. Remember those beautiful goblets that you would win at the fair or carnival for pitching pennies? You know the ones that are a quarter of an inch thick, and they have nice stems at the base and some even have a circle of red stars. When it broke, it shattered into pieces, leav-ing only the stem and a sharp, V-shaped, jagged piece of pointed glass attached. Still continuing to laugh and taunt me, Mark pushed me against the sink and went to snatch the glass out of my hand, telling me how foolish I looked. I thought he was going to try to take it and cut me with it. Without further warning, fear consumed me and I felt like I was trapped in a corner. Before I knew it, I was fight-ing my way out by striking back and slicing him like he was a piece of cake. For the first time in months, I had come to the realization that

I was truly afraid that this man might kill me. I was fighting for my life, afraid that if he got a hold of the glass he was going to harm me first. We tussled for what seemed like a long time without me wanting to let go of the glass. My mind snapped, and as I lie here thinking about it now and writing in my diary, I remember Mark begging me to put the glass down and telling me that I had cut him. Nothing he said at that moment mattered, for all that mattered to me was that I wasn't going to allow him to harm me or my children anymore, and today was going to be his last time ever putting his hands on anybody. I was tired, and enough was enough. Everybody gets to the point in their lives when they just can't take it anymore. And that day I could not take any more; I was fed up.

Horrific memories of all the terrible things he had done to me flashed before my eyes. This man had battered me physically, mentally, emotionally, financially, and let's not forget verbally, for three years constantly. Mark had no mercy for anyone, especially when I thought about how he had spat on me and watched me squirm when he did it. It gave him great pleasure to make me miserable and to see me frightened. If I didn't know any better, I would have thought that he was the devil himself. So many times I had asked God what it was that I was doing so wrong in my life that I deserved this kind of punishment. Believe me, it wasn't God; it was me and the choices that I was making without Him. So how could I blame God for something He didn't get me into? He didn't pick Mark for me; I chose Mark, and I also chose to continue to let him abuse me. No one twisted my arm.

Continuing to struggle with Mark and trying to push him off of me as he screamed that I had cut him, I felt no mercy and continued to swing at him, trying to scare him and keep him from grabbing the glass and cutting me with it. To me, I was defending myself; what else was I supposed to do? I couldn't just give in and let him kill me like he had already threatened. Mark begged out loudly for me to stop but I couldn't; I was too angry and furious, and to me, he needed a taste of his own medicine. Something he needed a long time ago. For a moment, it gave me pleasure to see the fear in his eyes for a change, and to know that I wasn't scared and that I was fighting back. Screaming out loudly that I had cut him badly, I still didn't believe him until he stopped trying to fight me and turned around to show me his hand, and it fell over, with blood gushing everywhere. That's right, I had injured him so badly until his hand was barely attached to his arm and he was bleeding profusely. Looking down at the freshly mopped floor, I could see where tiny speckles of bright red blood had dripped from Mark's hand as it dangled in front of me, appearing to be suspended from a string. Even looking at him with his hand dangling in front of me just made me madder, as I was out of control. Was I supposed to feel really sorry for him now? Look how this man had abused not only me, but also my children. It was time for him to pay for all the evil he had done, I thought to myself as I continued to cut him some more. Here I was, totally out of control of the whole situation. Watching Mark become weaker and weaker by the minute, almost passing out from the loss of blood, still didn't move me. Mark was so weak he fell onto the kitchen floor. It never crossed my mind that Mark would die if I didn't do something quick. I was so angry, angrier than I had ever been in my whole entire life. So angry I had lost it, and didn't care anymore; I didn't care about myself, my children, or what was going to happen next if I killed this man or this man killed me.

Please, somebody hear me, feel me; I lost control, and in losing control, I lost myself and what I believed in most. As I struggled to drag Mark's limp, frail, and bloody body from the kitchen to the living room, leaving behind a trail of freshly scented blood, I could hear the shivering and terrified cries of Mark's nephew Jonathan pleading mercifully for me to spare his favorite uncle's life. With the look of much disgusted anger and an uncontrollable rage burning in my eyes, almost appearing to be insane for a moment, I snapped at Jonathan, yelling from the top of my lungs that if he tried to stop me I would do the same to him. Fear gripped Jonathan's heart as he clenched his fist and fell to his knees screaming out for help, yet no one heard his cries. Whirling thoughts and flashes of horrific memories engulfed my mind as I watched Mark lying lifeless in a puddle of blood. Staring down at my white, open-toed sandals, all speckled with his blood, I felt no mercy, for he had given me so much pain. Never could I have ever imagined that I would be driven to this kind of madness in my life.

I knew within seconds that soon I would be carted off in a white car, the one that had the black stripes down the side and the blue lights that flashed on top of it, making it possible for anyone to see it for miles. To me, the men in blue saved my life that night, because if not, I more than likely would have gotten a life sentence. All the abuse Mark had taken me through drove me to the point of no return. Yes, I wanted to see Mark suffer like he had made me suffer time and time again. Each swing of that glass was meant to cause him much harm as I lashed out in pain from a broken heart, filled with many tears and so much hurt; there wasn't any medicine that could ever cure it. No glue to mend it, nothing but a hope chest. Hoping that he would change. No, I was the one that needed to change and believe enough in myself to trust God and to know that He controls our destiny, and through Him all things are possible.

Do you know that God can move mountains in our lives if we give Him a chance? Do you know God wants us to inherit the riches of the land? Ask me how I know God is real, and I will tell you, just like I am now. Thinking back, I could have killed Mark and gone to prison for a very long time, or he could have killed me.

Standing before the judge the next day after the tragic incident, I was waiting to hear how much my bail was going to be. Did you hear me? I said bail! Here I was, a black, twenty-eight-year old female with two beautiful children, a nice home, many wonderful friends, and a decent job, standing in the presence of a judge waiting to hear about my bail, trying to stand tall and proud as the judge called out my name and read my bail out loud. Clearing his throat, Judge Walters did not have a problem explaining to me why my bail post was so high. I was weaving back and forth, almost at the point of fainting, due to hearing the judge say, "Mrs. Davis, I understand in reviewing your record that you were an outstanding citizen and you've served three years in the military defending your country."

Smiling from ear to ear, I just knew that from all the great things that Judge Walters was saying about me that I would soon be released, and my bail would be a little of nothing, if any. And that the charges against me would be dropped. Especially after he was informed about the spousal abuse I had been subjected to from some of the officers who had spoken with some of my neighbors before I was arrested. Yes, that's right, *arrested* and charged with assault with a deadly weapon. Then Judge Walters announced before the whole court that even though I was an outstanding, law-abiding citizen, he had to set an example somewhere and that I could not get away with using spousal abuse as an excuse to cause bodily harm to someone else. I was totally shocked and knew that he was getting ready to throw the book at me. Judge Walters told everyone in the courtroom that he had just received a report from Mark's doctor at the hospital and that the doctor informed him that Mark has to undergo at least four to maybe six hours of surgery to reattach some of the arteries and tendons in his hand.

"Mrs. Davis, do you know that Mark has to undergo serious surgery and may never be able to use that hand again? So based upon the information I just gave you, I'm going to set your bail at $28,000 and no ten percent."

At that moment, I could have fainted on the floor. Tears flowed down my flushed face as I bared my soul, seeking the mercy of the court, pleading my innocence and describing the abuse I had endured from my spouse for many years. Judge Walters even saw the reports from when I had taken out a restraining order on Mark, and yet nothing mattered to him. Nothing was going to change Judge Walters's mind. Where was Judge Walters when I was being pushed down a flight of twenty steps at eight and a half months pregnant? Here I was, locked up in jail, being held under a $28,000 bail because an evil man had provoked me. All the tears in the world were not going to make Judge Walters change his mind. My body felt numb hearing the judge's words as they pierced a hole through my soul. Who had $28,000 just sitting around and was waiting to get me out of jail?

Here I was, in a town with my only blood relative being my brother. Who was I going to call? Most of my friends were struggling just like me and didn't even have a telephone. When this incident occurred last night, my brother was right in the next bedroom, but had his door closed and was sound asleep. He doesn't even know I'm locked up and that Mark is in the hospital. And the last thing I want is for my family to find out. Last night as I stood with my hands held out in front of me waiting for the officer to place the handcuffs on me, he motioned for me to put my hands down and informed me that it wasn't necessary for me to be cuffed. Surprised by the officer's response, it made me feel better knowing he respected me enough to know that I was a decent woman who had committed a crime in self-defense.

I never knew that any of my neighbors cared anything about me until that night when they saw me getting arrested. The outpouring of love and support from my neighbors gave me hope. One lady cried as she watched me being carted off to jail. As I walked toward the car to take the short ride to the jailhouse, I could hear whispers in the air amidst the crowd of people saying, "You'll be all right, and you'll be home tomorrow," and some saying, "She finally did it." Some people were walking around in shock; I could tell by the expressions on their faces. People were jeering at the officers and upset that I was going to jail, as was evident in the crowd of about two hundred people, some concerned and wishing me well by telling me that everything was going to be all right, that Mark finally got what he deserved, and some just plain old nosy. I couldn't help but look for the face of Mark's sister-in-law Joyce, hoping that she heard all the commotion that was going on outside and would go and get my baby so Child Protective Services would not take him.

Last night when the cops arrested me for cutting Mark, believe it or not, I felt free. Free that he could no longer terrorize me and my children. Free in knowing that for once, I could go to sleep and not have to worry about what he was going to do to me. Girlfriend, girl-friend, let me tell you something. No one, and I do mean no one, should have to go to jail just so they can feel free. Feeling free as a butterfly should be the way you feel each and every day and should be accepted as part of your everyday living. Practice and live by it, and you'll be forever rich.

Thinking back now, I know I'm truly blessed and that God was looking out for me and sent His angels to my rescue. Here I was, locked up in jail under a $28,000 bail and was clueless as to how or who was going to come up with the needed funds to get me out. After returning back to my cell from a long day in court, I was mentally drained as I lay down thinking and hoping that some miracle would happen, and someone would post my bail. For some strange reason or another, I stopped thinking about my situation and instead prayed for everyone else.

It had only been about an hour later when I heard the footsteps of one of the guards walking toward my cell, calling out my name, telling me to pack my things. Shocked and surprised at the officer's request, my heart raced in my chest as I jumped up to gather my things; none of which belonged to me other than the white, open-toed sandals that were attached to my feet. Before I had a chance to lay eyes on the guard, I asked loudly where I was being transported. Waiting for a response, I could hear the voices of the other cellmates surrounding me in the background trying to warn me that the only reason a guard would be coming to get me is one or two reasons, one being that maybe Mark had died during surgery and I was being transferred to another cell because they didn't know if he had family members that were in the same cell as me, and it would cause conflict. Upon hearing those shocking and chilling words, *that maybe Mark died*, almost made me go into a frenzy. For a moment, I thought I was going to lose my mind. I began to dread the thought of what was coming at me next and regardless of whether my cellmates knew it or not, they did a great job of scaring me silly. Before the cellmates could tell me what reason number two was, the guard had already arrived with the key to release me. Looking surprised at the officer as he opened the cell, I couldn't help but ask him for the second time where I was going. With a slight grin on his face, he told me that I was going home.

"Home!" I shouted, jumping up and down like a kid on Christmas morning. Grinning from ear to ear, I listened as the guard made the comment to me that I had a lot of people who loved me. Flattered by his comment, I was curious to know what made him say what he did. Turning toward the guard as we approached the metal electronic gate, I could see a female guard waiting to replace him and connect with me for the rest of my journey. Realizing that I only had a few seconds to ask him about the comment he had made, I finally broke my silence and asked him how did he know that I had a lot of people who loved me. Happy to respond to my inquiry, he told me that in order for anyone to post a $28,000 bail for me without a 10 percent reduction, they had to love me. Before releasing me into the custody of the other guard, he told me that he wished me much luck and that I would find out what he was talking about once I arrived at the court-house for my final release. I always thought that once you were re-leased, you were free to just walk out of the jail without having to sign anything. Oh boy, was I wrong! I signed paper after paper, one right after the other. My hands were tired from so much writing.

Arriving at the courthouse, waiting to be released, I wanted to find out who had performed this miracle in my life. Sitting patiently, waiting for the officer to call my name, I was anxious and curious to know who was the angel that God had sent to come to my rescue. Finally the moment had arrived for me to sign the last paper. I could feel my palm sweating as I grew nervous trying to guess in my mind who could have bailed me out. Suspense can kill you, and this night it was killing me mentally.

Hearing the voice of my brother Chad as he turned the corner at the end of the corridor, I could no longer contain myself and ran to greet him. My brother grabbed me and hugged me with tears in his eyes. As he stood with his arms around me, I noticed two other peo-ple approaching me, also reaching out to embrace me. It was none other than one of my co-workers named Kim whom I had only met recently. Kim was pleasant and polite as she greeted me with a smile and a hug filled with love. After she embraced me, her boyfriend, Donald, embraced me and told me that everything was going to be okay. Happiness filled my heart to know that someone thought enough of me to spare my life by posting my bail of $28,000. I could no longer resist saying thank you to all of them for coming to my res-cue in my time of need. As I thanked them graciously, no one uttered a word. Noticing the strange look on their faces, I could tell that something was wrong. Still waiting for a response, I asked what was wrong. Kim and my brother assured me that everything was okay but that they weren't the ones I should be thanking for getting me out of jail. Amazed at what I had just heard, I asked her to repeat it as if I didn't hear her the first time.

"Cee, you heard me right—we didn't have the money to get you out."

"Well, who did?" I demanded to know.

"Now that is something you'll just have to find out when you get home."

"When I get home? Why not now?"

"Because if we told you now, you may go into shock."

"Okay guys, stop playing games and tell me."

My curiosity was getting the best of me and making me mad as I wanted to know so badly. Chad laughed, watching me trying to guess who posted my bail. He told me to stop trying to guess, that I would know soon enough. Hearing him tell me that made Kim and her boyfriend Donald even more tickled.

The ride home that night seemed so long. Pulling up in front of my house, anxiety took control of my legs and feet as I hurriedly ran up to the gate, opening it and leaving everyone else behind. I wanted to see my precious baby Antwan and feel his touch. Running all the way upstairs, almost out of breath, I swung open the hallway door and entered into my house, hoping that Mark's sister-in-law would be there with Antwan. Disappointment filled my spirit, for she was not there.

Coming in the door behind me, I could hear my brother Chad talking with Kim and Donald, telling them that we needed to get some champagne so we could celebrate. Now, that was the last thing on my mind, as I wanted so badly to hold my baby boy. Breathing hard and too disappointed to move a step further, I could hear Kim's voice asking me to sit down and telling me that they had a surprise for me. Sitting down in my favorite chair, I waited for her to tell me what was going on. Just as she opened her mouth to speak, there was a knock at the door. Getting up to answer it, Chad motioned for me to sit back down. I was curious to know who it was and could barely sit still; as the sound of voices became clearer, I recognized who it was. It was my two newest tenants, Joanna and her husband, Dan, whom I had just rented to within the past two months. Joanna and Dan were the only two tenants I had that paid me their rent on time every month without fail, even though they smoked everything else up in crack. Getting up out of my seat to see what they wanted, my brother asked me to sit back down and that he had something he wanted to tell me in front of everybody.

"Cee, remember when you asked who posted your bail?"

"Yes and?"

"Well, Kim, Donald, nor myself can take any credit."

"What do you mean?" I asked.

"The persons you need to thank are Joanna and Dan." Stunned at what my brother said, I gasped out loud from shock, trying not to look obvious. It took a few moments for what he said to penetrate my brain. My legs could not move fast enough for me to run over and hug Joanna and Dan and thank them a million and one times for getting me out of jail, as they looked on proudly telling me that it was their pleasure and that they would do it over again. Learning that God had chosen these two people, who were strung out on crack cocaine, to be my angels in my time of need taught me to never underestimate the power of God, for He is awesome. Awesome in every aspect of the word.

Wondering how they came up with the money to get me out, my brother sat me down and told me the story of how he learned of my incarceration the day after the incident. Chad began to tell me how he was outside crying out loud as he sat on the steps, and Joanna and her husband, Dan, who were clueless as to my being arrested, approached him and asked him what was wrong. As he began to tell them that his baby girl was locked up, they asked him how much my bail was. My brother Chad said he told them not to ask that question, because no one he knew had enough money to get me out. Not wanting to be pushy, Joanna said she asked my brother again how much he needed to get me out. Screaming out loud, Joanna said Chad yelled, "If you want to know, Cee's bail is $28,000 and no ten percent, now you know," he said angrily, holding his head down and continuing to cry.

"That's when I told him that we would help get you out," Joanna said. "Dan had a lawsuit that had been pending for three years and it was for thirty thousand. We didn't have a checking account and couldn't find anyone to cash a check for that amount, so we told your brother Chad that if he took us to your lawyer and got the check cashed, we would get you out."

Crying as I embraced Joanna and her husband Dan, I could feel the spirit of God moving, for it was through Him that my angels were there for me. Just ask yourself what the chances were of someone strung out on crack cocaine coming into $30,000 the day after I was arrested, and being willing to sacrifice $28,000 up front to bail someone out whom they barely knew, and only receive $2,000 back in cash? How many people do you know who would have done this? I know it was an act of God. Every day I thank God for giving me a new chance in life.

Thinking back now, I have so many things to be thankful for. I'm thankful that I have learned to move on with my life by taking control and getting rid of the life that was poisoning me. I'm thankful that God gave me a forgiving heart so that I can heal and forgive others. I'm blessed that I'm still alive so I can help others to overcome abusive situations in their lives. For each step I have taken, I know my God has taken ten, if not more. One thing for sure is that I know God carried me. I'm so blessed to know that God is my friend and through Him all things are possible.

So many ripple effects could have taken place, such as contracting an STD (sexually transmitted disease), and let's not forget I could have been serving time in prison if Mark had died, and could have lost my precious, precious children to Child Protective Services forever. But instead I lost them for only two years when my oldest brother intervened and took custody. Maybe it's best that he did, even though at the time I didn't think so. Sometimes we have to think what's best for our children, especially after I went to jail and was convicted of assault with a deadly weapon.

God is real, because I'm alive and free today, sitting here telling you my story and what I went through and how *God brought me through the storm and the rain,* and now all I see is *sunshine. And you can, too!!! Just give God a chance and you will see for yourself. Whatever He did for me, He will do for you, too!* It took me a total of five years in an abusive relationship to wake up. Don't let this be you. Pray every day that God will give you the strength and courage to make the right choices for your life. Having God as my friend taught me to trust. For if I know nothing else, I know I can confide in Him. Life is for the living, so shoot for the moon and reach for the stars!

Crack Addict's Wife's Prayer

Dear Heavenly Father:

In my heart of hearts I pray—
that you'll protect our loved ones
addicted to crack cocaine,
so they won't go astray.

Please grant them the courage and
determination to stand strong,
so they can resist any temptation
to do any wrong.

Give them the will and desire
to do what is right;
please supply them with
all the ammunition
to win this terrible fight.

Oh Heavenly Father,
if what you say is true,
please show our loved ones
addicted to crack cocaine
exactly what they must do.

Take them by the hand
and guide them into the light,
fill them with much wisdom
to know what is wrong from right.

Please instill them with insurmountable faith
to know that they, too, can win,
but also remind them that if they refuse
to stop smoking crack cocaine,
death is surely the end.

Facts About Cocaine Abuse and Treatment

Source: Cocaine is a drug extracted from the leaves of the coca plant. It is a potent natural brain stimulant and one of the most powerfully addictive drugs of abuse.

Form: Illicit cocaine is distributed on the street in two main forms: cocaine hydrochloride, a white crystalline powder that can be snorted or dissolved in water and injected; and "crack," cocaine hydrochloride that has been processed with ammonia or sodium bicarbonate into a freebase cocaine called chips, chunks, or "rocks" that can be smoked.

Extent of Use: In 1999, according to the National Household Survey on Drug Abuse (NHSDA), an estimated 1.5 million Americans were current cocaine users; that is, they had used cocaine at least once in the past month. Of that number, an estimated one-half million were current crack users. As in the past, the rate of current cocaine use was highest among young adults in 1999—approximately 60 percent of current cocaine users were aged 18 through 34.

Methods of Use: Cocaine may be used occasionally, daily, or in a variety of compulsive, repeated-use patterns known as "binging." Major means of administering cocaine are snorting, injecting, and smoking. When snorted, cocaine powder is inhaled through the nostrils and absorbed into the bloodstream. Cocaine powder can also be dissolved in water and injected directly into the bloodstream. Crack cocaine is usually smoked in a pipe, and the cocaine vapor or smoke is inhaled into the lungs where it is absorbed into the bloodstream. Regardless of the route of administration, cocaine is addictive. Crack cocaine and injected cocaine reach the brain quickly and bring an intense and immediate high. Cocaine taken intranasally produces a high more slowly.

Effects of Use: Acute physical effects include constricted peripheral blood vessels, dilated pupils, elevated temperature, and increased heart rate and blood pressure. Some cocaine users reported feelings of restlessness, irritability, and anxiety. Prolonged cocaine use and smoking crack cocaine can also trigger paranoid behavior. Cocaine may also harm the health and development of infants born to women who use cocaine while they are pregnant. When addicted individuals stop using cocaine, they often suffer from depression and anhedonia, the inability to experience pleasure from normally pleasurable activities. This condition may lead to renewed cocaine use. Data from the Drug Abuse Warning Network (DAWN) (www.samhsa. gov/oas/ dawn.htm) shows that the number of cocaine-related emergency room visits increased by 25 percent between 1998 and 2002.

Treatment: Although NIDA's Medications Development Division has made considerable progress in the search for cocaine treatment medications, as yet no medications are approved for treating cocaine abuse and dependence. However, data from treatment programs using a variety of psychological and behavioral therapeutic approaches indicate that outpatient cocaine treatment can be successful. NIDA is supporting the development of new behavioral interventions that are showing increased effectiveness in decreasing drug use by patients undergoing treatment for cocaine abuse.

From "NIDA Notes," September/October 1995

Resource Guide for Drug Information and Treatment

If you like more specific information about drug addiction/ abuse and treatment options, please contact the following agencies:

Cocaine Anonymous (CA): (800) 347-8998 OR go to www.ca.org on the Internet to find a toll-free number for your state

Narcotics Anonymous (NA): (866) 802-6262 OR (800) 992-0401 OR go to www.na.org on the Internet to find a toll-free number for your state

Phoenix House: (800) 662-HELP or www.phoenixhouse.org

National Institute on Drug Abuse (NIDA): (301) 443-1124 or www.drugabuse.gov

National Clearinghouse for Alcohol and Drug Information (NCADI): (800) 729-6686 or www.health.org

Centers for Substance Abuse Prevention and Treatment: (301) 443-0365 or (301) 443-5700 or www.samhsa.gov

Office of National Drug Control Policy (ONDCP): (800) 666-3332 or www.whitehousedrugpolicy.gov

Internet Sites:

American Council for Drug Education: www.acde.org

Free Vibe (for teens): www.freevibe.com

Join Together: www.jointogether.org

Online Recovery (for ANY type of addiction): www.n2recovery.com

Web of Addictions: www.well.com/user/woa

Battered Women with Chemically Involved Partners

An abuser's involvement with chemical substances can have a significant impact on victims of domestic violence. Being in a relationship with an abusive partner requires considerable skill and resourcefulness and has a predictable effect on a victim. Victims learn to do and say those things that will help keep them and their children most safe. Becoming highly attuned to the pleasure and displeasure reactions of the abuser is a survival strategy. A victim's own needs, wants, desires, dreams, and goals become irrelevant, because what will help keep the victim most safe is intimately connected to the abuser's moods, wants, likes, and dislikes. As a result, victims may know more about the abuser than they do about themselves. In fact, victims will often adopt these survival strategies regardless of whether their partners are involved with chemical substance abuse or not.

The following statistics are taken from the National Clearinghouse for the Defense of Battered Women (September 1995):

- Among all female murder victims in 1992, 30 percent were slain by husbands or boyfriends.
- The American Medical Association estimates that over 4 million women are victims of severe assaults by boyfriends and husbands each year. About 1 in 2 women is likely to be abused by a partner in her lifetime.
- Females are victims of family violence at a rate of at least 3 times that of males. Based on domestic crime data kept by 17 states, experts estimate that 1.37 million domestic violence offenses were reported to the police in 1991, women the victims in an estimated 85% of the cases. The average age of the offender is 31 years old.
- Studies reveal that domestic violence occurs in 2 million families in the U.S. However, this figure is substantially understated because battering is usually not reported until it reaches life-threatening proportions. In the *National Crime Victimization Survey* in 1992, 51% of the victims were attacked by a boyfriend/ girlfriend, 34% were attacked by spouses, and 15% were attacked by ex-spouses.
- Results of the *National Family Survey* indicate that all forms of marital violence occur most frequently among those less than 30 years of age. The

rate of marital violence among those under 30 years of age is more than DOUBLE the rate for the next group, ages 31 to 50.

- About 1 in 5 women victimized by their spouse or ex-spouse reported that they had been the victim of a series of similar crimes. They had sustained at least 3 assaults within 6 months of the interview, and the assaults were so similar that they could not remember them distinctly. Of the husbands who batter their wives, 47% do so three or more times each year.

Domestic Violence Resources

National Domestic Violence/Abuse Hotline: 1-800-799-SAFE (7233) or 1-800-787-3224 (TDD) or www.ndvh.org on the Internet.

24-HOUR HOTLINE staffed by trained counselors ready to provide immediate crisis intervention assistance. Callers can be connected directly to help in their communities, including emergency services and shelters, as well as receive information and referrals, counseling, and legal assistance in reporting abuse. Calls are confidential and callers may remain anonymous if they wish. Tell them Stop Abuse For Everyone, or SAFE, referred you at www.safe4all.org on the Internet.

Cybergrrl "Safety Net" Site for Women: www.cybergrrl.com on the Internet. Find domestic violence survivor stories, test your knowledge about domestic violence and how to tell if you or someone you know might be in an abusive relationship. Find links to national resources and Web sites.

Growing.Com Internet Site: www.growing.com/nonviolent/research/dvlinks.htm on the Internet. More than 1200 links to domestic violence resources on the Internet.

National Resource Center on Domestic Violence: 1-800-537-2238 or www.pcadv.org on the Internet. Although located in Pennsylvania, this domestic violence coalition does advocate on behalf of battered women nationally through the development and passage of legislation strengthening legal protections. It offers promotion of public policies that meet the needs of battered women and the pursuit of additional funding for programs and a network of services to respond adequately to the ever-increasing requests for services, protection, and safety.

Final Thoughts

In life, no matter what we go through, good or bad, one thing is for sure, and that is that we need God. Life isn't always easy or fair, nor will it ever be. But it's up to you to make the best of it. It is only through our true-life experiences that we gain the wisdom and knowledge to proceed to a higher plateau. Remember, knowledge is power and power gives us the strength to conquer the greatness within. So why not go out and conquer the world!

Remember, it only takes the smallest seed to produce the ripest fruits from the blossom of a tree that was already fruitful and multiplied.

Wishing you many, many blessings!

The Turning Point Advantage—
Succeeding Against the Odds

Stop dreaming about the life you dare to live and start living the life you dare to dream about. Cindy has mastered the blueprint for successful living. Take the journey as she enlightens your spirit and warms your heart with her touching, but true, life story. Learn how to live and have the win-win attitude that exudes confidence whenever you step into a room. Gain insight into God's true purpose for your life. Get prepared to rise to greater heights by taking the necessary steps in order to enrich your life forever. Sit back and relax as Cindy captivates your heart and stirs your soul with her spiritual way of thinking.

A best-selling author, Ms. Hunter is also available to speak to your organization. Cindy Hunter is at ease addressing universities, religious gatherings, and book clubs as well as corporate audiences on diverse topics such as spousal abuse, drug addiction, and codependency in the workplace.

Also Learn How To:

* Take control of your life * Master positive thinking * Step out on faith!
* Set obtainable goals * Mold and shape your destiny * Gain confidence
* Become a leader * Succeed against the odds! * Dream BIG!
* Focus through any complex situation

Contact Information

It is always a pleasure to hear from people who have read ***Diary of a Crack Addict's Wife***. If this book has added value to your life or someone you know, please write and let me know. I would love to include your story in my next book or on my Web site.

If you would like me to speak at your organization please do not hesitate to e-mail me at mochaexpress22@yahoo.com I look forward to hearing from you soon. For more information, please go to my Web site: www.cindyhunter.com

ANTWAN'S ADDICTION

Dear Readers,

After writing this book, *Diary of a Crack Addict's Wife,* and going on tour from city to city across the nation, I started meeting other women who had faced similar situations with the addiction of their newborns. These women were also accused of being crack addicts. Most of them were just like me: drug-free but involved with or married to a spouse who had a drug addiction.

I was totally surprised by the number of women who would approach me after reading the earlier self-published edition of my book to share their experiences.

For many years it's been medically stated that the only way a child can be born with an addiction is if the mother herself is indulging in the use of an addictive drug. Reviewing all the controversy centered around this issue of whether a baby can actually be born addicted if the mother is not smoking crack but the father is, made me search for a better understanding in an effort to educate other people.

My first step was to contact one of the leading genetic specialists at Emory University in Atlanta, Georgia. All the information gathered from this specialist still left unanswered questions in my mind, so I continued to research and research. The more I searched for answers the more confusing it became, because what I found was a medical society that was unsure. Most of the medical professionals could not tell me that it was known one hundred percent that the mother had to be an addict for the unborn child to be affected in any way. Therefore, if there is a one percent uncertainty still lingering, who is to say that the little one percent couldn't be you or your child.

I'm more than certain that there are other women out there who are just like me as well as many others who are afraid to come out of the shadows for fear of ridicule. It's time that we challenge the medical association for a better understanding concerning this particular issue, for there are so many women who need to be freed from thinking that it was their fault when in fact it wasn't.

Believe me, I know the feeling all too well since I was once accused of this.

Sincerely,

Cynthia D. Hunter

DIARY OF A CRACK ADDICT'S WIFE

CYNTHIA D. HUNTER

ABOUT THIS GUIDE

The suggested questions are intended to
enhance your group's reading of
this book.

DISCUSSION QUESTIONS

1. What do you think about the title of the book?
2. How would you rate the title on a scale of 1 to 5? (With 1 being the lowest and 5 being the highest.)
3. Would you tell a friend about *Diary of a Crack Addict's Wife*? Please explain why you would or would not.
4. Did *Diary* hold your attention and why?
5. What audience do you think *Diary* will attract?
   a. Older and mature group
   b. Younger age group 18-29
   c. All ages
   d. African-Americans only
   e. All nationalities
6. What was your favorite part of the story and why?
7. What part of the story made you laugh?
8. What part of the story made you sad?
9. What part of the story made you mad?
10. Were the descriptions of the characters in the story clear?
11. Do you know anyone in real life who reminds you of any of the characters?
12. Do you feel that *Diary* will be helpful to others in similar situations?
13. Are you anxious to read *Diary 2*? Please explain why or why not.
14. Could you identify personally with any of the situations in the book? Why?
15. What part of the story do you remember the most?
16. Did you like the illustration for the cover? Why?
17. Have you gained any insight into a crack addict's wife's life by reading this book?
18. What things do you envision in the future for *Diary*?
19. What would your reaction be if you were reading the *New York Times* and read that *Diary of a Crack Addict's Wife* made the #1 Best-sellers list?
   a. Totally shocked
   b. Slightly shocked
   c. Absolutely knew it would
   d. Unsure
20. Would you be willing to help promote *Diary*? Why?
21. Why did you want to read *Diary*?
22. Did each page make you want to read more?
23. Would you like to share any personal comments or suggestions?